Wonderfully Made

Loved by God

Mark Huffman
Tanya Eustace Campen
Leigh Meekins

Wonderfully Made: Loved by God

ISBN: 9781501842795

Mark Huffman, Writer
Tanya Eustace Campen, Writer
Leigh Meekins, Writer
Marjorie M. Pon, Associate Publisher and Editor of Church School Publications (CSP)
Jones Zimmerman, Editor
Kellie Green, Designer

Art Credits:
Cover, i, iii and fireflies throughout, 3, 15, 41, 57, 79, 87: Shutterstock
Pages 1, 7-8, 11, 16, 19, 22-26, 28-31, 33-36, 42-43, 45-49, 51, 65, 70-73, 75: John White, Neis Group

17 18 19 20 21 22 23 24 25 26—10 9 8 7 6 5 4 3 2 1

PACP10041284-01

Contents

Introduction

Welcome to Wonderfully Made: Loved by God.

You are embarking on an exciting adventure. As you go through this book, you will find questions that you are invited to consider carefully. We also encourage you to share with your parents or guardians what you're learning about yourself.

The Wonderfully Made Participant Book is a workbook and an informational book. You may wonder why we wrote this book. The authors of this book believe strongly that God loves us and gives us sexuality as a gift. We also believe it is important for older children to learn about their bodies. We believe you need this information to make good decisions for yourself. The decisions you make about sex, sexuality, and your faith in God will have a significant impact on your life.

This book focuses on prayer and your relationship with God. God created us in God's image. It is OK to bring God your thoughts and feelings about your body and sexuality. Take time to be prayerful.

This book is your book. But we hope you have some trusted adults in your life to talk to as you work through this book. Your parents or guardians know what it is like to go through puberty. Trust them to be with you and to support you during this time.

Remember that every preteen is on a different journey through puberty and adolescence. You may be excited and ready to work through this book, while other preteens may not be ready to have these conversations. Be respectful of everyone's journey by not sharing this information with those who aren't ready for it. On the other hand, if you hear others sharing incorrect information, it might be appropriate for you to take a moment to share with others what you've learned. You always can ask a trusted adult if you're not sure what information is good to share.

Enjoy learning about your body and how you have been wonderfully made by God!

P.S. Parents/Guardians: On page 91, there is a page designated for you to write a note to your child. This is an opportunity for you to encourage your child and to express your love.

Wonderfully Made

Scripture:

Genesis 1:26-31

Matthew 5:14

Hello! Welcome to Wonderfully Made, a guide to understanding who you are and how loved you are as God's wonderfully-made creation!

Did you know that you are God's good creation? In the very first book of the Old Testament, Genesis, we hear how God created the world, including humans like you and me! In Genesis 1:26-28, God created and blessed humanity. This means that you are blessed! The Bible doesn't stop there. In Genesis 1:31, God looked at everything God had made, including humans, and declared Creation supremely good. As a part of Creation, you are supremely good.

As we grow, we experience lots of changes. These changes occur in our bodies, minds, emotions, and responsibilities. Maybe you can kick a soccer ball into a goal, write a letter to a friend, make a layup with a basketball, play a difficult piece on the piano, read a chapter book, multiply numbers in your head, or dance on your toes. You developed those talents over time as you practiced, grew, and experienced bodily changes.

You are not the same today as you were when you were 1 year old or 5 years old. You are also not the same today as you will be when you are 18, 21, or 30 years old.

As we grow, our bodies change and affect how we look, feel, think, and relate to other people. When you were a baby, people probably referred to you as an infant. Then you were a toddler, then a child. You may hear people refer to you as a preteen or a tween. These are all words that help identify where a person is in the growing process. Another word that you may hear is *adolescent*. **Adolescence** is the time when your body transitions from childhood to adulthood. Your body does this work over many years. In fact, your brain will not be fully developed until you are about 26 years old!

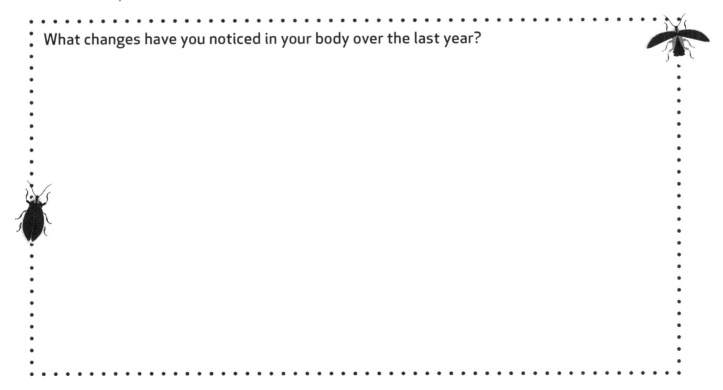

What changes have you noticed in your body over the last year?

We are all growing and changing on different paths. Your body might go through changes at a different pace than your friends. The good news is that God is with you as you change and grow.

The people who love you are with you as you navigate these changes. The purpose of this book is to help you learn more about your body and what changes to expect, and to remind you that you are not alone during this important time in your life.

Who loves you and is with you on this journey? Write in the box provided the names of adults you love and trust. These are people you can talk to when you have questions about something as you read this book, or when you are curious about the changes your body is going through.

It is also important to pay attention to how you feel as you read this book. Feelings help us understand whether we are ready for various conversations. As you read, you may have a variety of feelings. There is a feelings chart on page 7 showing examples of various emotions. You can use this chart to help you figure out what you're feeling as you work through this book!

Start by drawing your own emojis that reflect how you feel. You might choose one from the feelings chart, or make your own.

At the end of this chapter, we'll introduce you to something called GLOWS. This is a way for you to connect to God, to listen to what God and others are saying, and to explore how you feel in response to everything you are learning. In the church, we call this prayerful process *liturgy* or "the work of the people." You are not alone, and you can talk to God and the people you trust at any point on this journey. In fact, throughout this book, question boxes are placed for you to write and record your feelings. Use these spaces to record your thoughts and your questions as you read.

ANGRY

DISGUSTED

HAPPY

HOPEFUL

EXCITED

RELAXED

OVERWHELMED

JOYFUL

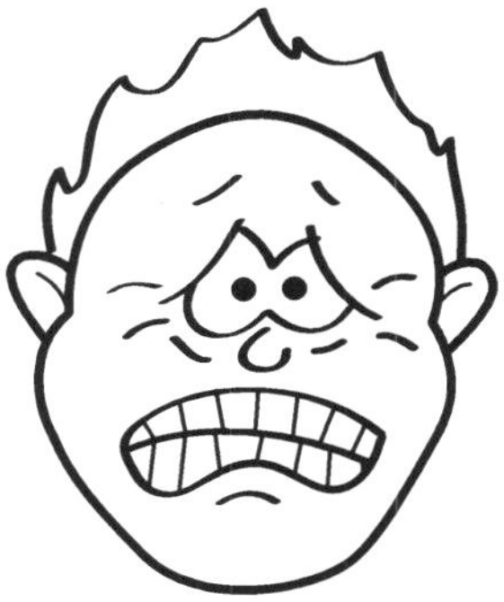
AFRAID

NERVOUS

CONFUSED

CURIOUS

Let Your Light Shine

Have you ever seen a firefly or lightning bug? Some people enjoy watching lightning bugs at night. People of all ages are fascinated by the glow of fireflies' bodies. Some people even try to catch them and store them in glass jars so they can watch them glow. There are more than 2,000 species of fireflies, and they come in a rainbow of colors. Fireflies light up in shades of yellow, red, green, or orange.

Firefly lights serve an important purpose. Did you know that fireflies use their glow to attract mates and prey? In fact, some call fireflies "flashy flirts." They shine their lights into the world.

Just like fireflies, we, too, have a light that shines in and through us. As humans, our light is different than that of fireflies. While a firefly's light helps it survive, our light helps us shine God's love into the world. Our light is a gift from God. Your light shines so brightly that others can see God's love in and through you!

In Matthew 5:14, we read that Jesus said, "you are the light of the world." Our work as we change and grow is to let our lights shine before all people. The first step in this work is to recognize that God loves us. God created each of us wonderfully. We don't ever need to be ashamed of our bodies, because God made them and saw that they were good. When we love God, love ourselves, and love others, our lights shine. When our lights shine brightly, others are drawn to us and want to know more about God's grace and love.

Is This Book About Sex?

The word "sex" can mean different things. It can describe a biological category, as in "female," or "male." It can describe a behavior between people. Those three letters, s-e-x, also begin a number of other words, such as "sexy," "sexual," and "sexuality." Let's take a moment to define and explain what we're talking about.

This book is about the broadest of the words: *sexuality*. Sexuality is about sexual feelings, puberty, reproduction, and much more. Sexuality involves:

1. **Our bodies and senses.** Our bodies were created to feel some special sensations. By adulthood, our brains, genitals, reproductive organs, and hormones *(chemical messengers)* develop in a way that enable us to form sexual sensations and connections with others. Most people start to become aware of these new sensations as they enter puberty. **Puberty** is the period during which human bodies mature and become capable of making babies.

2. **Emotional intimacy.** Care, nurture, and acceptance help us feel connected to others. We call this type of connection **intimacy.** Intimacy is not just about sexuality or romance. There are many types of emotionally close relationships. In fact, the first of these start when we're born, with parents, caregivers, and family members. Later, emotional intimacy creates a safe and healthy connection in which romantic and sexual feelings can be expressed.

3. **Who we are, and the categories we use to describe our sexuality.** Different ways of describing ourselves are:

   - By sex—biological categories based on genitalia, reproductive organs, and chromosomes. While sex is typically categorized as female and male, it's not always that simple. *(More on that in Module 4.)*

   - By gender identity—a person's internal sense of their own gender, most commonly "woman," "man," "girl," and "boy," but it's not always that simple. *(More about that in Module 4.)*

   - By sexual orientation—who we're attracted to, for example, people of a different gender *("straight")*, people of the same gender *("gay/lesbian")*, people of multiple genders *("bisexual")*, and so forth.

4. **Reproduction and sexual health.** It's important to become familiar with the reproductive and sexual parts of our bodies to keep our whole selves healthy. Sexual touch carries some health risks. This means we need to make smart decisions about the ways we choose to share our bodies. Smart decisions help protect ourselves and our partners. This book will help you learn more about yourself and decide how you want to protect your body, and when you want to share your body with someone in the future.

5. **God's love for us and our response to God's love.** Our sexuality is wonderfully made by God. As God's children, all aspects of our lives have the capacity to shine with God's love. That applies to our sexuality, too.

Though God wants all expressions of sexuality to reflect God's love, the sad reality is that not all sexual connections do. Unfortunately, many people experience sexual abuse, such as sexual touch that they did not choose, which leads to pain and shame. *(We will talk about this in more detail in Module 4.)* If you've experienced unwanted sexual touch, we encourage you to talk to a trusted adult. It's not your fault, and you are not alone.

The changes we experience as we grow are physical, emotional, spiritual, mental, and relational. That is a lot of changes! You might be curious about the changes you are experiencing, and that is OK! You might begin to feel attracted to another person. This is good and healthy because God created us for relationships.

We have many different types of relationships. We have relationships with our families, our friends, other adults, and other kids. We get to decide how we participate in these relationships; how we talk, how we act, and whom we can trust. This is part of being human.

We all have different relationships and every relationship has its own set of boundaries that should be respected. **Boundaries** are guidelines that we and others set to define how we treat each other. Our families might set boundaries on where we can go and when. Friends set boundaries about what information to share and what information to keep confidential. You get to determine your own boundaries in relationships.

Spend a few minutes thinking about what you have read. Jot down any thoughts or questions you have.

Road Map

Each chapter in this book has Scripture to read, information to consider, questions to ponder, and spiritual disciplines to practice. Spiritual disciplines are practices that help us connect with God. Some might feel familiar, and some might be new.

Wonderfully Made contains four different modules, and each focuses on a different aspect of development and sexuality.

- Module 1 introduces you to the whole book and what to be looking for throughout.
- Module 2 focuses on the typical reproductive systems of male and female bodies.
- Module 3 focuses on the changes bodies experience during puberty. This module also will discuss sex and the decisions you will begin to face as you go through puberty.
- Module 4 talks about your body, boundaries, and intimacy.

As you will see, some words are **bolded.** These words are defined in the glossary at the back of the book.

If you are participating in a Wonderfully Made Experience at church, we invite you to bring your questions and discoveries with you to small- or large-group discussions. The leaders of these experiences are trained in this information and are ready to join you in conversation. You will find boxes containing questions for you to consider. There will be space for you to write your thoughts privately, and if you choose, you can share them with your group.

We hope you will discover throughout this book how wonderfully made you are. Take time to explore your body as you go through this book! Inspect your toes, check for hair under your arms, feel your genitals in the shower, or flex in front of the mirror. Take time to wonder, learn, and discover the intricate details of what makes you you!

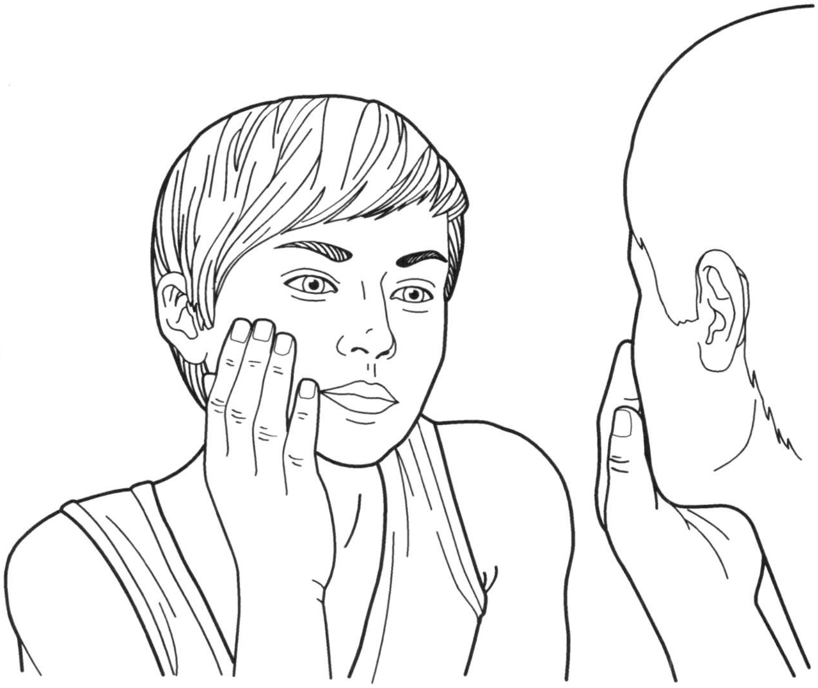

GLOWS

As you read through this resource, you will be invited to connect, listen, reflect, wonder, and respond to God through a process called GLOWS.

You might want to identify a safe space to practice the GLOWS liturgy. This might be in your room or a special place outside. You might choose to place something in your space to remind you that God is with you, such as a candle, a glow stick, glow-in-the-dark modeling clay, a photograph, or a cross. *(The recipe for glow-in-the-dark modeling clay can be found at the end of this module.)* You might bring special items with you to this space: your Bible, a journal, pens, and markers, crayons, or other creative items. Decide whether you want to practice GLOWS alone or with your family or a trusted friend.

Finally, be sure to give yourself 10-15 minutes in this space. This will give you enough time to connect with God, to listen, to open your heart to what God is saying, to wonder about what you hear, and to consider steps you want to take when you leave this special space.

GLOWS

Connect with **G**od. Pray and light a candle *(with your parent's or guardian's permission)*, or use glow-in-the-dark modeling clay, then say:

"God, you know me! I am wonderfully made! I come to you with an open mind and an open heart as I listen for what you might say to me today."

Listen. Read a section in this book or one of the suggested Bible verses at the beginning of the module.

Open your heart. Think about what you heard in silence or with quiet music playing. There are many ways to process what you are learning. You might choose to journal, draw, or create something with modeling clay. Take time to record questions or insights you have.

Wonder. Consider writing in a journal or notebook your responses to the following questions:

What did I learn in this chapter?

What was difficult to read or see?

What gifts has God given me?

What questions do I have?

Steps. Write what steps you want to take in response to all you have experienced in this time of prayer.

Closing Prayer:

"God, I praise you, for I am wonderfully made. Thank you for being with me as I change and grow. Amen."

Glow-in-the-Dark Modeling Clay

Let your parents help you make this recipe.

Supplies: bowl, large spoon, parchment paper, plastic wrap

Ingredients

- 3 cups flour
- 1 cup salt
- 2 teaspoons oil
- 2 teaspoons cream of tartar
- 2 cups boiling water
- 6 ounces glow-in-the-dark paint in the color of your choice

Directions

1. Mix the flour, salt, oil, and cream of tartar together in a bowl.

2. Add the boiling water and mix well.

3. When the mixture has cooled to the touch, turn the clay out onto the parchment paper and knead until the clay is smooth. Add the glow-in-the-dark paint, and continue kneading until it is mixed throughout.

4. Return the clay to a bowl and cover it with plastic wrap. Place it in a well-lighted area to activate the glow-in-the-dark paint.

Tips: *The paint can be purchased in two-ounce bottles at arts and crafts stores; keep the clay in an airtight container so it will last a few weeks.*

What God Created

Scripture:

Psalm 139

John 1:1

Psalm 8:1a, 3-5

Genesis 1:28

We are wonderfully made. How do we know? The very first book in the Old Testament, Genesis, has a story about how God created every part of this world. After creating humanity, God looked at all of Creation and said it is "supremely good" (Genesis 1:31). We are supremely good!

As we grow, our bodies change. That's part of God's "supremely good" plan. We get taller, our hands and feet get bigger, and our brains learn more difficult skills. Some tasks, such as tying our shoes and getting dressed, now seem super easy, but they were difficult 5 or 10 years ago.

During puberty, our bodies transition from childhood to adulthood. Our bodies might start to look or feel different than we're used to. This is normal; this is part of growing up. As our bodies change and as we grow, we learn how to move, play, and live in the bodies that God has given us.

Sometimes it feels like our bodies don't cooperate. Sometimes we might not feel good about the bodies God gave us. Sometimes we are not as fast as our friends, or maybe we are not as good at math as another student in our class. However, Scripture reminds us that no matter who we are, no matter what we are good at or what we struggle to do, we are "supremely good." We can celebrate what God has given us, and use our bodies to share God's love with others.

The good news is that we do not have to do this hard work by ourselves. God is with us. Psalm 139:1 says:

"LORD, you have examined me. You know me."

God knows us. From the very beginning, God is with us and loves us. Some Christian traditions refer to this truth as **prevenient grace.** Prevenient grace reminds us that there was never a time when we weren't loved by God. Psalm 139:13 describes it this way:

"[God] created my innermost parts; [God] knit me together while I was still in my mother's womb."

Look in the mirror and find something to celebrate. Maybe you like your new haircut or the color of your eyes. Maybe your big hands help you to catch a basketball or your long fingers help you to play more difficult pieces on the piano. As you look in the mirror, what do you see that you're thankful for? Take time to thank God for making you "supremely good." At night, or when you wake up in the morning, read Psalm 139. Think about how it feels to know that God is with you, and that God loves you.

No two people are exactly alike, but we share some similarities. Every person's sex organs may look slightly different, but they are also similar to other people's.

Before we go further into this information, let's take a minute to think about how it feels to be talking about sex, body parts, and so on. When someone is talking about sex or you see a couple kissing, how do you feel?

Draw a picture of how you react or what face you make when you hear someone talk about sexuality.

Sometimes, when we hear people mention body parts, we giggle, feel our face flush, or feel awkward. As you read this chapter, you may feel awkward, uncomfortable, or even embarrassed. That's all normal. If you find yourself feeling this way, it can help to pause and take a few deep breaths. Giggling a little can help us get over being uncomfortable. And by all means, feel free to look away from illustrations if you feel really awkward, and return to them later when you feel ready. They'll still be here!

Though you may feel a little uncomfortable, remember that God created all of us, wonderfully. That includes all of our body parts. God made us in the image of God. From Psalm 139:14-15,

"I give thanks to you that I was marvelously set apart. Your works are wonderful—I know that very well. My bones weren't hidden from you when I was being put together in a secret place, when I was being woven together in the deep parts of the earth."

How does it feel to know that every part of your body is wonderfully made?

God made sex as a gift for us to enjoy and share. This gift needs to be shared wisely and is best shared as an adult. Choosing to wait to have sex is called **abstinence.**

Sex is not just a physical action; it is spiritual. God created sex, and created you to be in healthy, loving relationships. The gift of sex is best shared in an emotionally intimate, healthy relationship between adults. Waiting to share the gift of sex until you are in a committed relationship like marriage gives your body, mind, and spirit time to grow and mature. Then you may be ready for the intimacy and responsibility that comes with sex.

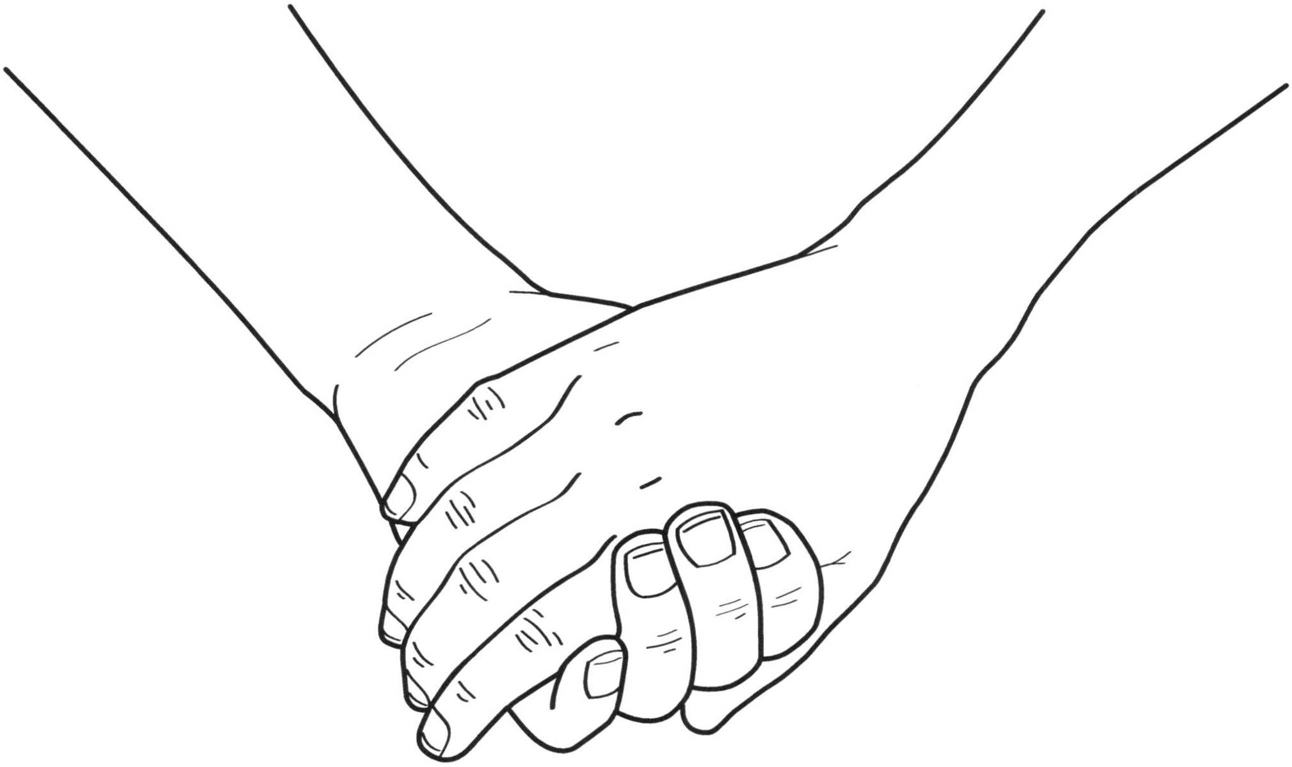

How do you feel about sex being a gift from God?

Our Sexual Identity: "Who We Are" in Our Sexuality

In the news, in our communities, and on the Internet, people often talk about the aspect of sexuality that deals with "who we are," that is, our gender identity and sexual orientation.

One thing that makes this area complicated is that health experts have come to understand that many of the words and categories we have used historically, such as *male, female, boy,* and *girl* are not as simple as they seem. Following are some definitions to guide you.

Sex and Gender Identity

A person's **sex** refers primarily to biological features, such as genitals, reproductive organs, genes, and hormones. Typically, the term *female* refers to bodies that have a uterus, ovaries, vagina, vulva, and a higher dose of a hormone called estrogen. Typically, the word *male* refers to bodies with a penis, scrotum, testicles, and a higher dose of a hormone called testosterone. The term *intersex* refers to bodies that have some male and some female biological characteristics. Though the term is relatively new, we know that there have always been intersex people.

The term **gender** refers to the behaviors, traits, and characteristics typically associated with one sex. The term **gender identity** describes our deep sense of our own gender. The words *boy, man, girl,* and *woman* are used by many people to describe their gender identity. A person's gender identity often aligns with the biological sex they were assigned at birth. That is, a person with male biological features will typically feel like a boy, and a person with female biological features will often feel like a girl. When a person's gender identity matches their biological features, they are **cisgender.**

There are some people whose gender identity doesn't match the biological features of their body. People whose gender identity differs from the biological sex they were assigned at birth are **transgender** or **trans.** A transgender man might have a vagina, uterus, and ovaries, but know deep down he is a man. A transgender woman might have a penis and testicles, but know herself to be a woman.

Some people don't identify strongly with either gender. They feel themselves to be both or neither gender. Sometimes people who feel this way refer to themselves as **gender fluid, gender non-conforming, or genderqueer.**

Whether a person is cisgender, transgender, gender fluid, gender non-conforming, or genderqueer, people may express themselves in a variety of ways. There's no one way to dress, talk, or behave in order to express your particular gender.

Sexual Orientation

Another aspect of "who we are" when it comes to our sexuality has to do with who we tend to be attracted to as we develop romantic and sexual feelings. This is called **sexual orientation.** Following are some of the labels people use to describe their sexual orientation.

Heterosexual (or straight) refers to people who are attracted to people of the other gender; for example: men who are attracted to women, and women who are attracted to men.

Homosexual (or gay or lesbian) refers to people who are attracted to people of the same gender, for example, men who are attracted to men *(gay)*, women who are attracted to women *(lesbian)*. The term "gay" can refer to both men and women. The word "lesbian" always refers to women. The word "homosexual" is still used by some, but historically this term was used in a negative way. So most prefer other terms *(gay, lesbian)*.

Bisexual refers to people who are attracted to people of multiple gender identities, such as men, women, transgender people, and/or gender fluid people.

Asexual refers to people who do not experience sexual attraction in the way most others describe it.

Discussion and Disagreement

There is a long history in our faith, and in society, to think about sex and gender as two categories, male and female. At the same time, there have always been people who don't fit into these categories. Christians are called by God to love all of God's children and welcome everyone with dignity and respect.

Regardless of one's opinions about these categories, God commands us to be kind to one another. This means that we do not insult, tease, or do anything to hurt someone physically or emotionally. If we see someone being treated badly by others, we should do what we can to help that person.

Which of these terms have you already heard? Which were new to you? What questions do you have about sex, gender identity, and sexual orientation?

Bodies

What are our body parts? What makes bodies male or female?

Every body has: genitals, pubic hair, an anus, a urethral opening, a shaft, a glans, a mons, skin, a brain, breasts, and nipples. What are these parts?

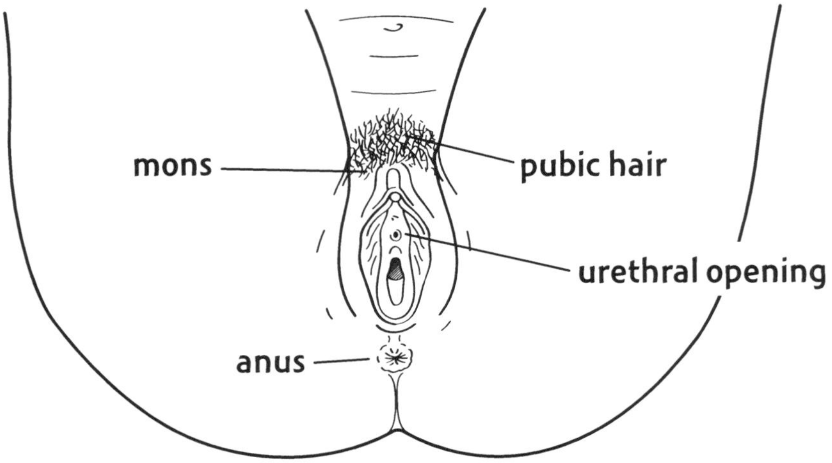

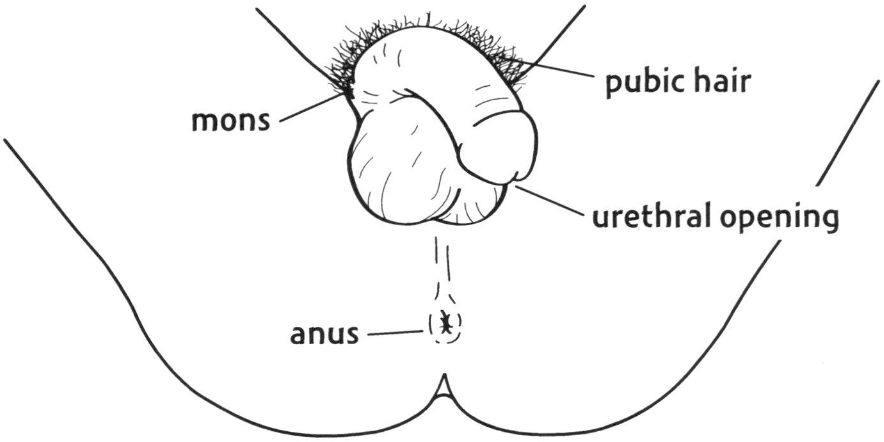

Pubic hair is hair that covers the genital area. Pubic hair is usually dark and curly. It protects and keeps the area clean. Pubic hair is a little like nose hair. Without nose hair, much more dirt would get into your lungs and make you sick. Pubic hair protects your genital area like nose hair protects your lungs. Pubic hair usually grows around the whole genital area.

The **mons** area is a mound of skin just under the pubic hair along the pubic bone for both male and female. The mons releases hormones, or chemicals, which are important for sexual attraction.

The **anus** is the opening for solid waste, or feces, to leave the body. The **urethral opening** is where the liquid waste, or urine, comes out. Both of these openings are important for all bodies. The urethral opening connects to the bladder by the urethra.

All bodies have a cylinder-shaped organ called a **shaft.** For typical male bodies, the shaft is the **penis;** for typical female bodies, the shaft is the **clitoris.** The **glans** is the tip of the shaft. On male bodies, the glans is at the top of the penis and looks like a hat; on female bodies, the glans is like a small ball attached to the tip of the clitoris.

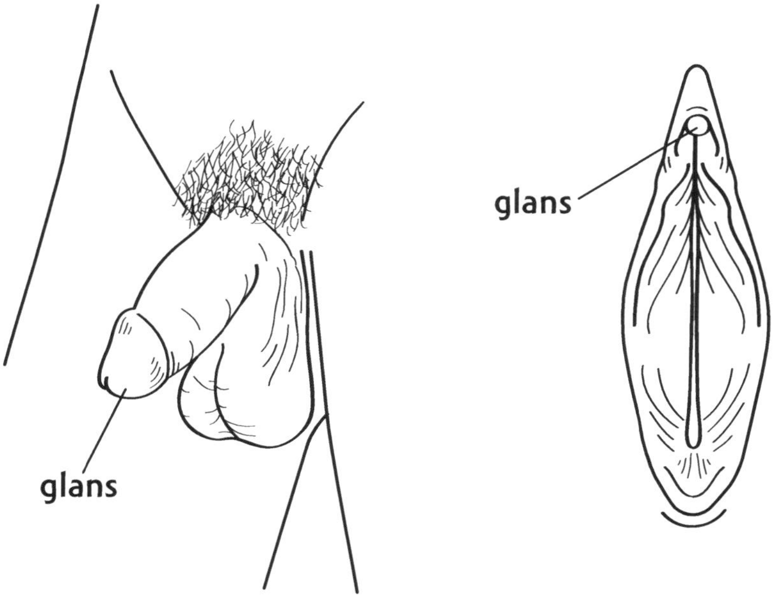

All bodies have **erections.** An erection is when the tissue of the shaft *(the penis or the clitoris)* fills with blood during arousal. **Arousal** is a state of strong sexual stimulation. When the shaft fills with blood, it becomes larger, firmer, and erect. When the shaft is not aroused, it is not erect. A shaft that is not erect is called **flaccid.**

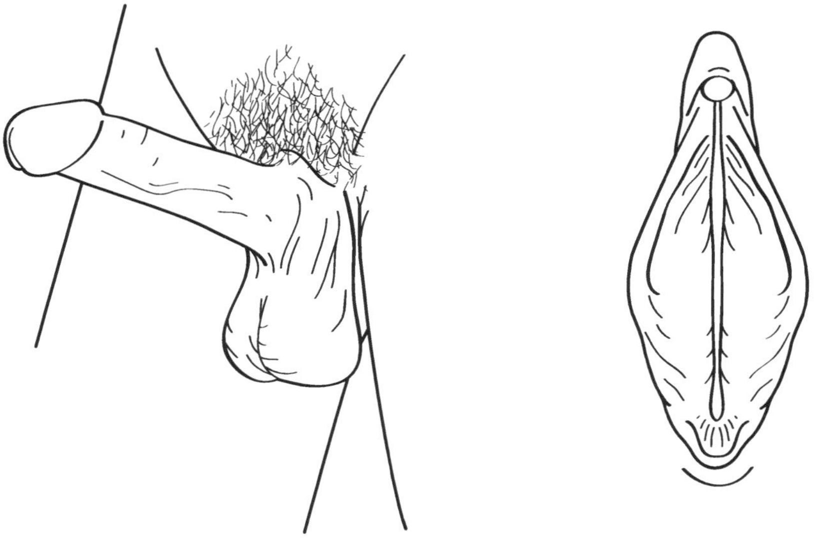

Both female and male bodies experience orgasm. During sexual touch, blood vessels in the genital area swell and become more sensitive. There are fluids present in and around the vagina and the penis. If sexual arousal continues, orgasm can occur. **Orgasm** is the muscular contractions or quick, pleasurable squeezing sensations that occur at the peak of sexual excitement. Both female and male bodies can enjoy the experience of sexual touch.

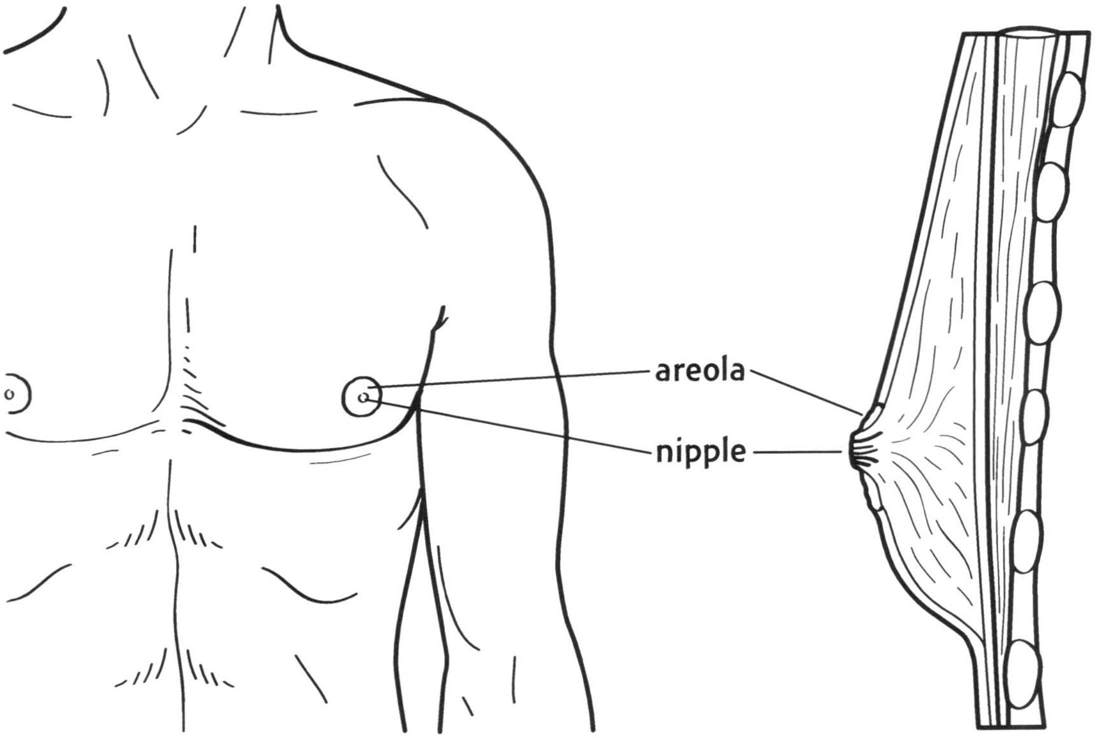

All bodies have **breasts** and **nipples.** Yes, you read that correctly. Surrounding the nipple is a circular area of skin called the **areola.** The areola is usually darker and thicker than the rest of the breast. Female breasts and nipples are typically able to lactate, or provide milk for a baby. We'll talk more about breasts when we talk about the female body.

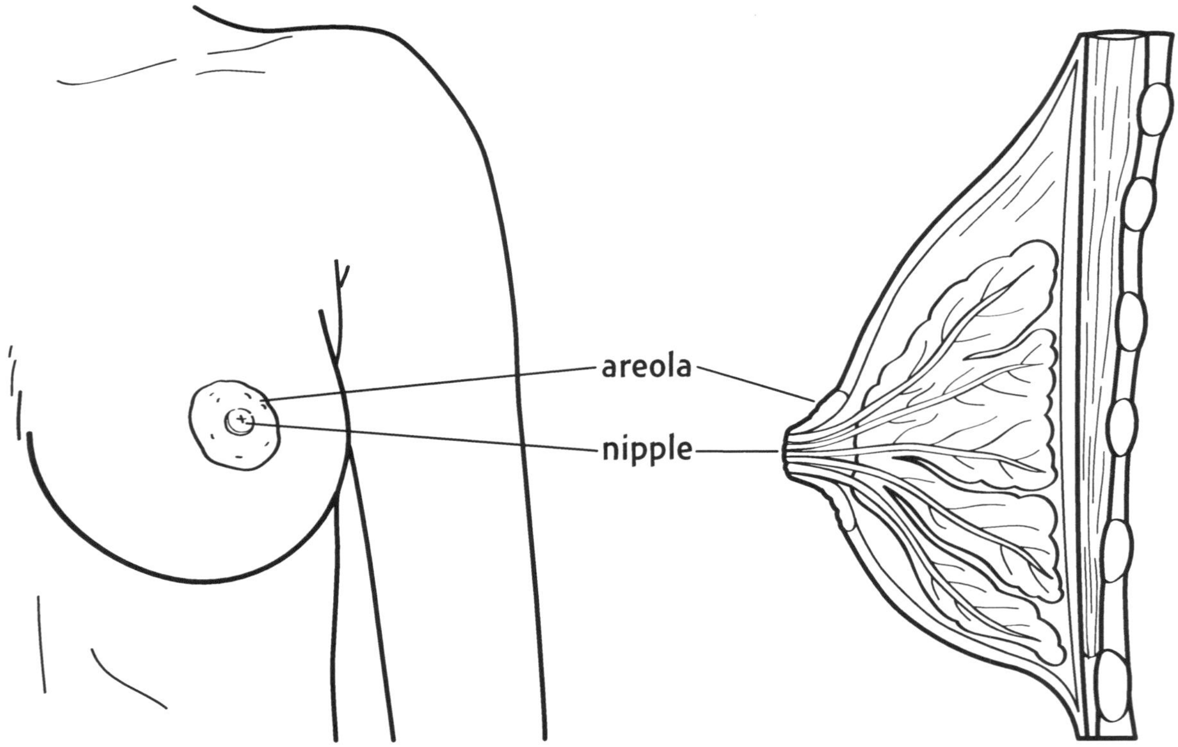

Everyone with breasts, whether male or female, should practice breast self-examination. To perform a breast self-examination, touch your breasts all over while lying down and standing up. Check the way the breasts feel and look. If you feel a knot or lump, or the breast has a very different appearance, talk with your parents or doctor.

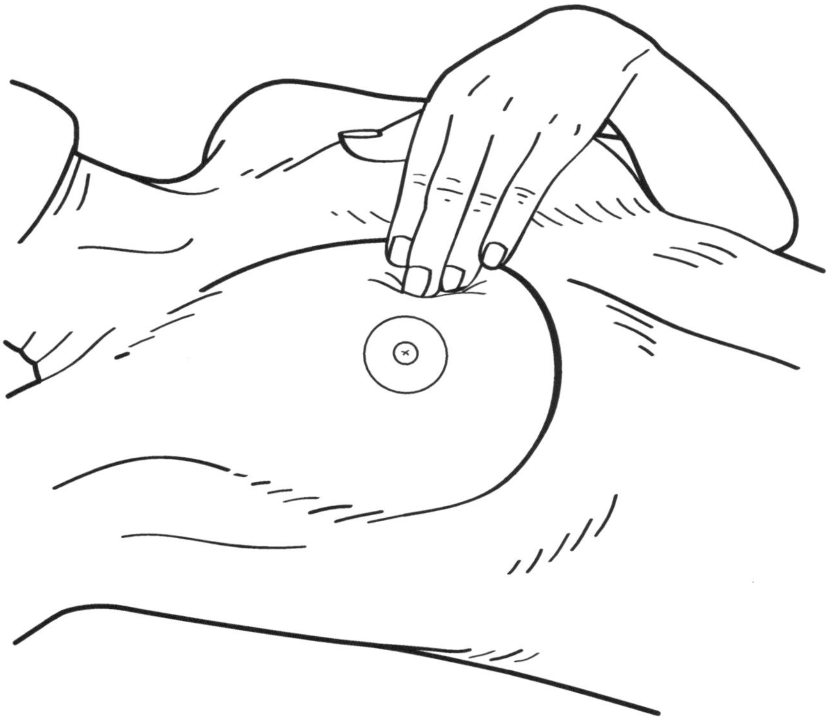

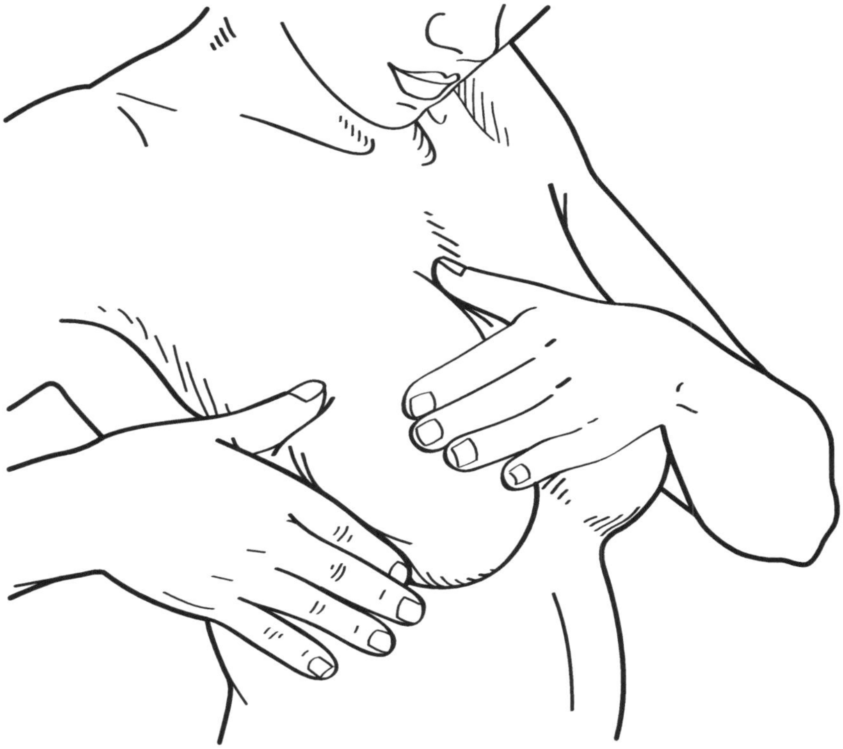

The largest sex organ in a body is the skin. The skin is sensitive and reacts to touch. For all bodies, the skin becomes more sensitive to touch during arousal.

Another very large sexual organ is the brain. Emotions begin in the brain. Emotional connections are very important for a positive sexual experience. Your brain also controls your senses, such as smell, and your nerve endings, which respond to touch. Your brain helps you understand what is good touch and what is bad touch, what is safe, and what is enjoyable. Your brain gives you the ability to express your feelings and communicate with your sexual partner.

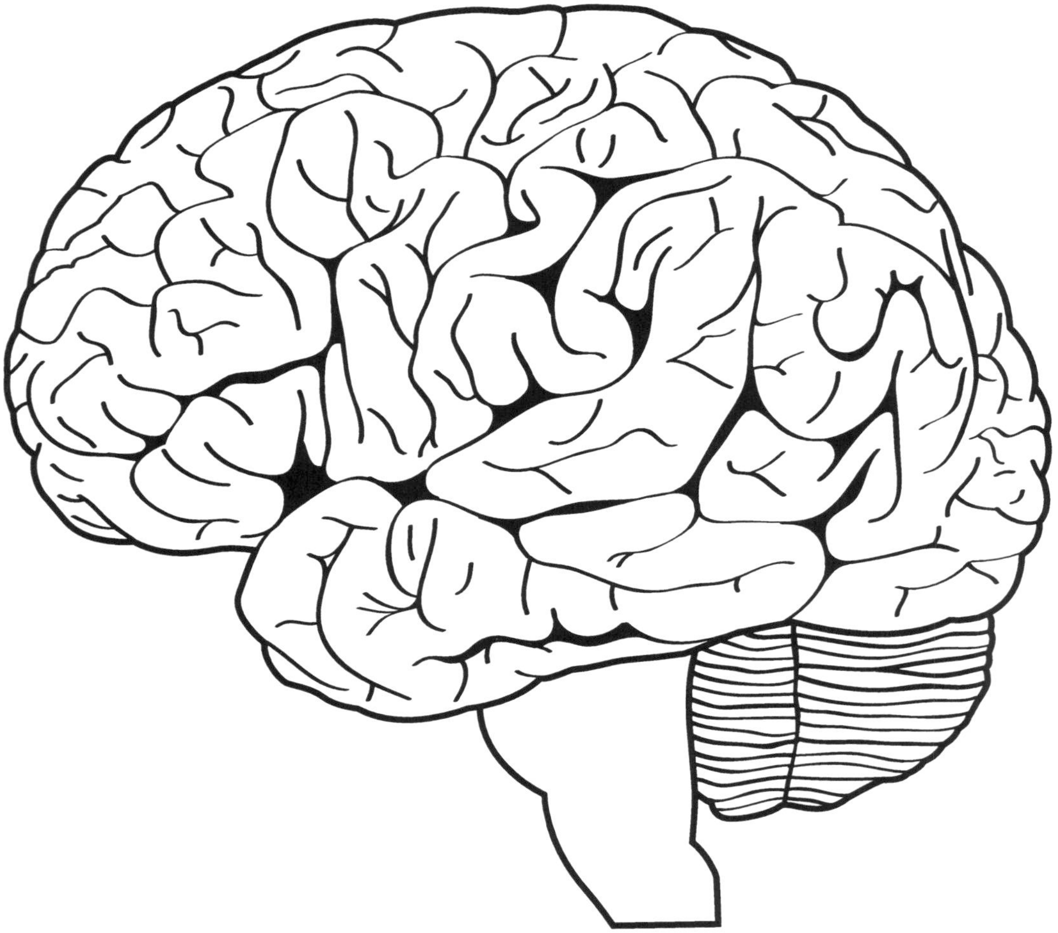

This is a lot of information. What questions do you have? Below is a place for you to write your questions and draw a picture of how you are feeling after learning about these body parts.

Male Bodies

Let's talk about bodies that have male biological features.

The picture below shows male genitals. Pubic hair grows above the penis, and covers the mons, the scrotum, and the area around the anus.

The penis is the male shaft. It has a tip called the glans. At the tip of the glans is the urethral opening. This opening is where urine and **semen** come out of the body. The male genital area has two openings: the anus and the urethral opening.

The penis is made up of nerves and tissue that fill with blood during sexual arousal. Most of the time, the penis is in the limp or flaccid state. When it's flaccid, the penis rests in front of the body. During arousal, the penis becomes **erect** or stiff because the tissue and vessels have filled with blood. The penis grows longer and becomes more sensitive than usual. When the penis is erect, it is "hard." In this case, the word *hard* means "stiff or unbending." It does not mean hard like concrete.

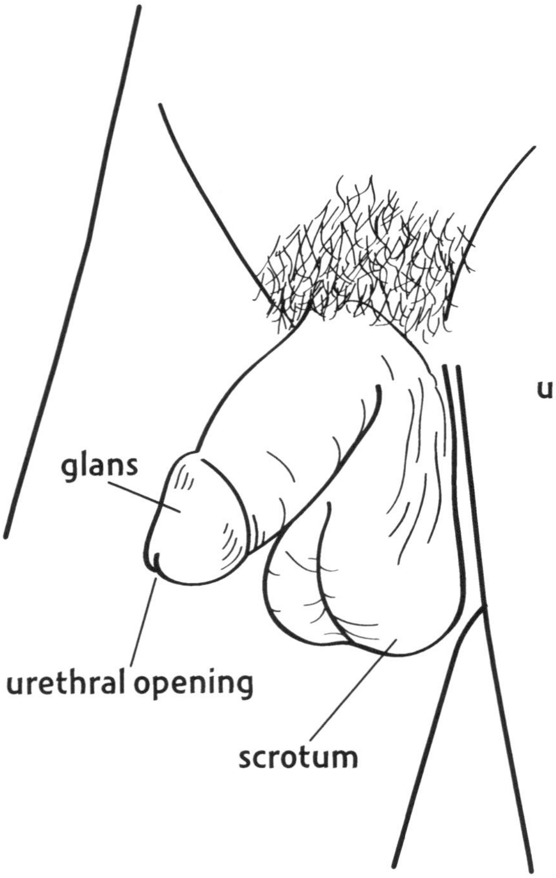

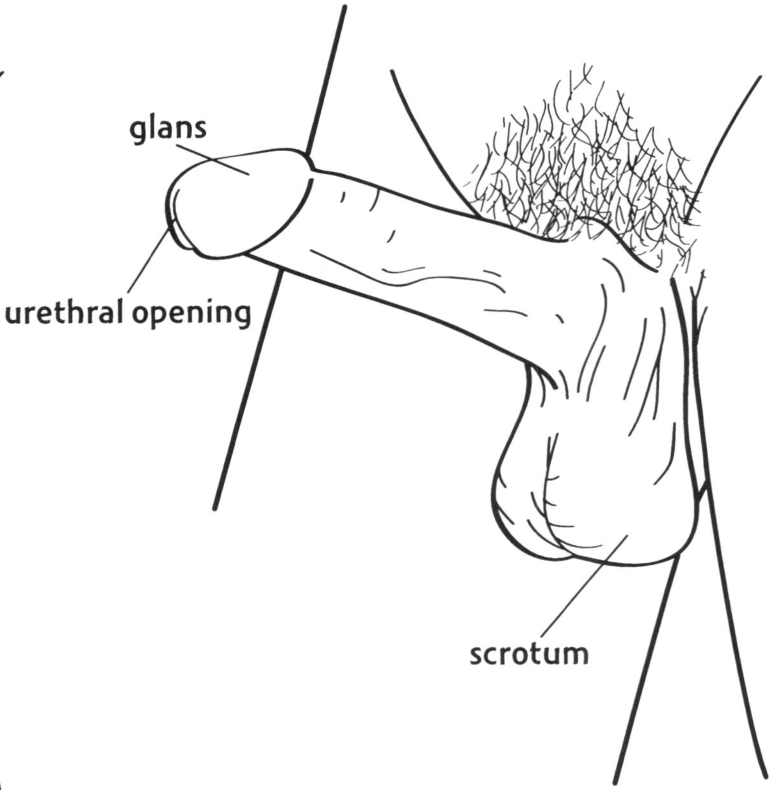

At birth, there is a skin covering the glans of the penis. This skin is called the **foreskin.** For many in the United States, the foreskin is removed a few days after the baby is born. The removal of the foreskin is called **circumcision.** In the United States, about 60-70 percent of newborn males are circumcised; around the world, around 20 percent have the procedure performed.

Throughout the Bible, there are references to circumcision. The Hebrew people used circumcision as a sign that they were God's people. Check out Genesis 17:9-11. In the New Testament, the apostle Paul said circumcision was not necessary to be a child of God. Read Colossians 3:10-11 to see how God loves all people. Today parents are able to choose whether or not to circumcise their newborn babies.

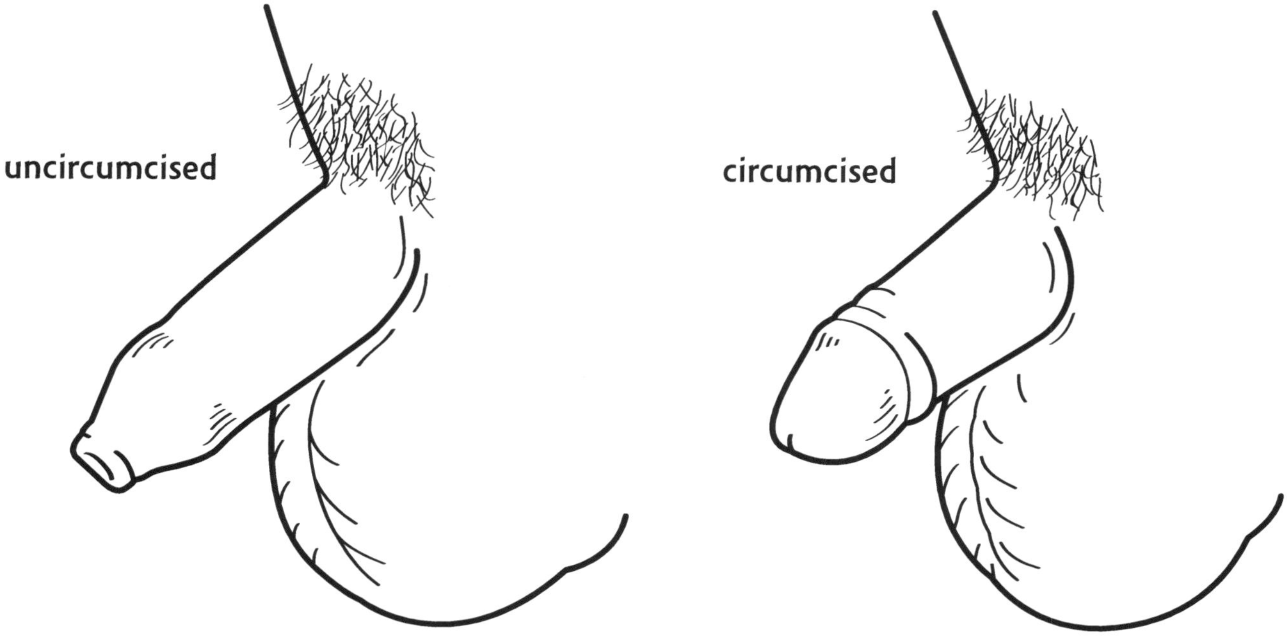

Some people worry that it's more difficult to keep an uncircumcised *(or **intact**)* penis clean and healthy, and wonder if special care is needed. Early in life, the foreskin usually stays over the glans, and does not naturally pull back ***(retract)*** from the glans. During this time, washing the outside of the penis is usually enough to keep it clean. It is also important not to forcibly retract the foreskin, as it can be painful and poses some health risks. At a later age, usually during puberty, the foreskin naturally begins to retract. At this stage, pulling the foreskin back during bathing can help keep the penis clean.

Behind the penis is the area called the **scrotum,** which is a sack of skin holding the **testicles,** or **testes.** The scrotum is small during childhood, and grows larger through puberty. As an adult, the scrotum is usually about the size of a pear. There are typically two testicles, which sit side by side in the scrotum. They are usually about the size of walnuts, and one is typically larger than the other. The testicles produce the male reproductive cells, **sperm.** At birth, the testicles do not produce sperm. The testicles begin making sperm during puberty, and continue to produce sperm until death.

Because sperm are very sensitive to temperature, the testicles hang below the body inside the scrotum. This allows the testicles to move toward and away from the heat of the body, so that the sperm stays at a comfortable temperature.

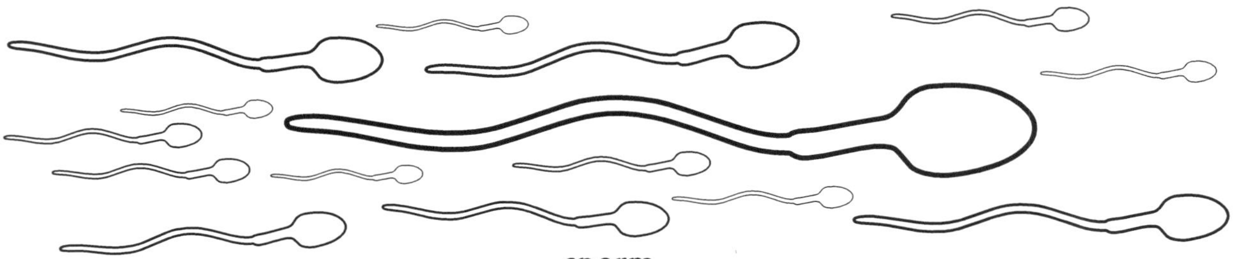

sperm

It is important to examine the testicles regularly, through **testicular self-examinations.** Testicular cancer is not very common, but those who have it are most commonly between the age of 15 to about 35. So it is good to begin self-examinations at a young age. Testicles tend to feel like ripe grapes. Examining the testicles on a regular basis makes it easier to notice changes. If the testicles feel different than normal, like a hard rock inside the scrotum area, or if they look different than usual, then it is important to tell your parents or your doctor.

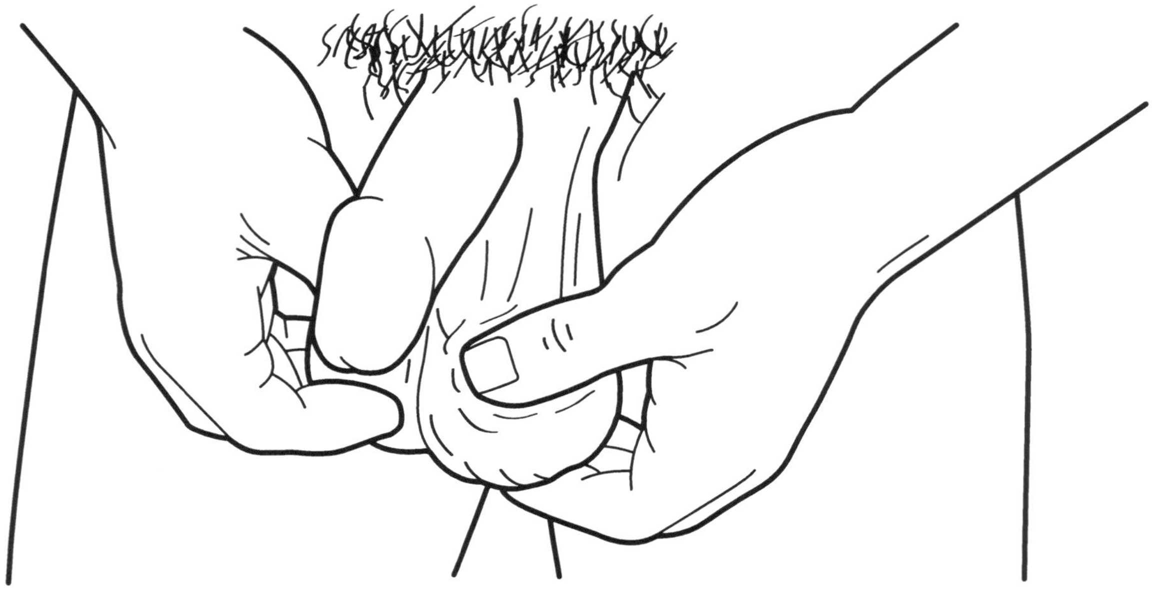

On the back side of each testicle is a coil of tiny tubes, called the **epididymis,** which will store the sperm for approximately 8 days while they mature. After about 8 days, if the sperm are not **ejaculated,** they are absorbed into the body while the testicles continue to make more sperm. Sperm is constantly produced. A sperm cell is very small. About 500,000 sperm could probably fit on the tip of a very sharp pencil.

When a male body becomes aroused, the sperm stored in the epididymis travel up a tube called the **vas deferens.** The vas deferens carries the sperm from the epididymis into the body and through two types of glands, which provide liquid that helps keep the sperm living and moving. The first type of glands are **seminal vesicles,** attached to the back of the bladder, which provide a clear, sugar-rich and sticky fluid. The second type of gland is the **prostate,** a very sensitive, walnut-sized gland that encircles the vas deferens where it attaches to the urethra. The liquid from the seminal vesicles and prostate gland, together with the sperm, is called **semen.**

During arousal and before ejaculation, a male body may produce a clear fluid called **pre-ejaculate/pre-cum.** This fluid lubricates the penis and neutralizes any acid present in the urethra. Not all male bodies produce pre-cum. The pre-cum may or may not have sperm present; if the person has an STI, the virus or bacteria may be present in the pre-cum.

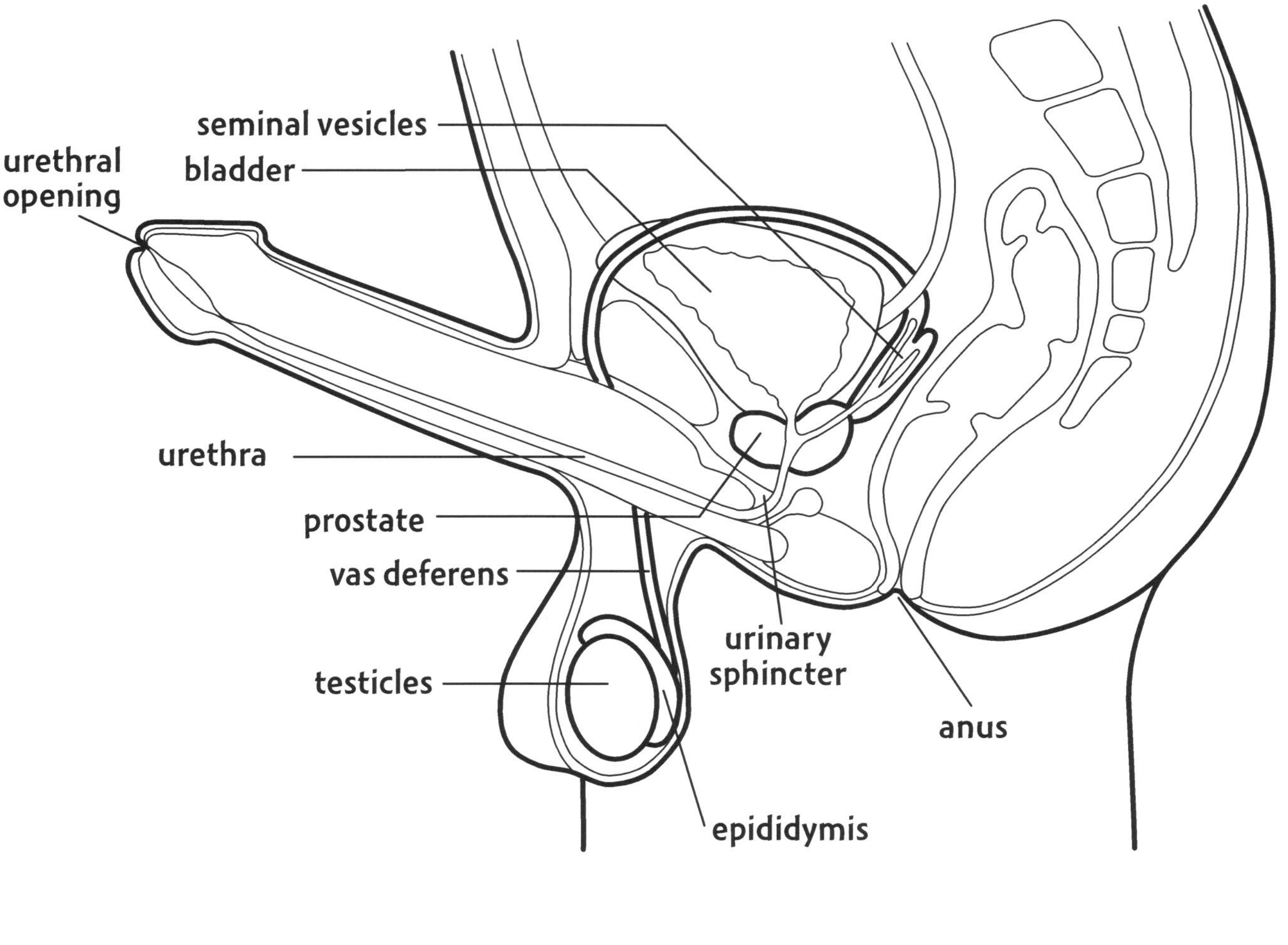

During ejaculation, muscles at the base of the penis push the semen out through the urethra, and through the opening of the penis. There can be as many as 130 million sperm present in an ejaculation.

You may recall that the urethra is used for carrying two things from the body: semen and urine. Beyond the point where the vas deferens joins the urethra, the urethra continues upward to attach to the bladder, where urine is stored. At the top of the urethral tube is a muscular gate called the **urinary sphincter.** This closes off the bladder from the urethral tube during arousal and ejaculation so that the sperm doesn't come into contact with urine, which can kill sperm cells.

This is a lot of information at one time. It's OK if you cannot remember all of this information. What questions do you have? The box below is a place where you may write any questions you may have.

Female Bodies

Now let's talk about bodies with female biological features.

The female **breasts** have **glands** that make milk to feed a baby. The glands have ducts that carry the milk to the **nipple** to feed the baby. During puberty, the breasts begin to grow. As they grow, they sometimes feel tender and sore. They change in both size and shape. Sometimes one breast is a little different in size from the other. There is not one perfect size for breasts.

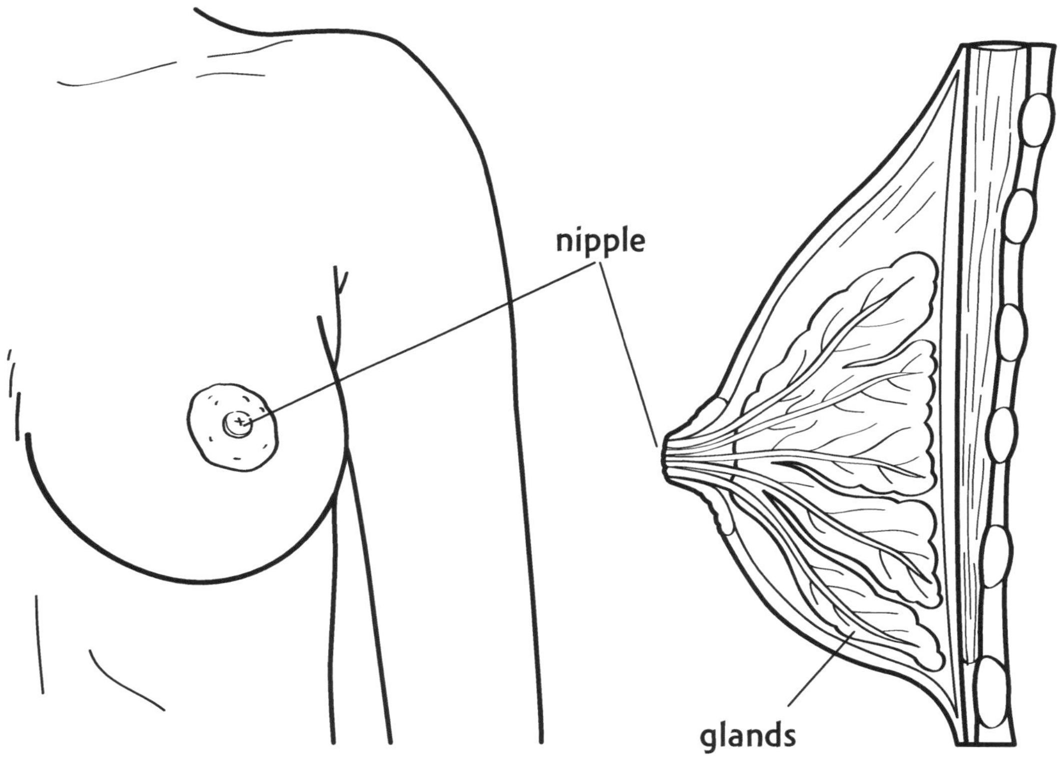

During puberty, the pubic hair of female bodies grows around the mons and the **labia.** The genital area of female bodies has several layers of sensitive tissue. There are two lips that surround the genital area called the labia. There are larger lips and smaller lips: the major and minor labia. The area surrounding the labia is called the **vulva.** The vulva and the labia are made of tissue and vessels that fill with blood during sexual arousal. Inside the labia is the urethral opening, which is a very tiny opening for urine. Just above the urethral opening is the clitoris. The clitoris is a small shaft that has a ball-like glans at the top. The only purpose of the clitoris is for pleasure. The clitoris is a very sensitive organ that becomes erect when aroused. When the clitoris becomes erect, it fills with blood and becomes very sensitive to touch. This erection may or may not be visible.

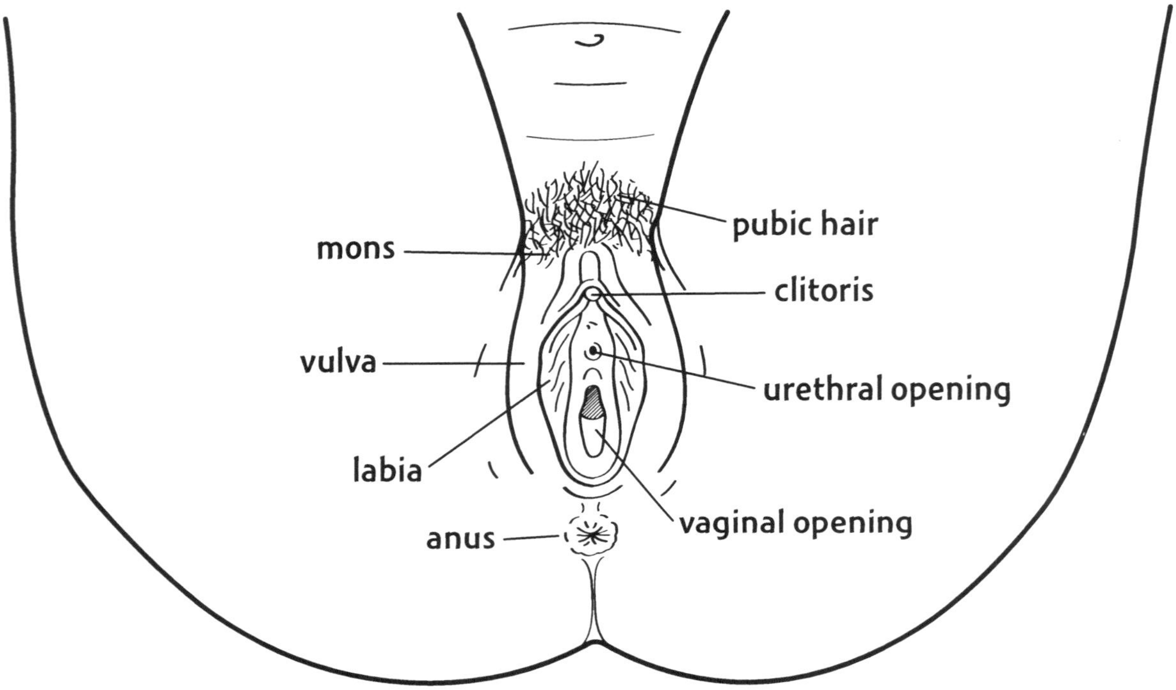

Below the urethral opening is the **vaginal opening.** The vaginal opening leads into the **vagina,** which is the beginning of the internal female sex organs. At birth, the vaginal opening might be slightly covered by a thin membrane or skin covering called the **hymen.** The hymen only partially covers the vaginal opening and is not a barrier into the vagina. The hymen usually dissolves or is slightly torn during childhood, and some female bodies don't have them at all.

The vagina is a muscular tube-like organ. The vagina is only about 3 inches long. The vagina regularly releases some fluid to keep the area clean and moist. During sexual intercourse and childbirth, the vagina can extend and lift up to be longer. The walls of the vagina rest together like a closed umbrella when there is nothing inside the vagina. When something is placed inside the vagina, the walls stretch to fit. Also, when a baby is born, the vagina walls stretch so that the baby can be pushed out.

At the top of the vagina is a circular, ring-shaped organ called the **cervix.** The cervix is the entrance into the **uterus,** where a fetus can grow. The cervix typically stays closed so that only sperm can enter, about .8 centimeters in diameter, which is about the size of a pencil point. During childbirth, if a baby is to be delivered through the vagina, the cervix usually stretches to approximately 10 centimeters in diameter so that the baby can move from the uterus to the vagina to the outside world.

Above the cervix is the uterus. The uterus is a pear-shaped, muscular organ that is only about 8 centimeters or 3 inches long. It is a small organ that will stretch to fit if a fetus is developing inside. After the birth of a baby, the uterus will return to a smaller size.

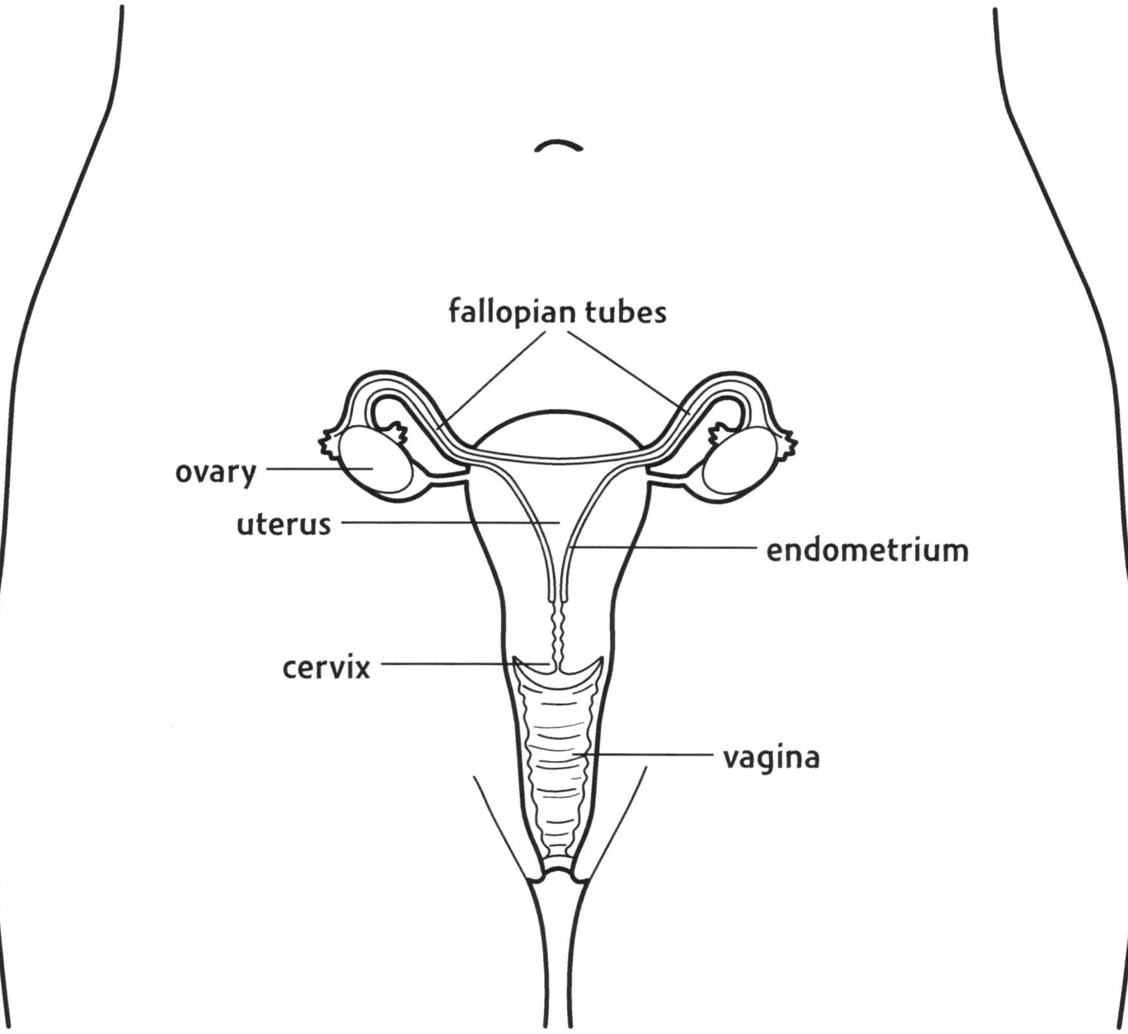

The uterus has a lining called the **endometrium.** During puberty, the endometrial tissue begins filling with blood each month to provide for a fetus if pregnancy occurs. If pregnancy does not occur, the endometrium will **slough off,** or separate from the uterus and fall away. The endometrium is slowly discarded by the body through the cervix and the vagina. This process is called menstruation or a period. A period typically lasts between 4 and 7 days; some periods may be fewer than 4 days, and some more than 7.

At the top of the uterus are two tubes that go off to the right and left. These tubes are called the **fallopian tubes.** The fallopian tubes have tiny hairs called **cilia** inside. The cilia help to move the ovum, or egg, along the tube.

At the end of each fallopian tube is an almond-sized and -shaped **ovary.** The two ovaries are not attached to the tubes but are connected to the outside of the uterus. Ovaries store the female reproductive cells, **ova** or eggs.

Female bodies, at birth, already have all the eggs they will ever have. The female body typically has about one million eggs at birth. Between the age that menstruation begins and the end of menstruation, called *menopause*, a female body will only release about 500 eggs.

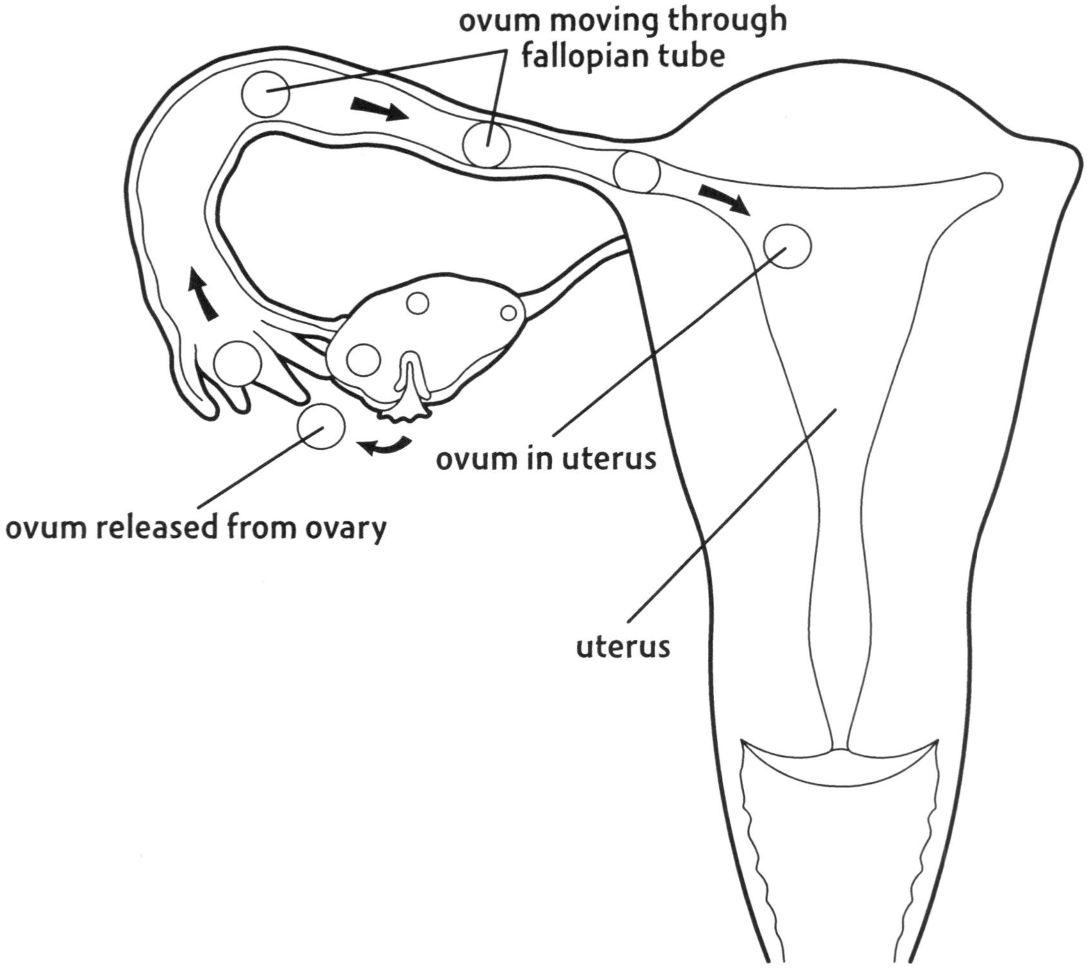

One of the major events of puberty for the female body is the beginning of the menstrual cycle. After each period, the endometrium prepares itself again for pregnancy. When the endometrium is thickened and the egg has matured, **ovulation** occurs. During ovulation, an ovary releases an egg. Ovulation occurs once during a menstrual cycle, typically every four weeks. It varies from person to person, and can vary at different times in a person's life. Before ovulation, the egg matures in a small sac called the *ovarian follicle*. When the egg is mature, the ovarian follicle bursts and releases the egg into the fallopian tubes. The cilia at the end of the fallopian tubes pull the ovum into the tube to make its way toward the uterus.

If the ovum encounters a sperm and pulls that sperm into itself, **conception** or **fertilization** occurs. If the ovum is not fertilized, it moves into the uterus and is sloughed off with the endometrium during the period.

This has been an important module. You have heard all about how God created you wonderfully. Take a deep breath. Remember, your parents or guardians know all of this information. You can ask them any questions.

It is time to take a few quiet minutes to think about all you have learned. Following are the directions for GLOWS. This might be a good time to invite your parents to join you. You can sit quietly with them or you can ask questions. Prepare your heart and mind for GLOWS.

GLOWS

As your body grows and changes, remember that God loves you, God is with you, and you are supremely good. If this is hard to hear or to believe, talk to your parent, an adult mentor, your small group leader, your pastor, or another adult you trust. Ask them to share with you the gifts they see in you. Ask them to help you see and celebrate your goodness.

Connect with **G**od. Light a candle, or use glow-in-the-dark modeling clay, and say:

"God, you know me! I am wonderfully made! I come to you with an open mind and an open heart as I listen for what you might say to me today."

Listen. Take time to read a section in this book or one of the suggested Bible verses from the beginning of the module.

Open your heart. In silence or with quiet music playing, think about what you read or heard. There are many ways to process what you are learning. You might choose to journal, draw, or create something with clay. Take time to write down questions or insights you have as you ponder what you have heard.

Wonder. Consider writing in a journal or notebook your responses to the following questions:

What did I learn in this chapter?

What did I already know?

What was difficult to read or see?

What gifts has God given me?

What questions do I have?

Steps. Record what steps you want to take in response to all you have experienced in this time of prayer.

Closing Prayer.

"God, I praise you, for I am wonderfully made. Thank you for being with me as I change and grow. Amen."

Spiritual Discipline: Prayer

Prayer is one way we can connect to God. Through prayer, we acknowledge that God is with us and that God is listening to us. You might choose to read Scripture (Psalm 139 or John 1), then sit silently as you ponder what you read. Or you might choose to say a breath prayer, repeating a few words over and over again as you breathe:

(Breathe in): *God created me. God loves me.*

(Breathe out): *I am supremely good.*

Prayer is simply communication between us and God. There is not a one-size-fits-all way of praying. Our bodies are great tools for prayer. Here's a body prayer for you to try:

Take in a deep breath and say:
Thank you, God, for my body.
Thank you for my fingers, hands, and arms.
Thank you for my toes, feet, and legs.

Take another deep breath and say:
Thank you, God, for my brain, my heart, my skin, my lungs, and my stomach.
Thank you for my sexual organs. For my (name the parts that belong to you):
 breasts, nipples, vulva, labia, clitoris, vagina, ovaries, and uterus.
 breasts, nipples, penis, scrotum, and testicles.
Thank you for my eyes.
Thank you for my ears.
Thank you for my nose.
Thank you for my mouth. Thank you for my body.
Help me to remember that this is my body, your gift to me.
Help me to protect and care for my body. Amen.

You are invited to move through this body prayer three times. Each time, try something different; maybe point to each part of your body as you say it, or wiggle or move the different parts of your body. You might choose to speak the words aloud or read them quietly. How you move through this body prayer is completely up to you. See what feels right to your own body as you say these words.

A Conversation with Your Parent/Guardian

Sex may be a new topic for you to talk about. Sometimes it is very difficult to talk about sex with your parents, guardians, or other adults. You may not know what to ask or how to ask your questions. Sometimes it's just scary to begin the conversations. Did you know that sometimes your parents, guardians, and other adults feel the same way?

Here are some questions for you to ask your parents, guardians, or other important adults in your life. Find a comfortable, private place to talk in which you won't be interrupted. Take your time and know that even if both of you are uncomfortable at first, you will grow to respect and trust each other.

Questions:

1. How did you feel when you first met me?

2. How have I changed in the last year?

3. What do you remember about going through puberty?

4. What do you want me to know about puberty?

5. How can I let you know when I need to talk about growing up?

Puberty and Growing Up

Scripture:

Luke 2:41-54

Romans 12:1-2

Just like us, Jesus grew and changed. There's one story in the Bible about Jesus as an adolescent. You can read it for yourself in Luke 2:41-52.

In this story, Jesus, a 12-year-old boy, talked with the teachers in the temple, impressing them with his wisdom. When you read this Scripture, you might forget that Jesus was just a kid in this story. Then his mom and dad showed up. Jesus' conversation with his parents reminds us that adolescents are sometimes very wise and sometimes seem to forget important things, such as telling their parents where they've gone!

Jesus knows what it's like to grow up. Jesus knows what puberty is like. We are blessed to have a God who knows us so well. God knows that puberty is not a simple, overnight experience.

Puberty happens during adolescence, the time when we transition from childhood to adulthood. During puberty, the body goes through a lot of changes. Many of those changes involve the body's sex organs, as they mature and become capable of making a baby. Each body goes through puberty at its own pace. This means that some bodies begin to look like adults very quickly and others take longer. Whatever pace a body takes through puberty is normal for that body.

The average age for female bodies to begin puberty is between 8 and 10 years old. The average age for male bodies to begin puberty is between 10 and 12 years old. Most of the time, it takes anywhere from 2-6 years to complete puberty.

Puberty starts in a tiny gland in the head. The **pituitary gland** is in the base of the brain and is about the size of a small marble. This gland tells the body to start puberty by sending out chemicals in the blood called **hormones.** Every body begins puberty on the inside before any changes show on the outside.

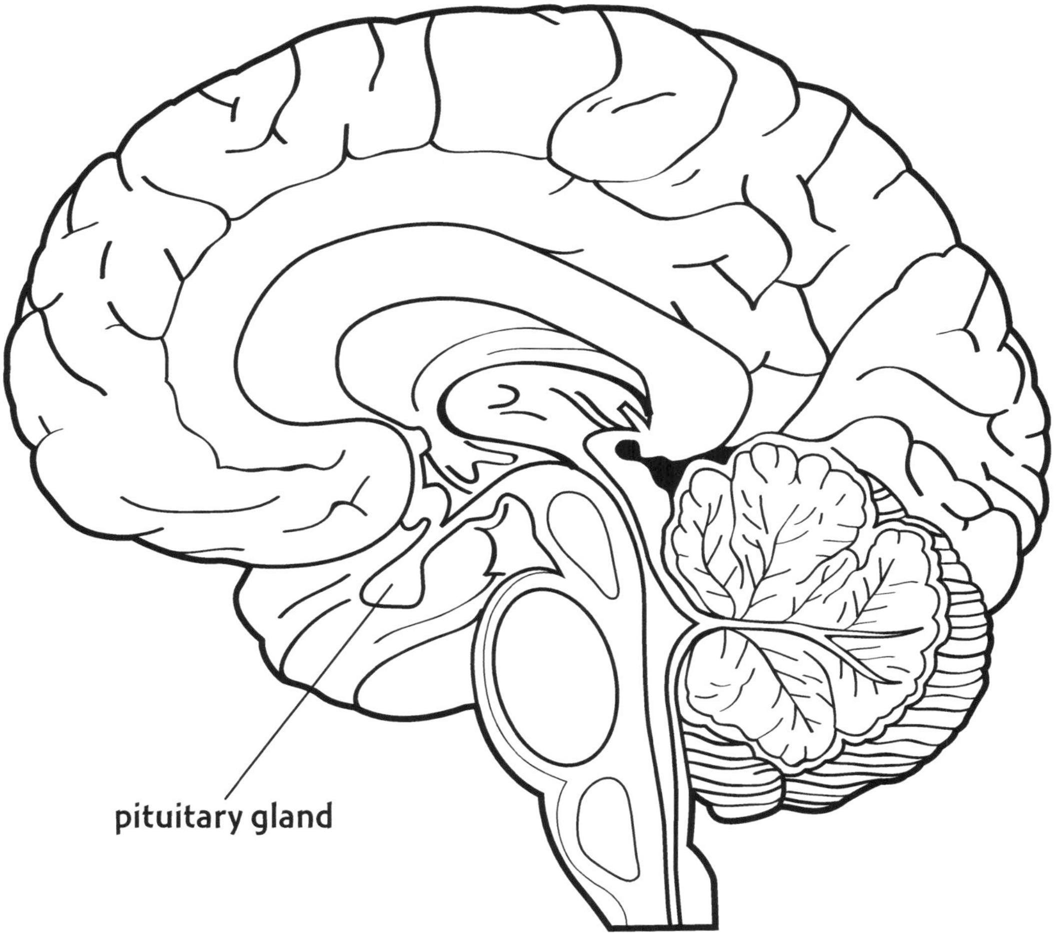

There are a couple of hormones you need to know about: **estrogen** and **testosterone.** Every body has both hormones. Typically, female bodies have more estrogen than testosterone, and male bodies have more testosterone than estrogen. These hormones are important to a healthy body. Every body needs both hormones to be healthy and to grow up.

During puberty, every body needs more sleep to have time to recover and to grow. Puberty also brings changes in emotions and attitudes. Some people experience anger or frustration. Some people cry more or laugh at inappropriate times. A lot is happening in the body, and sometimes the hard work the body is doing during puberty also can be hard for our emotions.

Many people experience **acne** during puberty. Acne is pimples, blackheads, and bumps on the skin of the face, upper back, and chest. Some acne is easily treated, and some acne needs to be treated with medications from the doctor. Acne occurs when the pores of the skin become infected due to bacteria combining with the oils produced during puberty.

During puberty, bodies need more water and, as always, good nutrition. While you may not think your body needs water, drinking water is always a good way to keep your body healthy.

During puberty, hygiene becomes more important. Teenagers need to begin taking regular baths and using deodorant. It sometimes may feel that no matter how many baths you take, your feet always smell. It's OK! This is part of growing up and going through puberty.

Puberty also is a time when bodies grow and change. The face changes shape and looks more like the face of an adult than that of a child. Hair grows in the armpits and becomes darker on the legs and arms. For some bodies, hair grows on the back and chest as well.

The body also changes shape during puberty. Some bodies grow taller and some bodies develop more curves.

During puberty, young people may **masturbate,** or touch their own genital area for sexual pleasure. Both male and female bodies can become sexually aroused through touch, and sexual arousal can lead to orgasm. Masturbation is one way young people begin to learn about their bodies. Some people masturbate and some people don't. Both choices are OK and normal. It's your body, and you get to decide what to do with it. Masturbation is a personal experience. Masturbation is something that should be done in a private place, not with other people around. Sometimes people wonder how much masturbation is too much. Most experts agree that a person should be only concerned if masturbation is interfering with other activities, such as homework, family time, or hanging out with friends, or if it causes physical discomfort or pain.

Female Bodies

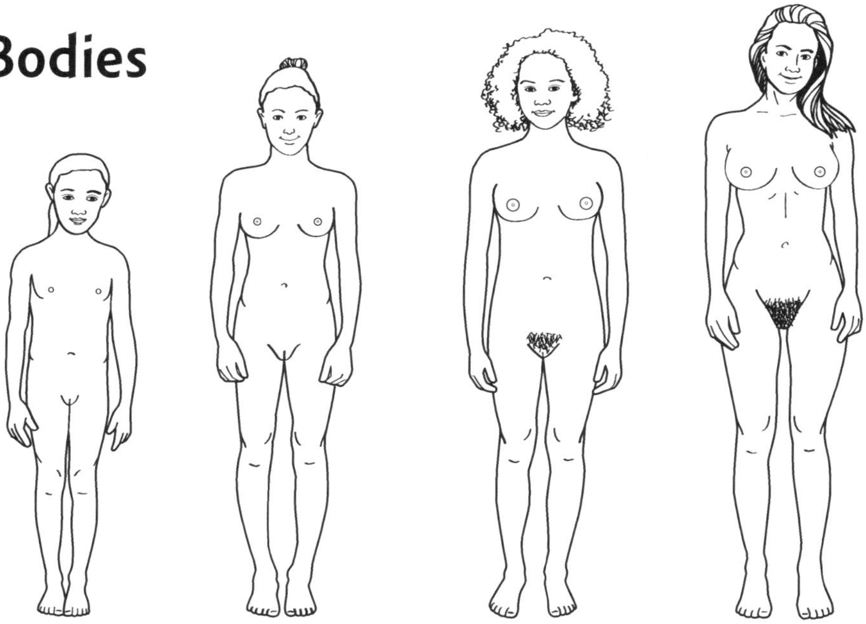

Let's talk about the changes a female body typically goes through during puberty. As the pituitary gland begins to send messages through the hormones, the ovaries grow and mature *(each ovary grows to about the size of an almond)*. While the ovaries grow in size, the eggs begin to mature as well. The uterus grows during puberty as well. The uterus doesn't change shape, but becomes slightly larger.

Early in puberty, female bodies begin to grow taller. Female bodies often experience growth spurts before male bodies of the same age. Female bodies also begin to change shape. For many, the shoulders begin to narrow, and the hips begin to widen. Wider hips are helpful if a female body carries and delivers a baby.

About a year into puberty, most female bodies begin having a menstrual cycle, which is also called having a period. The menstrual cycle is a continuous series of events that begin when an egg matures. The mature egg is released from the ovary during ovulation, and travels through the fallopian tube. If the egg does not encounter a sperm and is not fertilized, it travels into the uterus and is absorbed into the uterine lining *(the endometrium)*. The endometrium is full of blood, and if the ovum is not fertilized, the endometrium begins to slough *(pronounced "sluff")* off. The blood and the tissue flow out of the body through the vagina. This part of the cycle is called the period or menstruation.

When a female body prepares to menstruate, other changes take place as well. The body begins to hold water, which will be used if pregnancy occurs. The body may ache, and hormones may cause grumpiness or irritability. Sometimes this process is called PMS or Pre-Menstrual Syndrome. Not everyone who menstruates experiences PMS.

People who menstruate typically use hygiene products to collect the menstrual blood, such as pads, tampons, or menstrual cups. Everyone is different and will choose to use what is most comfortable for them. A pad is a cotton liner that fits in the person's underwear. A tampon or menstrual cup can be placed in the vagina to collect menstrual flow.

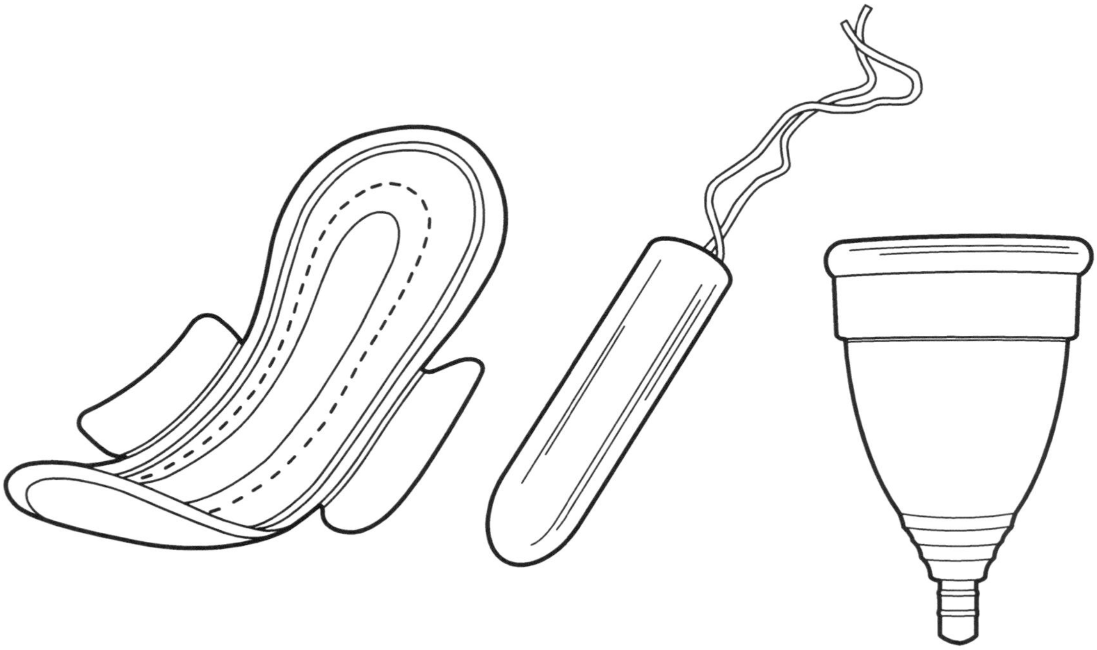

Puberty brings on the development of pubic hair. Pubic hair grows in gradually, and is often dark, curly, and coarse by the time puberty is complete. Hair also begins to grow in the armpits, and leg hair begins to darken. In the United States, some begin to shave their armpits and legs during this time. Not everyone chooses to shave; shaving is a personal choice.

The vulva and vagina grow during puberty. Additionally, the clitoris grows and becomes more sensitive to touch. Remember, the clitoris is present for pleasure only. The vagina begins to release a liquid to keep the area clean and moist. During sexual excitement, glands around the vagina also produce a fluid to lubricate the vagina.

During puberty, female breasts begin to grow. Breast growth might start with a little bud, then breasts begin to take on a more mature shape. Breasts are all different sizes and shapes. During puberty, the breasts may be more sensitive and tender. Many people begin to wear a bra during this time, though some choose not to wear one. This is a personal choice.

As female bodies change and grow, the way we see ourselves also changes. Remember, we are all wonderfully made, and greatly loved by God.

Male Bodies

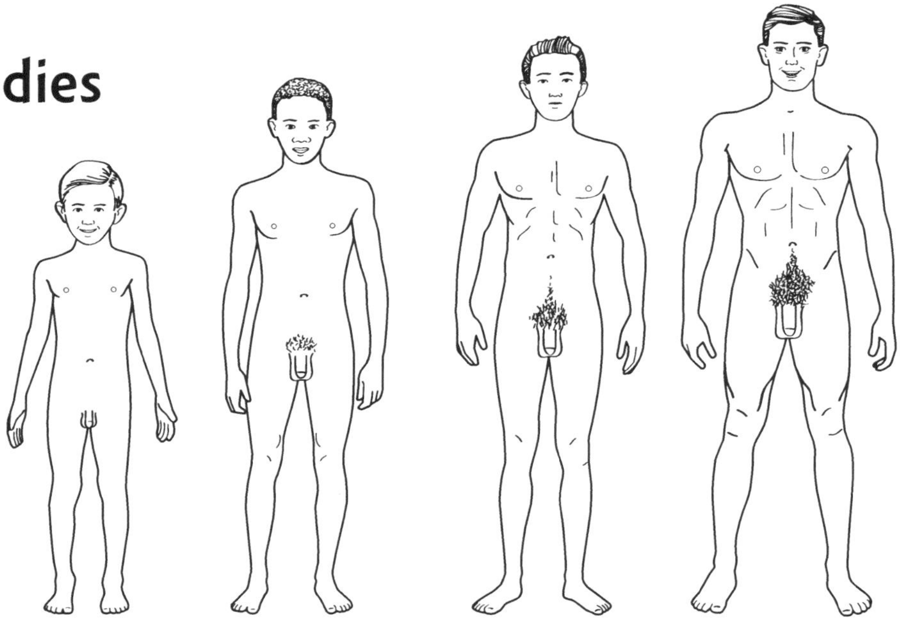

Now let's talk about the changes a male body goes through during puberty. When puberty begins, hormones direct the testicles to grow before the scrotum begins to grow. The testicles begin to produce sperm, the male reproductive cell.

During puberty, the male body often grows taller, the shoulders widen, and the hips narrow.

The penis grows during puberty to the length and width it will be at the adult stage. The average length of an adult male penis is about five inches—some are longer, some are shorter. Each male body is different, which includes the penis. If a penis isn't circumcised, the foreskin will begin to be able to retract in puberty.

The penis and scrotum area are very sensitive. During sports activities, wearing protective cups or compression shorts can help protect the penis and scrotum.

Puberty is typically the time when **ejaculations** begin. Most of the time, the first ejaculations happen as **nocturnal emissions,** or **"wet dreams."** The morning after a nocturnal emission, the bed sheets may be sticky and damp. These ejaculations may cause embarrassment, but they are completely normal.

Puberty also brings hair growth on the face, in the armpits, on the chest and back, and in the genital area. Some male bodies have lots of hair, and some have little hair. Not everyone grows hair on the chest, back, or face. The facial hair begins to get darker and become coarser. About this time, some people begin to shave their faces, if they choose.

Male bodies also have a vocal change during puberty. The change can cause the voice to crack and squeak before it settles into its new normal sound. Sometimes the voice will crack several times in just a few minutes, and sometimes it won't crack much at all. While it takes a few months for the voice to change, every body is different. After the change, the voice is usually deeper and lower in pitch than it was before.

Conception

The process of puberty allows human bodies to reproduce. When a female body ovulates, an egg is released into the fallopian tube. If there are sperm in the fallopian tube, there is an opportunity for conception.

Conception is when the egg encounters sperm, and pulls one sperm into itself. At this point, the egg and the sperm become one, creating an **embryo.** The embryo travels through the fallopian tube into the **uterus.** The embryo settles onto the endometrium, the lining of the uterus, to grow into a fetus—a term used for a baby still in the uterus or womb.

It only takes one sexual encounter, when an ovum and sperm are present, for pregnancy to happen.

When people have sex in committed relationships such as marriage, they are able to share emotional intimacy and support each other if there is a pregnancy. Sex within marriage is the best way to experience the gift of sex.

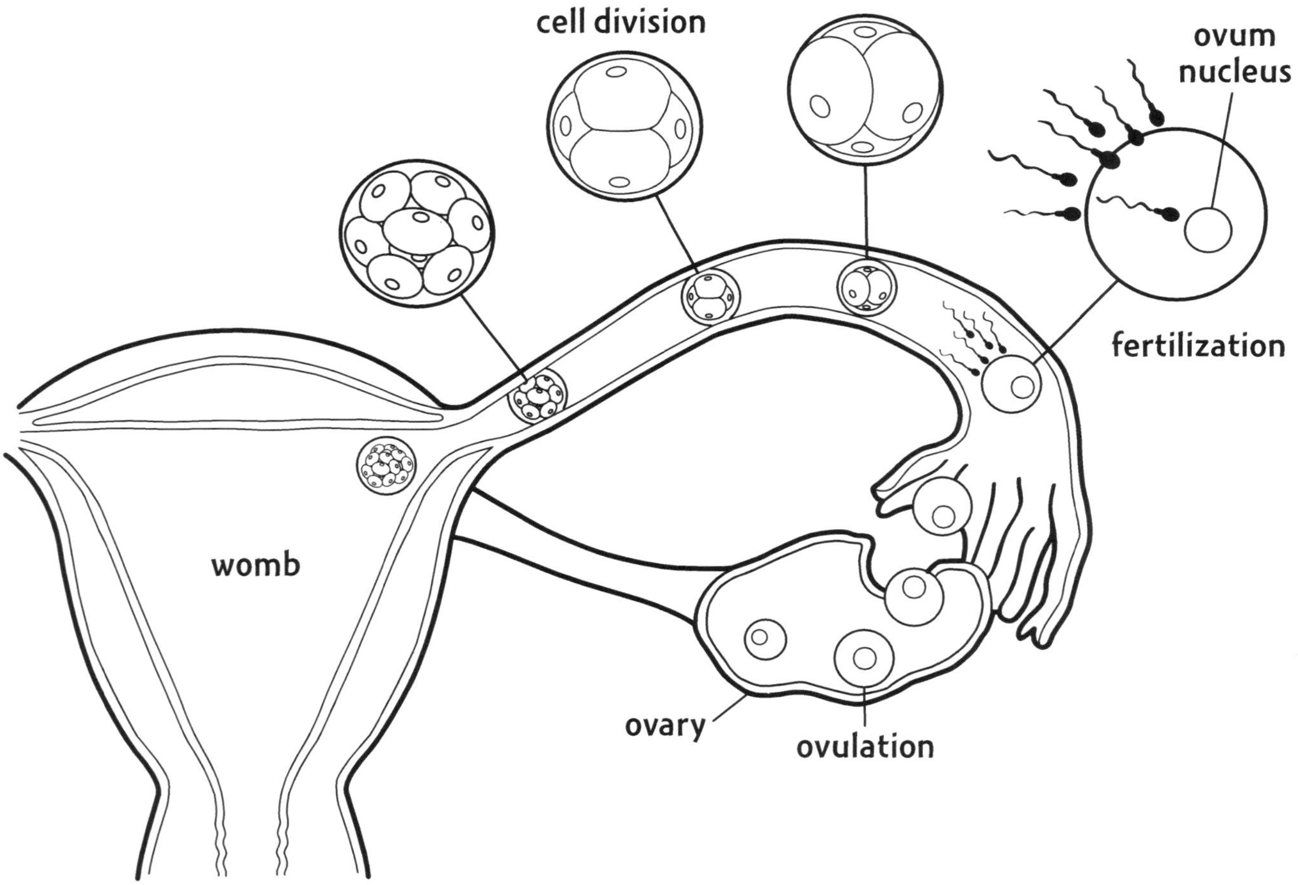

Pregnancy

When a fertilized egg, called an embryo, arrives in the uterus, it attaches to the endometrium. The embryo then grows a tissue sac called the **amniotic sac,** or the **placenta,** around itself, and the sac is filled with a fluid called **amniotic fluid.** This fluid helps protect the embryo as it grows. The embryo also grows a tube, called the **umbilical cord,** which connects to the amniotic sac. The umbilical cord provides oxygen and nourishment to the embryo. The embryo grows each day for approximately 40 weeks. After the first 2 months of development, the embryo is called a **fetus.**

While the fetus grows in the amniotic sac, the fetus experiences anything the parent carrying it eats, drinks, or inhales. People who are pregnant are encouraged to eat healthy foods, drink lots of water, avoid cigarette smoke, and refrain from alcohol.

As the embryo develops, the cells begin to divide. As the cells divide, the embryo develops lungs, a heart, kidneys, fingers, toes, a brain, and more. Sometimes during this time of division, a twin is formed. If an embryo begins to divide after landing on the endometrium, the division creates another identical embryo, resulting in an **identical twin.** If the separation is not complete and the two embryos remain attached, it can result in **conjoined twins,** or twins who are physically connected after birth.

Fraternal twins come from two eggs and two sperm. If an ovary releases two eggs, then there is the opportunity for each egg to be fertilized by a separate sperm. Then both embryos move into the uterus, attach to different places on the endometrium, and begin to grow.

As the fetus grows, the uterus stretches. The pregnant person may feel the fetus moving around, kicking, and having hiccups. A full-term baby is born after approximately 40 weeks. When it is time for the baby to be born, the uterus begins to tighten and release. These rhythmic squeezes

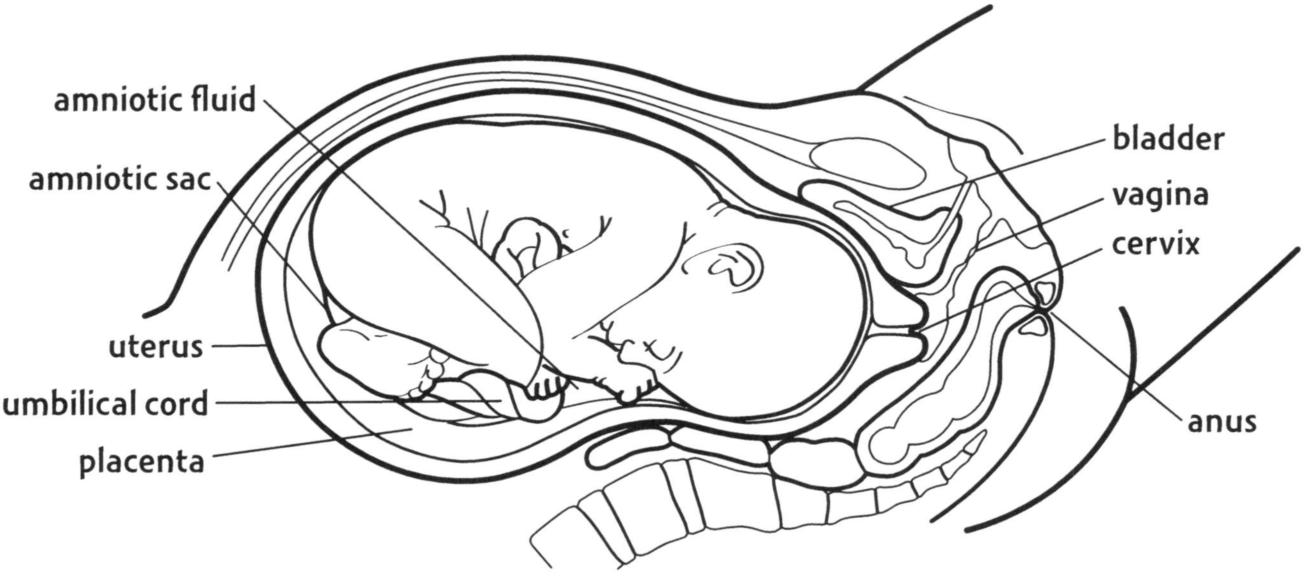

are called **contractions.** In the case of a vaginal birth, the uterus works to push the baby into the cervix and vagina, which is called **labor.** Labor helps the cervix stretch from .8 centimeters to a full 10 centimeters, almost 4 inches wide. Labor is encouraged by the baby's head resting on the cervix and pushing against it. When the cervix is open, the baby is pushed out of the uterus through the vagina. Babies also can be born by caesarean section *(C-section)*, an operation in which a doctor surgically removes the baby directly from the uterus. After a baby is born, the amniotic sac is then delivered.

When a baby is born, the parent may nurse the baby. The baby sucks on the nipple for milk. Not all parents with female bodies are able to nurse, or choose to nurse. In that case, the baby is fed formula *(a milk-like substitute)* from a bottle. Either decision is OK.

Avoiding Pregnancy and Sexually Transmitted Infections

The term **birth control** refers to a wide range of methods people use to prevent pregnancy or the spread of **Sexually Transmitted Infections (STIs)** during sex. Birth control is the responsibility of anyone who is sexually active, whether they have male or female biological features. Abstinence, or refraining from sex, is the only completely reliable way to prevent pregnancy and the spread of STIs, but other forms of protection can be very effective too. There are a variety of different forms of birth control.

One group of birth-control methods are called **hormonal methods,** which release hormones to prevent the ovaries from releasing an egg. Examples of hormonal methods are: the **birth-control pill,** taken daily; the **implant,** inserted by a doctor or nurse under the skin; the **patch,** placed on the skin; some kinds of **Intrauterine Devices *(IUDs)*,** inserted in the uterus by a doctor or nurse; and the **morning-after pill,** taken within a few days after intercourse.

Another group of birth-control methods are called **barrier methods,** which work by preventing sperm from entering the vagina or uterus. Examples are: the **male condom,** placed on the penis before sex; the **female condom,** a loose sheath placed inside the vagina before sex; the **diaphragm,** inserted to the top of the vagina against the cervix; and the **sponge,** also inserted to the top of the vagina.

Spermicides, another group of birth-control methods, contain chemicals that stop sperm cells from moving. Spermicides are usually used in combination with another method. The most common forms of spermicides are foam, gel, or film that is placed inside the vagina near the cervix.

Surgical methods are permanent forms of birth control. Surgical methods block or remove part of the fallopian tubes in the female body, or vas deferens in the male body, so that the egg and sperm cannot join for fertilization.

The previous list does not cover every form of birth control. None of these are 100 percent reliable, though they are very effective.

It is important to remember that most birth-control methods do not protect against **Sexually Transmitted Infections (STIs)**. STIs are infections caused by bacteria or viruses, and can be transferred through contact with the genitals, mouth, or sexual fluids of an infected person. A list of STIs can be found on pages 55-56. To protect against STIs, a male condom *(latex or plastic)* can be used on the penis. A female condom can be placed inside the vagina or anus. For oral sex on a vulva, a **dental dam** *(a flat square of latex)* can help prevent the spread of infections. When used correctly, these methods are very effective, but not perfect.

Being sexually active is your decision. If you decide to be sexually active, you are responsible for taking care of yourself and your sexual partner by using birth control and STI protection. You also should talk with your parents, guardians, or trusted adults about this decision. Sexual activity stirs up deep emotions, so be sure you have safe people in your life to help you navigate sexual intimacy.

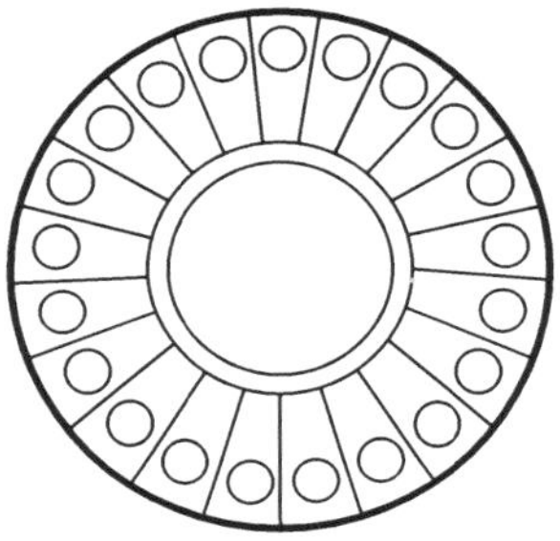

birth-control pills

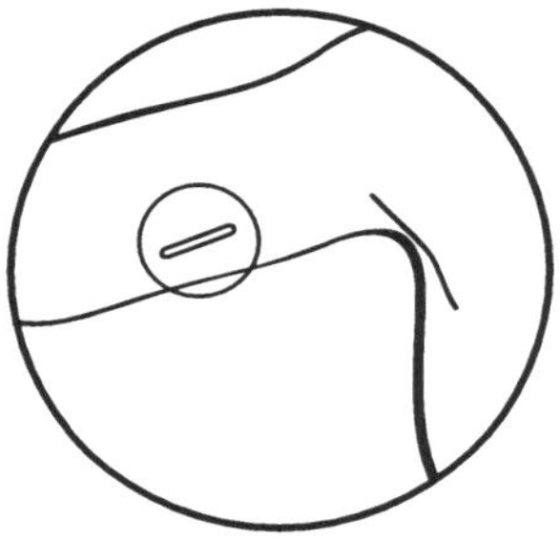

the implant

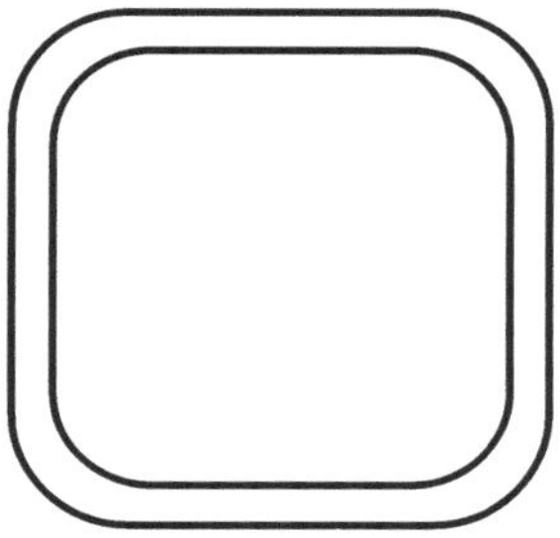

the patch

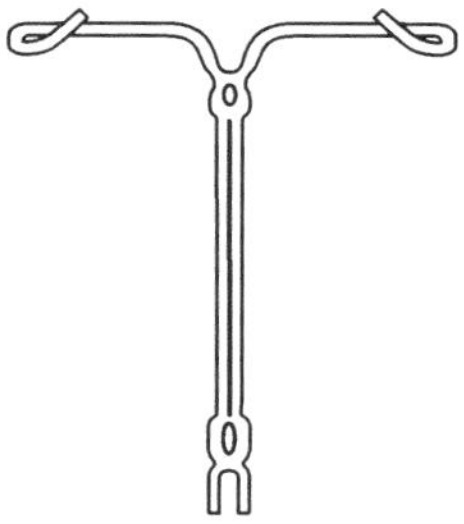

IUD

male condom

female condom

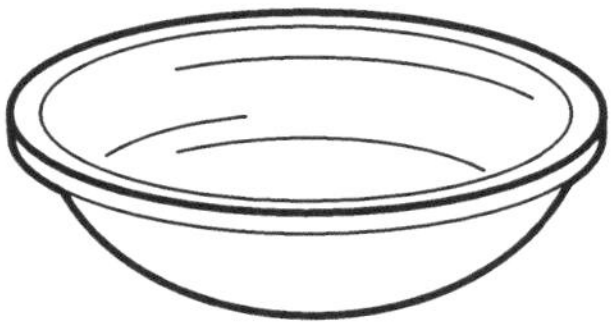

diaphragm

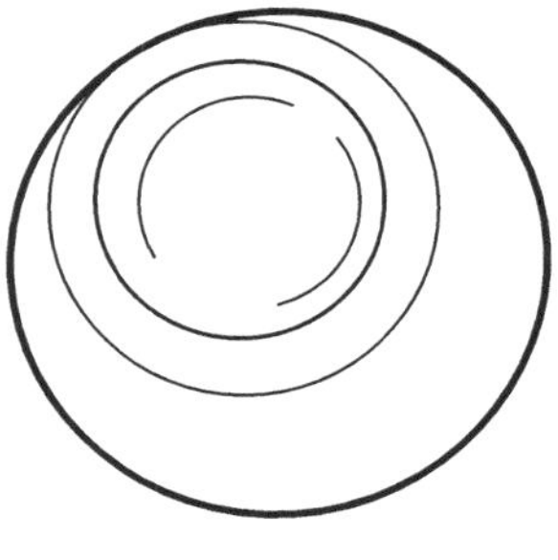

sponge

GLOWS

Sometimes growing up is hard. The things that happen during puberty might make us uncomfortable or embarrassed. Other times, puberty might make us excited about getting older and about all of the new things we get to do.

No matter how we feel about our bodies, God reminds us that we are wonderfully made and supremely good. God is with us through all of these changes. God wants to support, encourage, and help us through everything we experience as we grow and change.

God is with us, no matter what choices we make.

In Module 2, we talked about prevenient grace: God's love that is with us before we are born. Another form of grace is **justifying grace:** God's grace that brings us closer to God. God loves us and wants to be in relationship with us. You don't have to do anything to make God love you; God loves you just the way you are.

God wants to hear from you, and to know what's on your mind. Justifying grace enables us to be in relationship with God, to talk to God, to listen to God, and to lean on God when we need help or support. God is our partner as we grow and change.

GLOWS

Connect with **G**od. Dim the lights so your glow-in-the-dark modeling clay glows, and say:

"God, you know me! I am wonderfully made! I come to you with an open mind and an open heart as I listen for what you might say to me today."

Listen. Take time to read a section in this book or one of the suggested Bible verses.

Open your heart. In silence or with quiet music playing, think about what you read or heard. There are many ways to process what you are learning. You might choose to journal, draw, or create something with clay. Take time to write questions or insights you have as you ponder what you have heard.

Wonder. Consider writing in a journal or notebook your answers to these questions:

What did I learn in this chapter?

What did I already know?

What was difficult to read or see?

What gifts has God given me?

What questions do I have?

Steps. Record what steps you want to take in response to all you have experienced in this time of prayer.

Closing Prayer:

"God, I praise you, for I am wonderfully made. Thank you for being with me as I change and grow. Amen."

Spiritual Discipline: Journaling

God is with you as you grow and change. You can talk to God. In the last chapter, we practiced the spiritual discipline of prayer. This is one way to communicate with God. Journaling is another way to share your feelings. You can do this in a notebook, on paper, on your computer or phone, or in this book. You might choose to write, type, or draw your thoughts. You might take time every day to write thoughts about your day. You might choose to answer the following questions:

How do I feel?

What do I like about my body today?

What about my body makes me uncomfortable, sad, or frustrated?

What do I want to share with God today?

You can write/draw/journal about these questions or anything that's on your mind, and God will be with you, listening to you.

Sexually Transmitted Infections

Bacterial Vaginosis—an overgrowth of bacteria in the vagina that can cause discharge, itching, or odor. Treated with antibiotics.

Chlamydia—a bacterial infection that can cause genital pain and discharge from the vagina or penis. Some people don't develop symptoms, but still can pass the infection to others through sexual contact. Treated with antibiotics.

Chancroid—a bacterial infection that causes open sores on the genitals. Rare in the United States. Treated with antibiotics or clears up on its own.

Genital herpes—a viral infection that causes pain, itching, and ulcers or sores on the genitals. Can lie dormant for years between outbreaks. Medications can manage outbreaks.

Genital warts—small bumps on the genitals caused by a common STI *(human papillomavirus or HPV)*. Treated with prescription medication or surgery.

Gonorrhea—a bacterial infection that causes painful urination and abnormal discharge. Sometimes people do not experience symptoms. Treated with antibiotics.

Hepatitis B—a viral infection of the liver that causes abdominal pain, flu-like symptoms, and dark urine. Acute Hepatitis B often clears up on its own. Chronic Hepatitis B is more serious and can cause liver failure, cancer, or scarring.

Hepatitis C—a viral infection of the liver that causes abdominal pain and some flu-like symptoms. Treated with antibiotics.

Herpes—an infection caused by the herpes simplex virus *(HSV)*. There are two types of HSV. HSV-1 typically causes oral herpes, which can manifest in cold sores around the mouth. HSV-2 typically causes genital herpes *(see above)*. Oral herpes can be spread to the genitals through oral sex. Over 50 percent of the population in the United States have oral herpes, even if they don't exhibit symptoms.

HIV/AIDS—the Human Immunodeficiency Virus *(HIV)* is a viral infection that weakens the body's immune system. If left untreated, the virus can damage the immune system so much that it is unable to fight off infections and cancers. HIV at this stage is called AIDS *(or Acquired Immune Deficiency Syndrome)*. HIV is treated with drugs that control the progression of the virus. People with HIV can live nearly as long as people without HIV, if they have access to the proper medications. However, a person being treated for HIV still can spread the virus.

Human Papillomavirus *(HPV)*—a viral infection that may cause warts on the genitals or other parts of the body. Many people do not experience symptoms. Both men and women can carry HPV. Some forms of HPV can cause cervical cancer. Certain types are preventable by vaccine.

Lymphogranuloma Venereum (LGV)—a chronic infection of the lymph nodes that causes pain in the genitals and anus. Treated with antibiotics.

Mycoplasma genitalium—a bacterial infection that can cause painful urination and watery discharge from the penis for men, or pain and/or bleeding during sex for women. Sometimes no symptoms develop. Symptoms treated with antibiotics.

Molluscum Contagiosum—a viral infection that causes small bumps on the legs, abdomen, and groin. Sometimes the bumps are itchy, but often cause no problems. Often clears up on its own.

Pelvic Inflammatory Disease (PID)—a bacterial infection of the female reproductive organs that causes pelvic pain, fever, and sometimes discharge. Treated with antibiotics.

Pubic lice *(crabs)*—small insects that live in a person's genital area. Their bites can cause severe itching. Treated with creams and lotions that kill the parasites.

Scabies—a skin condition caused by burrowing mites. Extremely contagious from close physical contact. Treated with oral or topical medication.

Syphilis—a bacterial infection that progresses from a painless sore on the genitals, rectum, or mouth to a rash. The final stage can cause damage to the brain, nerves, eyes, or heart. Treated with penicillin.

Trichomoniasis—a parasitic infection that causes a smelly discharge from the vagina, itching in the genitals, and painful urination in women. Men typically do not develop symptoms. One of the most common STIs. Treated with antibiotics.

Zika—a virus that can be transmitted by a mosquito bite or sexual contact. Zika causes fever, rash, headache, joint pain, and muscle pain. As of 2017, there is no medication for the virus, but symptoms can be treated.

My Body

Scripture:

Luke 4:1-12

Ephesians 4:1-16

John 13:34-35

1 Thessalonians 5:11

Our bodies are God's gift to us. God gives us eyes to see the world, hands to work in the world, feet to move in the world, and many organs to keep our bodies breathing, playing, running, and creating. Our bodies are pretty amazing! God did not give us our bodies just for our own purposes; instead, God made us so that we can help others and make a difference in the world. In the New Testament, Ephesians 4:1-16 tells us that God not only has given us a body, but God also has given us unique gifts: different abilities that

"equip God's people for the work of serving and building up the body of Christ." Ephesians 4:12

We make millions of choices every day: when to get out of bed, what to eat, what to wear, whether or not to brush our teeth—the list is endless. We also make many decisions regarding how we treat our family and friends, what we say to people who seem different from us, and how we respond to bullies. Being an adolescent isn't easy, and there are many difficult decisions you will have to make.

It is hard to love ourselves, to love God, and to love every person we meet every moment of the day. Sometimes we make mistakes, we make poor choices, and we hurt people around us. The good news is that God forgives us and helps us find a new and better way forward. We aren't the only ones who face tough decisions every day. In the New Testament, Luke 4:1-12 tells the story of when Jesus was tempted to make poor choices. This story tells us that Jesus went into the wilderness for 40 days, where he was tempted. Jesus stayed focused and kept his heart set on God, telling the devil,

"It's written, *You will worship the Lord your God and serve only him.*" Luke 4:8

Jesus is our example and our guide. We too can stay focused on God when we make important decisions.

"I give you a new commandment: Love each other. Just as I have loved you, so you also must love each other. This is how everyone will know that you are my disciples, when you love each other." John 13:34-35

Jesus' commandment to us is to love one another. Most of the time, when we hear the word *love*, it is meant as a feeling. When God commands us to love one another, it has another meaning. This kind of love has more to do with our actions than our immediate feelings. God's commandment is that in all of our relationships, we treat one another with respect and kindness.

In this section, we will explore the many types of relationships we have with others. Before we begin, let's look at some central truths that help us embody God's love in any relationship:

- Each of us is wonderfully made by God, with our own uniqueness and worth.
- No two of us are exactly alike. Each of us has beauty. Each of us also has the ability to make mistakes. Each of us has talents, skills, and tastes.
- A big part of sharing God's love is encouraging one another and celebrating our uniqueness and sacred worth.

"Continue encouraging each other and building each other up." 1 Thessalonians 5:11

We don't always live up to this call. Two things that often get in the way of celebrating our uniqueness and worth are prejudices and stereotypes.

The word **prejudice** means to prejudge, or judge before we truly know someone. This means we make a decision about who a person is without getting to know them. An example:

> Beth, a new student, saw Kim sitting alone in the cafeteria. Beth walked up and introduced herself. Kim replied with a gruff and short "Hello." Beth decided, "Kim must be a stuck-up, mean person. I'm not talking to Kim again."
>
> Actually, Kim was very nervous about an upcoming math test, and was anxiously studying. If Kim didn't get a good grade on the test, it would mean receiving a D in the class.
>
> If Beth allowed her prejudice to guide her decisions about talking to Kim again, she may pass up an opportunity to form a friendship.

Stereotypes are assumptions about a group of people based on very little or wrong information. Examples are: *Kids are always messy*, and *Grown-ups don't know how to have fun*.

Harmful stereotypes are commonly based on groupings, such as race, culture, religion, age, physical ability, gender, and sexual orientation.

Gender is an area where stereotypes abound. Some common stereotypes are:

- Boys aren't very emotional.
- Girls are super emotional.
- Boys don't like dancing, fashion, or crafts.
- Girls aren't good at math or building things.

Gender stereotypes can be harmful because they can make us think that because we are a certain gender, we should be a certain way. For example, a boy interested in ballet may not want to take classes, because then he wouldn't be a *real boy*. A girl who's good at math may pretend she doesn't know the answers, so she can fit the stereotype of what a *real girl* is.

Prejudices and stereotypes get in the way of experiencing the wonderfully made uniqueness of one another. An important part of showing God's love is to do our best to look beyond stereotypes and prejudices, to get to know people for who they are, and to celebrate the differences among us.

Have you ever been treated unfairly because of a prejudice or stereotype?

Have you ever judged someone else because of a prejudice or stereotype?

How can you work to fight stereotypes and prejudices in your community?

Relationships

As children of God, we have many types of relationships with other people. There are various ways to show love in these different types of relationships.

1. *Community relationships:* As members of a community, we are called to show respect to others by obeying community rules and communicating kindly. All people can add to the good of the larger community by being informed about justice issues and participating in community activities. We all can show God's love through good works, such as volunteering, sharing our faith through our actions, and giving from what we have to others.

2. *Family relationships:* Family members have special responsibilities to one another. Parents and guardians are called to provide for their children, to teach them, and to give them guidance. Parents and guardians are also supposed to comfort and nurture their children.

3. *Friendships:* Friendships are wonderful opportunities to reflect God's love to others. We share many experiences with our friends. With close friends, we share our dreams, fears, and joys. Going through life's ups and downs with one another can create wonderful bonds that last a lifetime.

Intimacy

When we spend lots of time with someone, and share deep parts of our hearts and minds, we become emotionally intimate. The word *intimacy* is used to describe the quality in a relationship that makes us feel closely connected to that person. It involves sharing more than just casual experiences or thoughts—it means sharing a close familiarity.

There are various types of intimacy. Some relationships with friends and family can be described as intimate. These are the friends and family members with whom we share almost everything and who know us very well.

Some people hear the word *intimate* and think *sexual*. We are talking about emotional closeness, and that does not depend on sexual feelings. Emotional intimacy can happen between people in any type of relationship.

Healthy intimacy in any type of relationship doesn't happen automatically or quickly. It's built over time through many interactions. Building a healthy intimacy depends on two things: having a safe space to share our true, personal selves, and both people responding with acceptance, kindness, and love. This kind of personal sharing involves risk. When we share ourselves, the response of others can have the effect of building us up or hurting our feelings.

Imagine that in each of our relationships, there's a ladder of trust. As we get to know people, we share more personal things about ourselves. We climb up the ladder of trust. With each step, we get to decide whether we want to keep going, stay where we are, or go back down. As we reveal important parts of ourselves, the way another person responds helps us to determine if it is safe to share more of ourselves or to take a step back down the ladder of trust. Let's look at an example to see how this works:

> Ben has a fear of heights. Ben doesn't share that personal information with everyone. Imagine Ben is at an amusement park with some friends. Among them is a new friend, Sarah. Sarah runs up to Ben, firmly grabs his hand, and says, "It's time for the double Ferris wheel!" Ben, who can't think of a good excuse to say no, says, "Um, I've sort of got this thing about heights…"

A bit of Ben's true self has been revealed. Ben has taken a step up the ladder of trust, and shared some personal information. Sarah now has some options about how to respond to this information. Let's look at one way Sarah could reply:

> Sarah says, "What? A fear of heights? What are you? a baby? Should I go win you a stuffed animal to hold while I go on the Ferris wheel?"

In this instance, it's likely that Ben will choose to take a step back down the ladder of trust and not continue to share more personal things with Sarah.

Now let's imagine Sarah made a different choice in responding to Ben.

> Sarah said, "Oh, OK. No problem. I completely understand. Why don't you pick the next ride?"

In this case, because Sarah responded with acceptance, kindness, and caring, the friendship of Sarah and Ben increased in healthy intimacy. Ben could safely continue up the ladder of trust.

This is the way healthy intimacy is built: by sharing personal parts of ourselves with one another, and responding to one another with love and acceptance. Healthy intimacy allows us to climb the ladder of trust and connect with one another in a safe, loving way. Following are a few things you can do to build trust with others:

- Encourage other people by pointing out their strengths and what you like about them.

- Listen to people when they're sad or discouraged, and remind them you're there for them.

- Keep their confidence—don't gossip or share personal information about someone with other people. *(In some special circumstances, we may need to break confidentiality and share private information. If a friend indicates that they are in an abusive situation and/or considering harming themselves or others, tell an adult you trust.)*

Loving one another doesn't mean we always agree. We don't have to pretend we're happy with one another when we're actually upset or angry. Even when we're not happy with one another, we can still act in a way that respects the child of God in each of us. When things aren't going well in a relationship, consider taking these actions:

- Listen carefully to what the other person is saying.
- When you disagree, don't label the person or call them names (*"You're such a..."*).
- Be honest about your feelings, using the kindest words you can.

Building healthy intimacy can, and should, take time. Having a private self is normal, healthy, and important. It's wise to take our time as we create safety and trust with one another, sharing more over time.

This definition of healthy intimacy is true for whatever close relationships we have. You could imagine Ben and Sarah being siblings, friends, or romantic partners, and the same rules for intimacy would apply. Whenever people support and encourage one another, their intimacy can grow. Whenever people treat each other harshly, the relationship can become unhealthy.

God wants us to build healthy intimacy with one another. God knows each of our deepest selves, and holds that knowledge with love and caring. We are called to show one another that same kind of love, to the best of our ability.

What emotionally intimate relationships do you have?

What ideas do you have for encouraging trust in a relationship?

Romantic Relationships

A romantic relationship is a kind of intimate friendship that involves emotional and sexual intimacy. We are wonderfully made by God. God gave us the gift of sexual intimacy, a special type of deep, intense love for another person. Romantic love is more than a close friendship, though close friendship is the foundation of romantic love. A romantic relationship can involve physical sensations such as butterflies in the stomach or excitement in the sexual parts of your body.

Many people form romantic relationships during their teens. Others may not develop these relationships until much later in adulthood. Some people have several romances over the years, and some only have one. Some people choose not to have romantic relationships. No matter which path you take, you are wonderfully created and loved.

A romantic relationship may start with the two individuals spending time together at school, group dating with friends, attending school events, or going to movies. They may often talk on the phone, text, or message through social media. They may try out some romantic touch, such as holding hands, hugging, or kissing. For older teens, one-on-one dating may begin. For some, the ability to drive may provide more chances for a young couple to have private time together.

In the older teen years, romantic and sexual feelings can become increasingly intense. This calls for special thoughtfulness and attention on the part of the couple to decide together what behaviors they do and don't want to engage in. Sexual behaviors come with the risk of pregnancy or spreading infections, so it's important that couples have open and mature conversations before engaging in any sexual activity.

As young people enter puberty and develop romantic and sexual feelings, questions about sexual orientation may arise. Teenagers may feel attractions or crushes toward people of various genders, and wonder how to identify their sexual orientation. It's important to remember that sexual orientation is an established, ongoing pattern of attraction. Young people don't need to feel pressured to identify their sexual orientation based on a few experiences of attraction. No matter what your sexual orientation is, God loves you and you are wonderfully made. It can be helpful to talk to trusted adults if you have questions about your sexual orientation.

Have you had romantic feelings about someone? What questions do you have about romantic relationships?

Love, Intimacy, Romance: One Size Does Not Fit All!

In this section, we will talk about some very common experiences: romance, falling in love, and sexual attraction. But just like other aspects of God's Creation, there is much variation.

God created us all with the capacity for having loving, intimate relationships with others, though the exact feelings we have, and the ways we express those feelings, may differ. The capacity for these feelings emerges at different times in each of us.

Some people will find they do not have some of the common feelings and experiences we describe here. If you find yourself thinking that some of these feelings and sensations just do not fit your experience, that's OK.

If you are concerned about any differences you have, talking to your parents, a pastor, a trusted adult at school, a counselor, or medical professional can help.

Crushes

First, let's talk about crushes between peers, or people who are around the same age and equal in power. In many cases, the person with a crush doesn't take steps to start a close relationship with the other. Though the feelings can be intense and even agonizing at times, many people look back on these types of crushes with fond memories.

Some crushes will lead a person to take steps to get closer to the other person. If both people say "yes" to the relationship, that's great! If those feelings aren't shared by the other, it can cause very sad feelings. If that happens, talking to a trusted adult can help you deal with those feelings in a safe and healthy way.

Now, here's the tricky part: not all crushes are between peers. Some youngsters find themselves with a crush on someone much older than themselves. Sometimes the object of affection is someone the person will likely never meet, such as a popular singer or film star. But some crushes are closer to home. It is quite common for a young person to have a crush on a teacher, coach, or other authority figure, even a pastor.

The feelings behind these crushes are normal and healthy. But if these crushes are reciprocated *(returned)* by the adult or acted on by either party, they can become very damaging. That's because adults have more power than teens in a relationship. Power differences between people in sexual relationships often lead to abuse. As a result, it's legally considered abusive for an adult or authority figure to enter into a romantic relationship with a minor.

Romantic and Sexual Touch

A special characteristic of romantic relationships is the sexual feelings that come along with them. Sexual touch can bring a special sense of closeness and excitement.

Sexual touch can range from holding hands and kissing, to touching genitals and other sexual parts, to various forms of sex. Sexual touch requires us to make wise decisions about how we share our bodies with others and how we respect others' bodies.

The terms *sex*, having sex, or *sexual intercourse* can mean different things to different people, so here are some definitions for clarity:

Sexual contact refers to any kind of touch between people that involves either partner's genitals.

Penile-vaginal intercourse refers to sexual contact in which a penis is inserted into a vagina.

Anal intercourse, or **anal sex,** refers to sexual contact in which a penis is inserted into an anus.

Oral sex refers to sexual contact between genitals *(either a penis or vulva)* and a mouth.

Deciding About Romantic and Sexual Touch

God put each of us in charge of our own bodies. Your body is yours. There may be times when a doctor needs to touch your body. But overall, no one has the right to touch your body without your permission. And we do not have the right to touch anyone else's body without their permission. Whether in a family relationship, a friendship, or a romantic relationship, we have the right to determine how we do and don't want to be touched. Always talk to a safe adult if someone asks or forces you to do something that you don't feel comfortable doing with your body.

Consent means giving permission to do something, or agreeing for something to happen. When it comes to romantic or sexual touch, consent isn't simply not saying no. Consent means saying yes in obvious ways, both verbally and through body language, such as gestures, facial expressions, and movements. The following is an example:

> Avery saw Rachel in the school hallway, and decided she wanted to give Rachel a hug. She came up behind Rachel, spun her around, and grabbed her.

Did Rachel give consent? No. Rachel had no option to say anything before Avery hugged her.

Let's try again:

> Avery said, "Hi, Rachel! I haven't seen you in forever! Can I have a hug?" Rachel turned to Avery, said, "Hey, Avery!" but stayed where she was, a few steps away. Avery stepped in and hugged Rachel.

Consent? No. Avery asked, which was good. But even though Rachel did not say no, she did not obviously say yes.

Let's try again:

> Avery said, "Hi, Rachel! I haven't seen you in forever! Can I have a hug?" Rachel turned to Avery, walked toward her with arms stretched out, and said, "Of course, Avery!"

Consent? Yes.

In romantic or sexual relationships, it's easy to get excited and forget to ask for permission to touch another person. But asking for consent is the only way to make sure you and your partner are both comfortable and excited about what's happening. You may have heard people say, "If they don't say no, then it's OK," but it's actually the opposite. Anything other than a clear yes should be taken as a no. People always have a right to say no, even if they have said yes before.

If someone offers, asks, or tries to touch you in a way you don't want, remember, you have the right to say no. If you feel uncomfortable around a person, one thing you can do is invite another person to be with you when that person is around. For example, if Rachel didn't feel comfortable with Avery, Rachel could always ask Samuel to hang out with her when Avery was around.

While reading this, you may be reminded of times when you were touched without your permission, or when you touched another person without consent. If you have painful feelings about this, or if you are in a situation in which someone else doesn't respect your wishes around touch, talk to a trusted adult.

Physical touch is one of the wonderful gifts God gave us to share our affection for one another, but only when both people are truly saying yes to that touch. It's our right to say no at any time to any touch, and our responsibility to make sure we have a true yes from another person before touching them.

With physical intimacy comes emotional vulnerability. The word **vulnerable** means "open to harm." Sharing personal parts of our bodies with one another is a special kind of intimacy. This kind of intimacy brings the opportunity for closeness and excitement, but also can bring about the chance of heartache. While each person differs in this area, it's important for us to decide the kinds of touch we're comfortable with and uncomfortable with. This decision is one that must be made with every relationship.

Sexual contact involves potentially serious health risks. It's important for a couple to know about potential health risks that the various types of sexual touch can bring. Dealing with these risks takes planning and effort, and for that reason sexual contact is best between adults who are in a committed relationship, like marriage. Couples need to be able to talk openly and honestly with each other about all of these issues. That's why intimacy is so important.

Pregnancy is one of the risks of sexual contact. Though mostly associated with penile/vaginal intercourse, any activity that allows semen to get inside or just outside the vagina has a chance of leading to pregnancy.

Another health risk is **Sexually Transmitted Infections (STIs).** There are many infections that can be spread through sexual contact. For information on birth control and methods for reducing the risk of STI transmission, see Module 3.

Our values are important guides. **Values** give us a sense of what's right and wrong, and what's good and bad for us. Our values come from many sources: family, church, school, community, and past experiences.

Figuring out our values, and learning to communicate them with partners, is not always easy, but it's worth the effort. Some ways to do this are by taking classes about sexuality, talking with parents and other significant adults, praying, and journaling.

Whether it's a young person holding hands with a special someone, or an adult having sex with a spouse, God wants our sexual touch to be loving. This means that it is:

- within the safety and security of an intimate relationship,
- appropriate to the level of commitment in the relationship,

- an expression of emotional closeness,
- kind and caring,
- pleasurable and safe for both, and
- wanted by both.

Living Out Your Values

You get to decide what kind of romantic touch you want to engage in. You might decide not to engage in any type of sexual touch until you're an adult in a committed relationship, like marriage. You may decide holding hands is OK. Later, you might decide you want to try kissing. You can decide what's right for you in each relationship and phase of life. It's helpful to think about what level of sexual touch you are comfortable with before you find yourself in romantic situations. Talk to a trusted adult who can help you make the best decision for yourself. You may find it helpful to date in groups or to have an adult be present or nearby. It is always best to be honest with the person you are dating by letting them know your boundaries regarding sexual touch. If you find yourself in a position in which you are uncomfortable, there are many adults in your life who will help you. Tell your parents/guardians or other trusted adult about the situation, and they will help you get out of it.

On the next page, there's space for you to write the names and contact numbers for three adults who can support you in making the best decision about romantic touch. These adults can be family, friends, or people at church who know you. Be sure to talk with your parents or guardians about these people in your life.

What are your values?

Who can help you live out your values?

Marriage

Many adults make a lifelong commitment to one romantic partner. Many Christians celebrate this commitment with a legal and religious ceremony of marriage. Christians consider this attachment to be symbolic of God's covenant with us. *Covenant* means a bonding or joining together, and it includes promises, agreements, and responsibilities toward one another. In the Bible, many stories speak of God's covenant always to be with us, God's children, with abiding love. In the same way, in the covenant of marriage two people make promises to love and support one another for the rest of their lives. They promise to be there for one another as they celebrate life's joys, and to offer support during difficult times. Entering into this deep bond or attachment allows a couple to develop deep intimacy and trust. For this reason, many people choose to limit sexual activity to such committed relationships.

Though marriage is often presented in stories and media as a happily-ever-after event, the truth is that most marriage relationships involve challenges. Maintaining healthy intimacy takes a strong commitment and lots of effort to communicate in healthy and supportive ways. This is not a bad thing: as a couple works through their differences, they experience an even deeper kind of love than they did in the falling-in-love phase.

Divorce

Some adults who marry find themselves ending that relationship through divorce. Though usually not a pleasant or easy decision to make, for most divorced families it is seen as the healthiest choice for the couple and, if they are parents, for their children. Divorced families may face certain challenges around finances or caring for children.

God's love is always present for all members of a family. Families going through a painful divorce often can find healing and support from loving friends and community. For the children, reaching out to non-parental, trusted adults can be very helpful.

Singleness

Not everyone chooses to marry or marry again, if divorced. For people who are single, there are many types of intimate and supportive relationships, romantic and non-romantic, through which they share and receive love. Some single adults choose to form families by having or adopting children, or by parenting children from a previous marriage.

Forming Families

Many adults regard the ability to form families as a major part of God's gift in making us sexual beings. Often this includes raising children. For many, forming a family involves biological reproduction, that is, people producing biological offspring from their own bodies.

There are many ways to create and carry babies. Following are some terms associated with the variety of options available to people wanting to become biological parents.

- **Penile/Vaginal Intercourse:** This is the most common way people create babies.
- **In vitro fertilization (IVF):** egg and sperm are joined outside the body, and fertilized ova are transferred to the uterus.
- **Surrogacy:** a third person with the ability to become pregnant carries and gives birth to a child for a couple. This commonly involves IVF with egg and/or sperm from at least one of the parents-to-be.

Those are the biological routes to forming a family. There are other ways families are formed. Some adults choose to adopt children, bringing into their family a child who was biologically produced by another. Many adults become stepparents, helping to raise children born previously to a current partner or spouse. Sometimes a child's adult relative *(such as an aunt, uncle, or grandparent)*, or a family friend will become a child's guardian.

Some families are formed without children or without a marriage partner. Regardless of how families come into being, raising a child is indeed a sacred duty.

Not All Secrets Should Be Kept

In abusive situations, the abuser often tells the young person to keep their relationship a secret. If you find yourself in any kind of abusive situation, you don't need to keep it a secret. If any type of touch, by anyone, makes you feel scared, uncomfortable, or worried, telling a trusted adult about it is OK.

One kind of sexual abuse is when an adult or older child touches a child in a sexual way, or asks them to do other sexual things, such as to look at pornography, pose for sexy pictures, or look at or touch their genitals. These behaviors are never OK. Remember: it is OK to say no to any touch that you do not want, and it is OK to talk about that with a trusted adult who can help you.

By trusted adult, we mean an adult who:

- Makes you feel safe and comfortable
- Is respectful of your feelings, opinions, and boundaries
- Does not ask you to keep secrets
- Will keep helping you in a troubling situation until you feel safe.

In any situation like those listed, if you tell an adult and they do not help you, you should keep talking to other adults until you find someone who will give you the help you need to feel safe.

Social Media

Our world is blessed with so many ways to connect with one another through technology. Through computers, tablets, smartphones, and more, we are able to share words, pictures, and videos in an instant. We have the ability to talk on the phone or have video calls with just about anyone, anywhere, any time we want.

On the positive side, technology allows us to be in touch with friends and loved ones instantaneously. The technology makes it possible to form wonderful friendships with people we otherwise would never meet. It gives people who are lonely or feel different a way to find supportive relationships that they can't find nearby. It allows romantic partners to share greetings, encouraging words, or loving messages at any time. People who are shy can try talking to others through technology as a way to warm up to face-to-face conversations.

At the same time, these technological wonders call for caution, especially when it comes to our sexuality. If the technologies are not used in ways that reflect God's love, they can cause harm.

There are important things to keep in mind when using an electronic device to communicate with someone. The first thing is that anything you send or post can become public, even if you don't intend it to be.

The second is that many electronic messages and posts, even if we deleted them, do not actually disappear. Our postings can leave electronic signatures that can be found by others later, even if we ourselves can no longer see it.

Additionally, unless you're messaging a specific friend who you know, the person on the other side of the media may not be who you think they are. Be careful of the information you share electronically.

Here are some specific uses of technology that can have negative consequences:

Cyberbullying is when someone uses an electronic device to post or send mean and hurtful messages to or about someone. Hurtful names, stories, and photos can spread to others in an instant, and can be emotionally devastating to the person being targeted.

Bullying of any kind is cruel, and against God's commandment that we love one another. If you are the target of hurtful messages or posts, tell a trusted adult who can support you emotionally, and can help you take steps to stop the bullying.

If you see or receive hurtful posts or messages about someone else, do not play along by responding, adding a post, or sharing the message. Instead, talk to an adult who can help you take steps to stop the bullying. If you know a person being targeted, it could help to reach out to her or him in a friendly, supportive way.

Another concern is commonly called **sexting.** One type of sexting is sending a text with sexual language, words, or phrases. Another type is sending sexually explicit pictures, that is, photos of sexual parts of your own or someone else's body.

For people in a romantic relationship, it is understandable that they might feel the urge to use their cell phones to send flirtatious messages or posts, much like an old-fashioned love letter. But because electronic images never truly go away, sending or posting sexual messages can be particularly dangerous. In most states, sending or having sexually explicit pictures of minors *(people under 18)* is against the law. The law includes pictures someone else sends to you, and even pictures you take of yourself. In many states, simply having one of these photos on a computer, phone, or other device, even if it was sent to you against your will, is illegal.

Do not use any electronic device to send or post photos of a sexual nature. If you receive a text or message of a sexual nature, tell a trusted adult immediately.

Thanks to the Internet, there are websites where one can get instant answers to questions about anything. When it comes to sexual matters, many people find that searching the Internet is a safe way to look for information without embarrassment. There are many websites that are written with the wellbeing of young people in mind, and that offer accurate, thorough information with no shaming or judging.

There are also websites where the information is not truthful, or the discussions are not appropriate for young people. Some websites are even designed to lure young people into dangerous exchanges.

One type of content that is widely available on the Internet, and is not appropriate for children or young people, is pornography. **Pornography** is language, photos, or videos that depict sexual acts for the purpose of causing sexual excitement in the viewer. It is not designed to provide accurate information about sexual development or health. Adults have differing views about whether some types of sexual images are OK for adults to view. One thing that's certain is that pornography is not appropriate for young people. Many scientists are concerned about potentially harmful effects of watching Internet pornography, in particular. Pornography can strengthen negative or harmful attitudes about sexuality that go against God's wishes for how we treat ourselves and one another.

It is actually quite easy for someone on the Internet to accidentally come across pornographic material, especially if they're looking for information about bodies or a sexuality related topic. If that happens to you, the best thing to do is to tell an adult what happened. They can help you find the information you want while staying away from inappropriate material.

With all the various websites out there, how can a young person tell if a website is a good source of information and support? The best way is to have a trusted adult check it out with you. A parent, caregiver, teacher, or clergy person can help you find websites that are of high quality, and appropriate for kids your age.

IRL (In Real Life) Contact

Another thing to think about regarding devices and communication: God created us with bodies for a reason. Our voices, facial expressions, and touch are ways in which we share with one another the richness of God's love. Electronic devices give us a way to reach out to those who aren't with us at the moment. But ultimately, there's an intimacy in face-to-face, body-to-body contact that can't be substituted by a computer, tablet, or smartphone.

Hugs feel good for a reason! While communicating with others electronically can be very important, we always want to make time for face-to-face, body-to-body contact with other people.

GLOWS

God gives us all we need to love ourselves, love God, and love our neighbors. God's sanctifying grace helps us grow and mature on our faith journeys. God's sanctifying grace stays with us throughout our entire life journey. This is not a one-time gift or event. We don't become perfect in one moment. We work toward perfection all the time. As we grow and practice making healthy decisions, we will make mistakes. When we do, God is there to support us, love us, and help us make better decisions.

Our bodies are God's gift to us:

> **"Therefore, as a prisoner for the Lord, I encourage you to live as people worthy of the call you received from God. Conduct yourselves with all humility, gentleness, and patience. Accept each other with love, and make an effort to preserve the unity of the Spirit with the peace that ties you together. You are one body and one spirit, just as God also called you in one hope. There is one Lord, one faith, one baptism, and one God and Father of all, who is over all, through all, and in all." Ephesians 4:1-5**

You are a beloved child of God. Your body is God's gift to you. You are an important part of the entire body of Christ. God created you, God loves you, God is with you. You have all you need to stand firm, to keep focused on God, and to live as a blessing to others.

GLOWS

G Connect with **G**od. Light a candle, or use glow-in-the-dark modeling clay, and say:

"God, you know me! I am wonderfully made! I come to you with an open mind and an open heart as I listen for what you might say to me today."

Listen. Take time to read a section in this book or one of the suggested Bible verses.

Open your heart. In silence or with quiet music playing, think about what you read or heard. There are many ways to process what you are learning. You might choose to journal, draw, or create something with clay. Take time to write questions or insights you have as you ponder what you have heard.

Wonder. Consider writing in a journal or notebook your responses to these questions:

What did I learn in this chapter?

What did I already know?

What was difficult to read or see?

What gifts has God given me?

What questions do I have?

Steps. Record what steps you want to take in response to all you have experienced in this time of prayer.

Closing Prayer.

God, I praise you, for I am wonderfully made. Thank you for being with me as I change and grow. Amen.

Spiritual Discipline: Practicing the Examen

The Examen is a spiritual discipline that helps us stop and assess how are we doing with the hard and holy work of loving God and loving our neighbor. The Examen has been used by Christians for many centuries. It's an ancient form of prayer that helps us to:

- Become aware of God's presence.
- Review the day with gratitude.
- Pay attention to our emotions.
- Focus on a few moments from our day/week.
- Look toward the next day.

You can use this tool once or twice a day, or you can pick one time each week to pray the Examen. You can practice the Examen alone or with others. Here are the steps to the Examen:

1. Identify 15 minutes when you can pray uninterrupted. This might be at lunch, after school, or at bedtime. You might want to bring your Bible, your journal, or some creative tools to help you talk and listen to God.

2. Invite one or two people to join you in this practice. You can take turns answering the questions, listening to one another, and discerning together.

3. Light a candle or use glow-in-the-dark modeling clay, get into a comfortable position and take a few deep breaths. Do what you need to do to connect to God, to breathe in God's love, and to prepare your heart and mind for this holy conversation.

4. Ask and reflect on the following questions:

When have I felt close to God today/this week?

When have I felt far away from God today/this week?

Who have I felt close to today/this week?

Who have I felt far away from today/this week?

What decisions have I made today/this week?

How do I feel about these decisions?

5. Give thanks for what you have experienced and what you have heard.

6. Pray: God, thank you for being with me, loving me, and listening to me. Help me to listen and to follow you in all that I do. Help me to remember that I am wonderfully made. Amen.

Glossary

Abstinence: the practice of not having sex for a period of time, primarily until one is in a committed marriage relationship

Acne: a skin condition that often occurs in adolescence, and causes pimples and blackheads

Adolescence: the time of life when a child develops into an adult

Amniotic fluid: the watery fluid surrounding the growing embryo and fetus

Amniotic sac/placenta: the membrane sac surrounding the embryo and fetus during pregnancy

Anal intercourse/anal sex: the sexual act of inserting a penis into a partner's anus

Anus: the opening for solid waste, or feces, to exit the body

Areola: the darker area of skin that surrounds the nipple

Aroused/arousal: to be stimulated, especially sexually

Asexual: not having or feeling sexual attraction in the way most others describe it

Barrier method: a form of birth control that prevents sperm from reaching an egg

Birth control: methods for preventing pregnancy

Birth-control pill: a pill taken daily to prevent ovulation

Bisexual: having sexual attraction to people of two or more genders

Boundaries: guidelines set in relationships that define how each member wants to be treated

Brain: the organ of the body that controls functions, movements, sensations, and thoughts

Breast: the part of the chest that contains a gland for producing milk for a baby

Breast glands: the glands in the breast that create milk

Breast self-examination: a regular monthly examination of the breasts for changes in feel or appearance

Cervix: the ring-shaped neck of tissue that connects the vagina and the uterus

Cilia: tiny hairs that pull the egg into the fallopian tube and move it to the uterus

Circumcision: a procedure that removes the foreskin from a penis

Cisgender: the state of a person whose gender identity matches the biological sex they were assigned at birth

Clitoris: the female shaft; becomes erect when aroused

Conception: the process of becoming pregnant in which an egg is fertilized by a sperm

Conjoined twins: twins whose bodies are physically joined together in some way

Contractions: the constriction of the muscles of the uterus before and during childbirth

Crush: an intense and short-lived attraction to another person

Cyberbullying: the use of an electronic device to send or post hurtful messages to or about someone

Dental dam: a piece of latex placed over a vulva during oral sex to prevent the spread of STIs

Diaphragm: a dome-shaped cup that is placed over the cervix before sexual intercourse to prevent sperm from entering the uterus

Ejaculate: to eject sperm from the penis; the semen released during ejaculation

Ejaculation: the act of ejaculating

Embryo: the fertilized egg as it develops during the first eight weeks

Endometrium: the lining of the uterus

Epididymis: the tiny tubes on the back of the testicles that store sperm

Erection: the state when the tissue of a penis or clitoris fills with blood and becomes firm and swollen during arousal

Estrogen: the female sex hormone

Fallopian tubes: the tubes that carry the egg from the ovaries to the uterus

Female condom: a latex or plastic cover that is inserted into the vagina to collect ejaculate during vaginal intercourse

Fertilization: the joining of an egg and a sperm to create an embryo

Fetus: a developing human in the womb, usually from two months after conception until birth

Flaccid: not erect, firm, or stiff

Foreskin: the fold of skin that covers the glans of the penis

Fraternal twins: twins born from two eggs, each fertilized by a different sperm, that developed simultaneously in the womb

Gay/homosexual: having sexual attraction to people of the same gender, especially for men

Gender: the behaviors, traits, and characteristics typically associated with one sex

Gender fluid/genderqueer: identifying with more than one, or no gender category

Gender identity: a person's internal sense of their own gender

Gender non-conforming: not conforming to the traditional behaviors, traits, and characteristics associated with one's biological sex

Genderqueer/gender fluid: identifying with more than one, or no gender category

Genitals: the external reproductive organs

Glans: the head of the penis or the tip of the clitoris

Heterosexual/straight: having sexual attraction to people of the opposite gender

Homosexual/gay: having sexual attraction to people of the same gender, especially for men

Hormonal birth control: birth control that prevents ovulation

Hormones: chemicals released in the body that affect growth and development

Hymen: the thin tissue that partly covers the opening of the vagina at birth

Identical twins: twins born from one fertilized egg that split into two embryos with identical genetic material

Implant: a small hormonal birth-control method that is implanted into the arm

Intact penis: uncircumcised penis

Intimacy: the quality of a emotional closeness in a relationship

Intrauterine device (IUD): a long-term birth-control device placed in the uterus by a healthcare provider

In vitro fertilization (IVF): the process of fertilizing of an egg removed from an ovary, then implanting the fertilized egg into a uterus to grow and develop

Justifying grace: the grace that brings us into closer relationship with God

Labia: the lip-shaped folds of skin that surround the vulva

Labor: the physical activities occurring in a human body during childbirth

Lesbian: a woman who is sexually attracted to women

Male condom: a latex, plastic, or lambskin cover worn over the penis to collect semen during ejaculation

Masturbation: the act of stimulating one's own genitals for sexual pleasure

Menstrual cup: a flexible, bell-shaped, silicone piece that is inserted into the vagina to collect menstrual blood

Menstruation/period: the monthly discharging of blood and tissue from the uterus when pregnancy does not occur

Mons: the mound of skin along the pubic bone

Morning-after pill: a pill that can be taken after penile-vaginal intercourse to stop a pregnancy before it starts

Nipples: a small, round, raised part of the breast where milk comes out during nursing

Nocturnal emission/wet dream: an ejaculation that occurs during sleep

Oral sex: the sexual act of using the mouth to stimulate a partner's genitals

Orgasm: the muscular contractions or quick, pleasurable squeezing sensations that occur at the peak of sexual excitement

Ova: the reproductive cells of the female body *(the singular is ovum)*

Ovary: the female reproduction organ that produces and stores eggs, or ova

Ovulation: the release of an egg from the ovary

Pads: cotton liners that many people use during menstruation to collect the blood

Patch: a hormonal method of birth control that sticks to the skin and is changed once a week

Penile-vaginal intercourse: the sexual act of inserting a penis into a partner's vagina

Penis: the male shaft; becomes erect when aroused

Period/menstruation: the monthly discharging of blood and tissue from the uterus when pregnancy does not occur

Pituitary gland: a gland at the base of the brain that produces growth hormones

Placenta/amniotic sac: the membrane sac surrounding the embryo and fetus during pregnancy

Pornography: language, photos, or videos that depict sexual acts for the purpose of causing sexual excitement in the viewer

Pre-ejaculate/precum: fluids that are present at the tip of the penis before ejaculation

Pregnancy: the time when an embryo/fetus is developing in the uterus

Prejudice: judgment or opinion about someone made before getting to knowing them

Prevenient grace: God's grace that is with us before we are even aware of it

Prostate gland: an organ that surrounds the urethra and secretes fluid that combines with sperm to create semen

Puberty: the period during which human bodies mature and become capable of reproduction

Pubic hair: coarse hair that covers the genital area

Retract: the ability of the foreskin to pull back and expose the glans

Sanctifying grace: the grace that helps us grow and become more Christ-like

Scrotum: the sac behind the penis that holds the testicles

Semen: the combination of sperm and fluids from the prostate gland and seminal vesicles

Seminal vesicle: two small glands on either side of the bladder that produce a fluid that combines with sperm to create semen

Sex: biological category based on reproductive organs, hormones, and chromosomes; sexual intercourse

Sexting: sending sexual texts, photos, or other electronic communications

Sexual orientation: a person's established pattern of sexual attraction to other people, in terms of gender

Sexual touch: any touch that involves sexual arousal and/or the sexual parts of the body

Sexually Transmitted Infections (STIs): infections that are shared through sexual touch. See pages 55-56.

Shaft: a cylinder-shaped organ

Skin: the largest organ of the body, which covers the muscles and bones

Slough off: to shed or cast off

Sperm: the male reproductive cell

Spermicides: a chemical form of birth control that works by immobilizing or killing sperm

Sponge: white plastic foam piece that is inserted into the vagina to prevent sperm from entering into the uterus during sexual intercourse

Stereotype: an often unfair or untrue belief about people with a particular characteristic *(such as skin color, gender, sexual orientation, and so forth)*

Straight/heterosexual: having sexual attraction to people of the opposite gender

Surgical methods: surgery that prevents pregnancy by blocking the vas deferens or fallopian tubes

Surrogacy: the practice of a person carrying and delivering a baby for another couple

Tampon: a piece of absorbent material placed in the vagina to collect menstrual blood

Testicles/Testes: the reproductive gland that produces sperm

Testicular self-examination: a regular monthly examination of the testicles and the area around the scrotum to check for any changes in feel or look

Testosterone: the male sex hormone

Transgender/trans: the state of a person whose gender identity does not match the biological sex they were assigned at birth

Umbilical cord: the cord connecting the embryo/fetus to the placenta

Urinary sphincter: muscle that controls the release of urine from the bladder

Urethral opening: the opening for liquid waste, or urine, to exit the body

Uterus: the pear-shaped organ in which an embryo/fetus grows and develops

Vagina: a tube-like organ leading from the vaginal opening to the uterus

Vaginal opening: the opening that leads into the vagina

Values: the principles that guide a person in living a good life

Vas deferens: the tubes that carry sperm from the epididymis to ejaculation

Vulnerable: open to physical or emotional wounding or manipulation

Vulva: the external female genitals

Wet dream/nocturnal emission: an ejaculation that occurs during sleep

Resources

Below are sources and resources for the WONDERFULLY MADE PARTICIPANT BOOK, FACILITATOR GUIDE, CHURCH GUIDE, and PARENT GUIDE. Websites are constantly changing. Although the recommended websites were verified at the time the WONDERFULLY MADE resources were developed, we recommend that you double-check all websites to verify that they are still live.

Participant Book

American Psychological Association. "Sexual Orientation & Homosexuality." *http://www.apa.org/topics/lgbt/orientation.aspx*.

American Psychological Association. "Transgender People, Gender Identity, and Gender Expression." *http://www.apa.org/topics/lgbt/transgender.aspx*.

Corinna, Heather. *S.E.X.: The All-You-Need-to-Know Sexuality Guide to Get You Through Your Teens and Twenties*. 2nd ed. Boston: Da Capo Press, 2016.

Dailey, D. "Sexual Expression and Aging" in *The Dynamics of Aging*, edited by Forrest J. Berghorn and Donna E. Schafer, 311-333. Boulder, CO: Westview Press, 1981.

Peck, M. Scott. *The Road Less Traveled: A New Psychology of Love, Traditional Values, and Spiritual Growth*. New York: Simon & Schuster, 1978.

Ritchie, James H. *Created by God: Tweens, Faith, and Human Sexuality*. Nashville: Abingdon Press, 2009.

Facilitator Guide and Church Guide

American Psychological Association. "Key Terms and Concepts in Understanding Gender Diversity and Sexual Orientation Among Students." *http://www.apa.org/pi/lgbt/programs/safe-supportive/lgbt/key-terms.pdf*.

American Psychological Association. "Sexual Orientation & Homosexuality." *http://www.apa.org/topics/lgbt/orientation.aspx*.

American Psychological Association. "Transgender People, Gender Identity, and Gender Expression." *http://www.apa.org/topics/lgbt/transgender.aspx*.

Feinstein, Sheryl G. *Secrets of the Teenage Brain: Research-Based Strategies for Reaching and Teaching Today's Adolescents*. 2nd ed. Thousand Oaks, CA: Corwin, 2009.

Schachter, C.L., et al. *Handbook on Sensitive Practice for Health Care Practitioners: Lessons from Adult Survivors of Childhood Sexual Abuse*. Ottawa: Public Health Agency of Canada. *http://publications.gc.ca/collections/collection_2010/aspc-phac/HP20-11-2009-eng.pdf*.

Schergen, Lisa and Hebert, Stephanie D. *Guide to Trauma-Informed Sex Education.* Cardea Services, 2016. *http://www.cardeaservices.org/resourcecenter/guide-to-trauma-informed-sex-education.*

Schladale, J. *A Trauma Informed Approach for Adolescent Sexual Health.* Resources for Resolving Violence, Inc., 2013. *http://resourcesforresolvingviolence.com/wp-content/uploads/A-Trauma-Informed-Approach-for-Adolescent-Sexual-Health.pdf.*

Substance Abuse and Mental Health Services Administration. *SAMHSA's Concept of Trauma and Guidance for a Trauma-Informed Approach.* HHS Publication No. (SMA) 14-4884. Rockville, MD: Substance Abuse and Mental Health Services Administration, 2014. *https://store.samhsa.gov/shin/content/SMA14-4884/SMA14-4884.pdf.*

Parent Guide

American Academy of Child & Adolescent Psychiatry. "Adolescent Development Part 1." *Facts for Families Guide* no. 57 (2015). *http://www.aacap.org/AACAP/Families_and_Youth/Facts_for_Families/FFF-Guide/Normal-Adolescent-Development-Part-I-057.aspx.*

American Academy of Pediatrics. HealthyChildren.org. "Kids & Tech: Tips for Parents in the Digital Age." *https://www.healthychildren.org/English/family-life/Media/Pages/Tips-for-Parents-Digital-Age.aspx.*

American Psychological Association. "Bullying." *http://www.apa.org/topics/bullying.*

American Psychological Association. "Developing Adolescents: A Reference for Professionals." Last modified 2002. *http://www.apa.org/pubs/info/brochures/develop.aspx.*

American Psychological Association. "Sexual Orientation & Homosexuality." *http://www.apa.org/topics/lgbt/orientation.aspx.*

American Psychological Association. "Transgender People, Gender Identity, and Gender Expression." *http://www.apa.org/topics/lgbt/transgender.aspx.*

Encyclopedia of Children's Health. "Puberty." *http://www.healthofchildren.com/P/Puberty.html.*

Federal Trade Commission. "Consumer Information: Protecting Kids Online." *https://www.consumer.ftc.gov/topics/protecting-kids-online.*

Georgia Campaign for Adolescent Power & Potential. "Family Communication About Sexuality: Technology." *http://www.gcapp.org/sites/default/files/images/family.comm_.tech_.pdf.*

Hofmann, Janell Burley. *iRules: What Every Tech-Healthy Family Needs to Know about Selfies, Sexting, Gaming, and Growing Up.* New York: Rodale Press, 2014.

Lucas, Cheri. "Spotting a Fake: Teaching Website Evaluation Skills." Education.com. *https://www.education.com/magazine/article/Website_Literacy*.

PACER's National Bullying Prevention Center. *http://www.pacer.org/bullying*.

Spano, Sedra. "Stages of Adolescent Development." ACT for Youth Upstate Center of Excellence. *http://www.actforyouth.net/resources/rf/rf_stages_0504.pdf*.

U.S. Department of Health & Human Services. "Bullying Definition." *https://www.stopbullying.gov/what-is-bullying/definition/index.html*.

Vogelaar, Amy. *Positive Encounters: Talking One-to-One with Teens about Contraceptive and Safer Sex Decisions: A Guidebook for Professionals*. Morristown, NJ: Center for Family Life Education, Planned Parenthood of Greater Northern New Jersey, 1999.

Ylvisaker, Mark; Hibbard, Mary; Feeney, Timothy. "Tutorial: Concrete vs. Abstract Thinking." LEARNet: A Resource for Teachers, Clinicians, Parents, and Students by the Brain Injury Association of New York State. *http://www.projectlearnet.org/tutorials/concrete_vs_abstract_thinking.html*.

A Note from the Adults Who Care About You

Made in the USA
Coppell, TX
06 January 2023

10389662R00055

Underst
Christianity 3

Sue Penney

Heinemann

Heinemann Educational Publishers
Halley Court, Jordan Hill, Oxford OX2 8EJ
a division of Reed Educational & Professional Publishing Ltd

OXFORD MELBOURNE AUCKLAND
JOHANNESBURG BLANTYRE GABORONE
IBADAN PORTSMOUTH (NH) USA CHICAGO

Heinemann is a registered trademark of Reed Educational & Professional Publishing Ltd.

First published in 1999

03 02 01 00 99
10 9 8 7 6 5 4 3 2 1

British Library Cataloguing in Publication Data
A catalogue record for this book is available from the British Library

ISBN 0 435 36796 X

Designed and typeset by Artistix, Thame, Oxon
Illustrations by Artistix, Thame, Oxon
Cover design by Aricot Vert Design
Printed and bound in Spain by Mateu Cromo

Acknowledgements
The publishers would like to thank the following for permission to reproduce copyright material: Christian Aid for the diagram from Time for Tea on p.60; The Corrymeela Community, 8 Upper Crescent, Belfast, BT7 1NT (website: http\\www.corrymeela.org.uk), for the quote on p.37; Kingsway Thankyou Music for the hymns 'God of glory we exalt your name' and 'Eternal God we come to you', by David Fellingham, copyright © 1982 and 1983 Kingsway Thankyou Music, PO Box 75, Eastbourne, East Sussex, BN23 6NW, UK. Used by permission on pp.13, 4; Lion Publishing for the map adapted from *A Lion Handbook to the History of Christianity*, copyright © 1977 Lion Publishing, on p.24; Oxford University Press for the hymn 'God is love, his the care' by Percy Dearmer (1867-1936) from *Enlarged Songs of Praise 1931*, by permission of Oxford University Press, on p.13; The Salvation Army for the extract on p.56, printed by permission of The Salvation Army UKT; The World Council of Churches, 150 Route de Ferney, 1211 Geneva 2, Switzerland, for the logo on p.40. Quotations from the Bible used throughout the book are taken from *The Good News Bible*, published by the Bible Society/HarperCollins Publishers, UK © American Bible Society, 1966, 1971, 1976, 1992.

The publishers would like to thank the following for permission to reproduce photographs: Agnew & Sons/Bridgeman p.20; AKG p.5, 12, 26, 27, 28, 29, 50, 51; AKG London/Stefan Drechsel p.28; AKG London/Erich Lessing p.45, 55; AKG/Munch/DACS p.44; Asian Christian Art Association p.23; Mark Azevedo p.43; Julian Baum/Science Photo Library p.6; Bridgeman p.22; British Library p.42; British Museum p.14; Canterbury City Council p.25; Chester Mystery Plays/Clint Hughes p.12; Circa p.4; Cobis-Bettmann p.9; City of Bristol Museum/Bridgeman p.26; Jerry Cooke/Corbis p.53; Corrymeela p.37; CTB/David Hastilow p.8; Jamie Drummond/Christian Aid/Still Pictures p.60; Mark Edwards/Still Pictures p.39; Catherine Emmerson p.33; EPA/Anatoly Maltsev/P.A News p.11; E.R. Degginger/Science Photo Library p.10; e.t. Archive p.21, 22, 48; Mary Evans p.38; Fine Art p.23; Fitzwilliam Museum/ Bridgeman p.19; Simon Fraser/Science Photo Library p.59; Galleria Dell Academia/Bridgeman p.4; Fiona Hanson/PA p.31; Hanan Isachar/Corbis p.18; John Rylands Library, University of Manchester p.47; Lambeth Palace Library/Bridgeman p.46; S. Leutenegger © Ateliers et Presses de Taizé, F-71250 Taizé-Community p.34, 35; Museo Nazionale/e.t. archive p.8; Museo De Bellas Artes/Bridgeman p.8; Northwest Photographers p.32; Richard T. Nowitz/Corbis p.15, 16; Eileen Orr p.12; Pictor p.57; PLI/Science Photo Library p.58; Stefan Rousseau/PA p.36; David Rubinger/Corbis p.17; The Salvation Army p.56; Michael St. Maur Sheil/Corbis p.30; Richard Hamilton Smith/Corbis p.7; Liba Taylor/ Corbis p.54; Tearfund p.61; Justin Williams/PA p.49; Gwyneth Windsor p.13.

The publishers have made every effort to contact copyright holders. However, if any material has been incorrectly acknowledged, the publishers would be pleased to correct this at the earliest opportunity.

Contents

1 Where and what is God?

Eternal God, we come to you
we come before your throne;
we enter by a new and living way,
with confidence we come.
We declare your faithfulness,
your promises are true,
we will now draw near to worship you.

Belief in God is an essential part of the Christian faith. Many Christians have their own ideas about where and what God is. This unit looks at ideas that most Christians would agree with.

What does the Bible say?

The Bible assumes that there is a God, and it does not really have any answers for people who are asking for proof. Christians believe that through the stories, songs and letters in the Bible, especially what they tell about the life and teaching of Jesus, they can learn what God is like. They believe that the Bible shows a loving God who cares so much about the people he created that he even sent his own son to die for their sake.

Where is God?

Hundreds of years ago, the popular idea of God was as a 'super-human' who lived in **heaven**. The Lord's Prayer, for example, begins 'Our father, who art in heaven.' Heaven was generally presented as a place of light and joy above the clouds, where good people went when they died (see unit 26). There were angels to carry out God's instructions, and the most important part of heaven was the throne where God was sitting. Today, Christians are more likely to talk of God as a force or power which is within them as well as beyond them.

This is not a new idea, however, as this simple prayer shows. It comes from a book of prayers which was printed in 1514.

God be in my head,
and in my understanding;
God be in my eyes,
and in my looking;
God be in my mouth,
and in my speaking;
God be in my heart,
and in my thinking;
God be at mine end,
and at my departing.

'God the Father Enthroned' (fourteenth century)

What is God?

All Christians would agree that it is not possible to describe God completely or accurately. If we could do this as human beings, it would mean that we could understand God. If we could understand God, then we would be equal with God, so we would also be God. This is clearly nonsense. When Christians think of God they usually use words which they say are as near as we can get to describing him. Words such as king, father, creator, holy one and love are often used by Christians to describe God. In John's Gospel Jesus says, 'God is Spirit, and only by the power of his Spirit can people worship him as he really is' (John 4, 24). Christians believe that Jesus gave them this power, even though what they are worshipping is also called the 'great unknown'.

A nineteenth century picture of God ruling the universe

Summing up

Believing in God is a matter of faith, not of proof.

Activities

A **1** In the hymn at the start of this unit, the writer talks about approaching God by a 'new and living way'. What do you think he means? Why is this so important for Christians?

2 Why do you think people used to think of God as an old man in the clouds? Why could most people not imagine this today?

B **3** 'To have faith is to be sure of the things we hope for, to be certain of the things we cannot see' (Hebrews 11, 1). Explain what you think this means. What things in your own life could you describe like this?

4 What are the reasons why Christians say it is not possible to describe God accurately? What do you feel is the best description?

C **5** The French philosopher Voltaire once said, 'If God did not exist, it would be necessary to invent him'. What do you think he meant? What arguments might people put forward to agree or disagree with him?

2 Is there anybody there?

Not everyone believes in a god or God. People who say that there is definitely no God are called **atheists**. Most atheists argue that the universe came about by chance. This follows the **big-bang theory**, that the universe began in a gigantic explosion. The explosion scattered matter, which eventually became planets and stars. This theory says that life developed on our planet because the conditions for life happened to be right. Many atheists say that the evil and suffering in our world means it is impossible that it could have been created by a God who cared about it.

Some people say that it is not possible to know whether or not there is a God. They are called **agnostics**. They argue that it is beyond the ability of human beings to understand any God. Since we cannot understand what God is, they say, it is impossible to be sure of anything about him. Therefore they believe that the only sensible course is to say that we cannot know whether or not God exists.

Believing in God

Ever since human beings began, most people have believed in some sort of power which was greater than themselves. They often call this power God. Everyone who believes in God would probably give slightly different reasons for their belief. It is something about which everyone has to make up their own mind. What one person thinks of as being as certain proof, someone else may regard as nonsense.
Here are some of the most important reasons that believers give for believing in God:

- They were told about God by people they trust (parents, friends).
- They can see God in beauty – in the natural world, in a painting or piece of music.
- They have experience of God's power – in creation, in nature.
- They have experience of God in an amazing event.

Stars forming

Amazing events

There are two sorts of amazing event in which people say they experience God. The first sort are often described as **miracles**, where the usual laws of nature seem to have been set aside. For example, someone is ill and expected to die, but they miraculously recover. Sometimes amazingly unlikely coincidences happen, and these are also called miracles. When Christians describe events like these as experiences of God, they usually see them as an answer to prayer. Sometimes the prayer is made by the person themselves, sometimes it is made on their behalf by a group of other people.

Some people experience God in music

The second sort of amazing event which often affects people's religious beliefs is some kind of personal encounter or meeting. Sometimes people have dreams in which they see or meet someone or something. Many people who have 'died' for a short time, then been brought back to life (for example, in an operating theatre), report similar experiences of travelling down a tunnel towards a bright light. Some say they saw a figure of light coming towards them.

Whole books have been written about apparently ordinary people who have been involved in this sort of extraordinary event. Some people feel that their life will never be the same again. Sometimes they say that the experience has persuaded them of the truth of religion. However, although experiences like these may mean a great deal to the people involved in them, they don't really answer any of the major questions about religion. The events can often be explained or traced back to other things that have happened in the person's life.

Summing up

Working out what to believe is a very personal thing. One person's reasons for believing in something may not convince someone else, but this does not mean that either of them is wrong.

Activities

A

1 Explain what the big-bang theory is. How could it support an atheist's views? What might a Christian's opinion be?

2 Some people say they believe in God because they have been told about him by someone they trust. What do you think of this? What advantages and disadvantages can you think of?

B

3 'Believe, in order to understand' (St Augustine). What does this tell you about faith in God? What answer might an atheist or agnostic give?

4 When 'miracles' are reported, crowds of sightseers and media reporters often flock to the scene. Why do you think people are so interested in this sort of event?

C

5 In a recent survey, over 60 per cent of people said that they had had a religious experience, but very few of them had any contact with a Church or organized religion. Work in groups to discuss why you think this is the case. What do you think you would feel about this if you were a Church leader?

3 Go on, then – prove it!

What is philosophy of religion?

Philosophers are thinkers, people who try to make sense of the world and of human beings by reasoning about them in an ordered and logical way. Philosophy of religion, as its name suggests, means thinking about God in this way. All through history, great thinkers have put together ideas to try to explain the existence of God, and what he might be like if he does exist. Many of these arguments are complicated and hard to understand. This unit is a brief introduction to the main ideas.

Philosophical arguments about God

Philosophical ideas about God can be put into four main groups. Each group is linked with the philosopher who first thought of it. For each group there are also arguments which disagree with the ideas.

The argument from God 'being'

This idea was really thought up by St Anselm, an archbishop of Canterbury who lived from 1093 to 1109. St Anselm argued that God must exist, because if he does not, he would not be God. To explain it another way: If God exists, he is perfect. If he does not exist, he is not perfect. Therefore he must exist. People who argue against this say that it dodges the question of whether God really exists. It only says what God must be if he does exist.

The argument from the world

This comes from the ideas of St Thomas Aquinas (1224–74). He argued that the world around us shows that God exists. Everything has a cause, which can be traced back to what happened before it.

St Thomas Aquinas

(You are reading this book because you are in school; you are in school because the law says you have to be, and so on.) But this tracing back must stop somewhere. St Thomas Aquinas said that where it stops – the basic cause of everything – must be God. The problem with this argument is that it does not work for anyone who does not wish to see God as the cause. Someone who does not want to believe that God is the basic cause of everything could equally say that things are as they are because that's just the way things are.

The argument from order

This idea goes back originally to Aristotle, a Greek philosopher who lived 300 years before the time of Jesus. However, it has been adopted by many Christian thinkers.

Did this world happen by chance?

Aristotle

It says that the world and the universe are so carefully organized that it is impossible that they came about by chance. For example, our world has a thin bubble of atmosphere which has exactly the right mix of gases, at the perfect temperature, to allow life to develop. Could this possibly have happened by chance? This is probably one of the most popular ideas today, but there are problems with it. Many things in the world do not seem to fit with a good design – natural disasters cause enormous suffering, freak accidents cannot be explained.

The argument from what is right

This idea came from Immanuel Kant (1724–1804). He said that the proof of God is in our conscience – the feeling that we *should* or *must* do, or not do, things. He argued that because these feelings come even when we do not want them to, they must come from God. The problem with this is that no two people have exactly the same conscience. What you believe to be right or wrong depends on what you have been taught, and many other things. Your conscience may tell you that you should not eat meat or that you should not pinch your little sister when she annoys you, but your friend's conscience may say something different!

Immanuel Kant

Summing up

No matter how many clever people try to explain the existence of God, in the end everyone has to make up their own mind about what they believe.

Activities

A

1 Philosophers have struggled to prove the existence of God for hundreds of years. Why do you think they feel it so important?

2 Despite the efforts of philosophers, no human being has ever proved that God exists. Write down as many reasons as you can think of to explain why millions of people believe in him.

B

3 Make a list of as many things in your life as you can, which require you to have faith in someone or something. In what ways can you prove your faith is justified?

4 Choose one of the four theories listed in this unit. Explain what it is (find out more about it if you can) and say:
(a) why people might find it helpful
(b) what problems there are with it.

C

5 Immanuel Kant said that conscience was very important. Write a story – real or imagined – about an occasion when your conscience 'spoke' to you. Did you obey it?

4 Good God! – the problem of evil

The problem of evil and suffering in the world is one of the most difficult that Christians have to face. On the one hand, Christianity teaches that God is good and that he cares about the world. On the other hand, Christians look at the world – the one that God is supposed to care about – and see suffering all around them.

Types of suffering

Many people think that suffering falls into two types. Some suffering comes from human beings. God did not invent war or bombs, he did not invent child abuse or bullying. The sufferings in this group can be explained by blaming them on the selfishness of human beings and their search for power.

The other group includes natural disasters. Most Christians would hesitate before saying that God actually invented earthquakes or volcanoes or painful diseases, but human beings did not invent them either. They are part of the way the world is – but Christians believe that the world was made by God. This means there are questions they cannot avoid:

- Why does God allow evil things to happen?
- Why do innocent, good people so often seem to be the ones who suffer?
- Why do some people seem to have been born evil?

The answers

No Christian would claim to have complete answers to questions like these. But some people have had ideas which they feel go some way towards giving an answer.

A volcano erupting in Hawaii

Some Christians believe that the key lies in the word trust. They would say something like 'God is way beyond our understanding, but we believe that he is good. He must have designed a purpose in suffering, even though we cannot understand it.' Other people, of course, would say that this is a cop-out! A similar idea is based on things being equalled out after death. No matter how great the suffering in this world may be, it will not be important in the life after death, because the joy of that life will be so great.

Why do innocent people suffer?

Another answer lies in the idea of contrasts. Life cannot be good all the time, because then we would not appreciate it, in the same way that we could not appreciate sunshine if it were not for rain. Suffering is necessary to give us something to compare it with. However, this leads on to another question, which is: Why does suffering have to be so great?

Human beings have free will – they can choose whether to do right or wrong. Pain and suffering are necessary to give people choices. For example, if God jumped in to stop cars crashing and people being killed, there would be no point in the drivers choosing to drive carefully. According to this theory, much of the suffering in the world would not happen if people lived in the way that God intended.

Being a Christian does not protect people from suffering. When Christians come across great suffering in their own lives they usually react in one of two ways. Some Christians find that they can no longer believe in a God who is good, and it destroys their faith. More often, people find that through their faith they can make sense of their suffering, and they become more deeply convinced that what they believe is true.

Summing up

The problem of suffering is one to which every Christian struggles to find an answer.

Activities

A

1 Work in pairs. Think of as many examples as you can of suffering in the world. Then divide them into the two groups of 'natural' and 'people-made'.

2 Some people believe that pain is a punishment from God. What reasons would they give?

B

3 Choose one example from your list of 'people-made' sufferings in question 1. Write a paragraph explaining what causes the suffering, and what changes would be necessary for it to be prevented. Do you think the changes come under the heading of 'people living in the way that God intended'?

4 Explain why suffering has to result from human beings having free will. Think of a situation where a caring God could prevent suffering by taking over. Write a paragraph or draw a cartoon to describe what might happen.

C

5 List as many ways as you can think of in which Christians are working to make the world a better place. Find out about one person or organization, and put together a short profile explaining their work.

5 What do Christians say about God?

Many books have been written about who God is, what he is like and what Christians believe about him. In the history of Christianity, there are thousands of descriptions of God. They range from majestic poems, through long, complicated essays to snatches of prayers. This unit only has space to look at a few of them, but they are descriptions with which most Christians would agree.

St Augustine

St Augustine of Hippo was a great Christian writer and thinker who lived from 354 to 430CE. He was Bishop of Hippo, in what is now Algeria. He had a great influence on Christian thinking, both in his lifetime and afterwards. His two most famous books are The Confessions and The City of God. This quotation is from one of the most famous paragraphs in The Confessions.

Man is one of your creatures, Lord, and his instinct is to praise you … The thought of you stirs him so deeply that he cannot be content unless he praises you, because you made us for yourself and our hearts find no peace until they rest in you.

Mystery plays

During the Middle Ages, **mystery plays** were put on by tradespeople in many towns. They were plays telling stories from the Bible. This is part of one of God's speeches in The Tanner's Play, from the York Mystery Plays.

A scene from the Chester Mystery Plays, as performed in 1997

I am gracious and great,
God without beginning;
I am maker unmade, all might is in me;
I am life and way unto wealth-winning;
I am foremost and first, as I bid it shall be.

John Donne

John Donne was a priest and poet who lived in England in the seventeenth century. This is part of one of his Divine Meditations:

Wilt thou love God, as he thee? Then digest,
*My **soul**, this wholesome meditation,*
How God the Spirit, by angels waited on
*In heaven, doth make his **temple** in thy breast … .*
'Twas much, that man was made like God before,
But, that God should be made like man, much more.

Modern hymns

These two quotations are both from hymns written in the twentieth century. Both are often sung in churches, and both show Christian beliefs about God. However, they describe God in quite different ways.

God of glory, we exalt your name,
You who reign in majesty.
We lift our hearts to you
And we will worship, praise and
magnify your holy name.
In power resplendent you reign in glory,
Eternal King, you reign for ever.
Your word is mighty, releasing captives,
Your love is gracious,
You are my God.

God is love: his the care,
Tending each, everywhere.
God is love – all is there!
Jesus came to show him,
That we all might know him:
Sing aloud, loud, loud!
Sing aloud, loud, loud!
God is good! God is truth! God is
beauty! Praise him!

Christians believe that praising God is important

Summing up

Christian beliefs about God can be expressed in many different ways.

Activities

A **1** Look at all the quotations in this unit. Which one do you think sums up best what Christians believe about God? Give reasons for your choice.

2 Using the quotation you used for question 1, or a different one, explain in your own words what it says about God.

B **3** The mystery plays were very popular in the Middle Ages. Write down as many reasons as you can why they were important.

4 Writing things 'to the glory of God' has been important to Christians all through history. In what other ways can Christians praise God?

C **5** Using your own ideas, or what you have learned in this section, write your own description of how Christians see God. You could write it as a poem or a prayer if you prefer.

6 Did Jesus ever exist? I

He never wrote a book – but countless books have been written about him.
He never founded a college – but his teachings have influenced people all over the world.
He never commanded an army – but for centuries volunteers have fought in his name.
He was never wealthy, but millions of people say he has given them riches beyond their wildest dreams.

Anon

If Jesus *had* written a book or commanded an army, it would probably be much easier to find out definite facts about his life. As it is, we don't know when he was born or when he died, what he looked like or how he spent the greater part of his life. Most of the information we do have about him comes from people who were his friends, and so it could be thought to be biased. Because of the lack of evidence, some people today reject the whole idea that Jesus ever lived. Many other people feel that the stories of Jesus' life might be based on fact, but have been exaggerated and are little more than fairy stories. This unit looks at the written evidence which Christians might use to support their belief that Jesus really lived.

Jesus in writings by non-Christians

Apart from the Gospels, the earliest writings which mention Jesus are by Roman authors. Tacitus, whose writings date from about 115CE, described the persecution of Christians in Rome by the Emperor Nero. His explanation of who Christians were says, 'the originator of that name, Christus, had been executed when Tiberius was Emperor, by order of the procurator Pontius Pilate'.

In 112CE Pliny, who was a governor of part of what is now Turkey, wrote a letter to the Emperor Trajan. It seems that he had been asked for information about whether Christians might cause trouble. In his letter he said that the Christians seemed to be harmless and met at dawn to 'sing hymns to Christ as to a God'. He described their beliefs as 'superstition carried to extreme lengths'.

Jesus is also mentioned several times in the writings of Josephus. He lived from 37 or 38 to 101CE. Some of the references to Jesus may have been added to his work by Christians, but it is unlikely that all of them were. Although he worked for the Romans and wrote about Roman history, Josephus was Jewish. The fact that he mentions Jesus means that a Jewish writer, who had lived in Galilee, was writing about Jesus in official records while people who could have known Jesus were still alive.

This is the earliest known picture of Jesus. It comes from a fourth century mosaic found in a Roman villa in Dorset

Studying ancient manuscripts requires a lot of care

Jesus in Christian writings

Most of the information about Jesus' life comes from the four Gospels in the Bible. Some people argue that the Gospels should not count as evidence, because they were written by Jesus' followers. However, many Christians would argue the opposite. They feel that the Gospels should be accepted as evidence *because* they were written by people who believed that Jesus was special. They would say that Jesus' followers had most reason to make sure that what was written down about him was true. Thousands of scholars have studied the Gospels over hundreds of years (see unit 20). They have not always agreed over how much of the Gospels should be thought of as true, but few have decided that they are totally false. Most Christians feel that the picture of Jesus which is shown in the Gospels is a real one, at least in the most important points.

Summing up

Christians believe that there is enough evidence to be sure that a historical Jesus existed.

Activities

A

1 Why do some people say that the Gospels should not be counted as evidence for Jesus really existing?

2 Why is it important that evidence about Jesus was written down while people who had known him were still alive?

B

3 What reasons might Christians give for believing that the Bible is accurate? Why do you think this is important to them?

4 Write down as many reasons as you can why so many scholars have spent their whole working lives studying the Gospels.

C

5 Find out more about one of the writers mentioned in this unit. Work in small groups to put together a wall display about their life and work, and their attitude to Christianity.

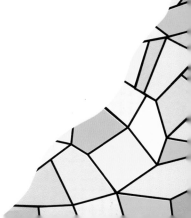

7 Did Jesus ever exist? II

Some Christians feel that finding out about how Jesus and his friends lived helps them to understand more about their own faith. One of the first people we know of who tried to do this was Helena, whose son Constantine was the first Roman Emperor to become a Christian. She visited Jerusalem in 330CE, and tradition says that she found and bought the cross and nails with which Jesus was crucified, and the robe he was wearing.

Archaeology

A few archaeologists have worked in the areas where Jesus is supposed to have lived so that they could 'prove' that the Gospels are true. More often, discoveries connected with the stories in the Gospels are made by chance. Jesus was not rich or important in the country, and there is no reason why anything from his life should have survived. But many discoveries have been made which show that details in the stories of Jesus' life in the Gospels are accurate. This unit looks at two of those discoveries.

Capernaum

In the last hundred years, archaeologists have discovered the site of the town of Capernaum. The place is no longer occupied, but the ruins of a synagogue which dates from the fourth century CE have been found. Beneath those ruins are the foundations of another synagogue, which goes back to the first century CE. This could have been the one where Jesus preached. Nearby, archaeologists have found the remains of a church dating from the fifth century CE. It was octagonal in shape, which in those days meant it was a special building. Beneath it were found the remains of an ordinary house, dating from the first century. Scratched into what was left of the walls of the house were Christian phrases such as 'Lord Jesus Christ' and 'Christ have mercy'. These 'graffiti' mean that the house must have been used as a meeting place for Christians. Probably no one will ever know, but the house is now often called 'St Peter's house'. Some Christians even believe that it might have belonged to Jesus himself!
Elsewhere in Capernaum, archaeologists have discovered the remains of Roman baths. They were large – over 20 metres long – which suggests there were large numbers of Roman soldiers in the town. This would fit with the mention of a centurion (a soldier in charge of 100 others) based in Capernaum (Luke 7).

The site of Capernaum (the octagonal shape at the bottom right is 'St Peter's house')

A fishing boat

In January 1986, a long drought in Israel caused the water level in the Sea of Galilee to drop. The remains of a boat became visible in the mud at the edge of the water, about eight kilometres away from Capernaum. Experts were called in when people realized that it was very old. Scientific tests have shown that it dates from between 40BCE and 40CE. It is just over eight metres long, just over two metres wide and a metre and a half high. The frame that remains suggests it had a covered area in the stern. In Mark's account of how Jesus calmed a storm on the lake, he says that Jesus was asleep in the back of the boat (Mark 4). Experts have worked out that the boat would have needed a crew of five, which fits with the story of how James and John 'left their father Zebedee in the boat with the hired men' (Mark 1, 19). It also suggests that the disciples were not as poor as some people have tried to make out, because equipment like this would have cost quite a lot of money. When the remains were found, newspapers all over the world were quick to call it 'the boat of Jesus and Peter', but of course this is not likely to be true.

The boat hull being excavated

However, the boat's discovery has added to what people know about the way of life at the time of Jesus.

Archaeological discoveries like these can never prove anything about Christian beliefs. But they have proved some of the details of the Gospels to be accurate, when many people had thought that the details were either made up by the writers or were based on misunderstandings.

Summing up

Many Christians feel that it adds to what they believe about the Gospels when the writers are shown to have been careful and accurate in the details they record.

Activities

A

1. Do you think it is likely that Helena really bought the cross, nails and robe of Jesus? What reasons can you give?
2. Why do you think newspapers labelled the discovery 'the boat of Jesus and Peter'? Why is this not likely to be accurate?

B

3. Why are people who set out to prove the Gospels are true likely to be disappointed?
4. Explain why some Christians feel that archaeological discoveries like these add to their faith.

C

5. Write your own newspaper report on one of the discoveries in this unit. Include a picture, and perhaps an interview with Christians about its importance. You could look up the Bible stories to add details.

8 Who do people say that I am?

The Transfiguration

Transfiguration means 'changing appearance'. The story of Jesus' Transfiguration is in all three **Synoptic** Gospels (Matthew, Mark and Luke). This is how Mark tells the story.

Six days later Jesus took with him Peter, James, and John, and led them up a high mountain, where they were alone. As they looked on, a change came over Jesus, and his clothes became shining white – whiter than anyone in the world could wash them. Then the three disciples saw Elijah and Moses talking with Jesus. Peter spoke up and said to Jesus, 'Teacher, how good it is that we are here! We will make three tents, one for you, one for Moses, and one for Elijah.' He and the others were so frightened that he did not know what to say.

Then a cloud appeared and covered them with its shadow, and a voice came from the cloud, 'This is my own dear Son – listen to him!' They took a quick look round but did not see anyone else; only Jesus was with them.

(Mark 9, 2–8)

The background

In all three accounts, the story of the Transfiguration comes soon after a conversation between Jesus and his disciples.

Mount Hermon, possibly the site of the Transfiguration

He had asked them who people said that he was. The disciples said that some people thought he was John the Baptist, others that he was Elijah (an important **prophet**), others that he was another prophet. Then Jesus asked who the disciples thought he was. Peter replied, 'You are the **Messiah**.' This was a stunning thing to say. Jews at the time were waiting for the Messiah who would be God's messenger to free the Jews and begin God's kingdom on earth. Peter's words show that the disciples believed Jesus was very special. For Christians, the Transfiguration shows that Peter was right.

What does the story mean?

The story of the Transfiguration is quite difficult to understand. It is important to realize that, like many other stories in the Bible, it probably includes picture language. The writer and early readers of the Gospel would have recognized this, but people today have to guess at it. An example is the description of Jesus' clothes shining brightly. At the time, shining light was often used as a **symbol** of God's glory. It describes the splendour and majesty of God. So describing Jesus like this would have been understood as Jesus sharing the glory of God.

Why are Moses and Elijah included?

Many Christians, of course, believe that they are included because they were there. However, there are also symbolic reasons why they were mentioned. Moses was the great leader who led the Jews out of Egypt when they had been slaves. Elijah is one of the first and most important prophets in the Jewish **Scriptures**. He was expected to return to earth before the Messiah came. Putting the two of them together is a way of summing up the whole Jewish faith. In other words, by putting them together, the Gospel writers are trying to show that the teachings of the Jewish Scriptures were looking forward to Jesus. The voice makes it clear that Jesus is the most important of the three.

A sixteenth century artist's idea of the Transfiguration

Why did Peter offer to build tents for them all?

There are several possible answers to this question, and no one is really sure. Most people think he was just so puzzled and scared that he said the first thing that came into his head.

Summing up

Christians believe that the Transfiguration was a special way of showing the disciples how important Jesus was.

Activities

A 1 Explain the importance of Jesus being seen with Moses and Elijah.

2 Why do you think Mark says Jesus' clothes became 'whiter than anyone in the world could wash them'?

B 3 Mountains, clouds and shining lights are symbols for the presence of God in many Bible stories. Why do you think this is so?

4 Look up the story of Jesus' baptism in Mark 1. What similarity do you notice? (See verse 11.) List as many reasons as you can why these two events may be connected.

C 5 Imagine that you are Peter, looking back on this day. Write down what you felt and what it meant to you.

9 The titles of Jesus

Jesus used many titles for himself and the Gospel writers, especially John, use others. Looking at the way Jesus described himself, and how early Christians described him, is important. It can show us more about what Jesus thought of himself, and what the first Christians thought about him.

Jesus

Jesus was given his name by the angel who announced his birth to Mary (Luke 1, 31). Jesus is the Greek form of the name. The **Hebrew** form, Joshua, means 'God saves'. Joshua was a very common name at the time, which is why Jesus is often referred to as 'Jesus of Nazareth'.

An eighteenth century painting of the vision of Daniel

Christ

This was not Mary and Joseph's surname! Christ is the Greek form of the Hebrew word Messiah. It means '**anointed** one' – that is, someone who has been chosen. For many Jews at the time of Jesus, it meant the person God would send to free them from the Romans whom they hated. The Messiah would begin God's kingdom on earth. Jesus appears to have avoided using this name.

Titles Jesus used for himself

Son of Man

According to the Gospels, the title which Jesus used most often was 'Son of Man'. It is only used by Jesus himself. Many Christians believe that Jesus intended people to be reminded of a passage in the Book of Daniel.

> *I saw what looked like a human being.* [This is often translated 'Son of Man'.] *He was approaching me, surrounded by clouds, and he went to the one who had been living for ever and was presented to him. He was given authority, honour, and royal power, so that the people of all nations, races and languages would serve him. His authority would last for ever and his kingdom would never end.*
>
> (Daniel 7, 13–14)

Son of God

Christians believe that this quotation from Daniel shows that Jesus intended 'Son of Man' to go together with 'Son of God'. According to Mark's Gospel, during Jesus' trial the High Priest asked him, 'Are you the Messiah, the Son of the Blessed God?' and Jesus replied, 'I am.' For Christians, the belief that Jesus is the Son of God is an essential part of their faith.

Jesus as the Good Shepherd (fifth century)

Summing up

The different titles used for Jesus in the Bible are ways of showing what his followers believe about him.

Titles used for Jesus

Lord

The word which is used for Lord in the New Testament is the same word which is used for God in the Old Testament. It is mainly used of Jesus after the **Resurrection**. 'Jesus is Lord' was one of the first statements of belief for Christians, and it is still one of the most important.

Son of David

This title is used most in Matthew's Gospel. Many people believed the Messiah would be a descendant of King David, Israel's greatest king.

Titles used in John's Gospel

John's Gospel is different from the others (see unit 22). Many titles used in it are not used anywhere else in the Bible. 'The Word' describes Jesus as the word of God. In the Old Testament, this is God's creative power. 'Lamb of God' reminds people of the lambs which were **sacrificed** in the Jewish Temple. It describes him as an offering for people's **sin**. The 'Good Shepherd' suggests Jesus looking after human beings, like a good shepherd looks after sheep. Many of these titles have been used in Christian art.

Activities

A

1 Why do you think so many different titles were used for Jesus? Which one do you think describes him best?

2 In the quotation from Daniel, who do you think the writer means by 'the one who had been living for ever'? Why might he use this description?

B

3 Look up Luke 1, 31. Explain as carefully as you can what it says about how and why Mary was told to call her baby Jesus.

4 Why do you think 'Word' is used as a way of describing the creative power of God? Look up the first chapter of Genesis in the Bible. How can you tell that God's words have power?

C

5 If you have a nickname, write a paragraph saying how you earned it and how you feel about it. If you don't have one yourself, use the example of a friend or someone famous. What do names like these tell you about the person?

10 Jesus in art

There are no pictures or paintings from the time of Jesus which claim to show what he looked like. There are no descriptions of what he looked like in the Gospels or other writings. Yet there is probably no other figure in the history of the world who has been painted so many times, in every century.

The shroud of Turin

The **shroud** of Turin is a length of cloth which shows the front and back images of a man just under two metres tall, who had been crucified and stabbed in the side. For hundreds of years, many Christians have believed that the shroud is an image of Jesus' body, miraculously transferred onto the cloth in which he had been wrapped after the crucifixion. Belief that the shroud was genuine was dented in 1989, when it was **carbon-dated** to about 1325CE. Recently this has been challenged by some scientists, who think that bacteria growing on the cloth may have influenced the results. Whether it is genuine or not, no one has ever been able to explain scientifically how the image came to be on the cloth.

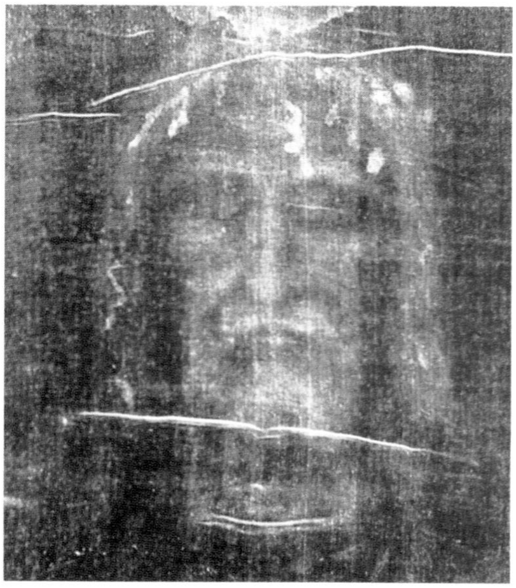

The face on the Turin shroud

Images of Jesus

Like all other paintings, images of Jesus reflect both the fashions of the time in which they were painted, and the abilities of the painter. In the Middle Ages, figures appear lifeless and not very realistic. In the sixteenth and seventeenth centuries, the fashion was for rounded, chubby people. The Victorians often painted Jesus as a romantic figure who looked very English. In the twentieth century, many artists have painted more 'realistic' portraits.

Icons

Icons are religious paintings, usually of Jesus or the saints. They are used by **Orthodox** Christians as part of worship. The painters of icons take great care, and follow strict rules, so that every icon of a particular person looks more or less the same.

An icon of Jesus

'Gentle Jesus, meek and mild'

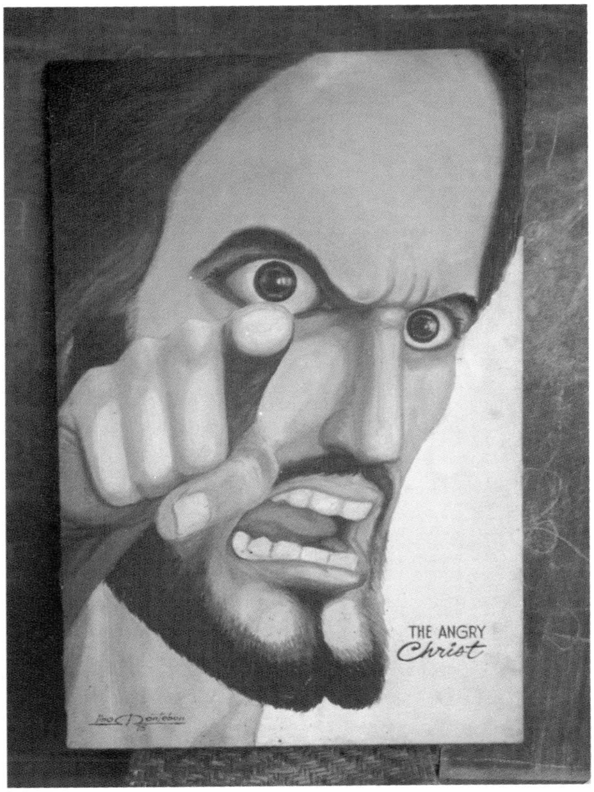

The Angry Christ (Lino Pontebon, 20th century)

Summing up

Pictures of Jesus are an important part of Christian tradition.

Activities

A

1. Write down as many reasons as you can think of why so many artists have painted pictures of Jesus.

2. Icons are used as part of worship. Why do you think there are rules about how they should be painted?

B

3. Artists have often tried to paint pictures of Jesus which show that Christians believe he was both a human being and God. Look carefully at the four pictures in this unit. Which do you think shows most 'God', which most 'man'? Why?

4. Do you think it would make any difference to Christians if the shroud of Turin were proved to be (a) fake or (b) genuine?

C

5. In pairs, look at the pictures in this unit and discuss what you think each artist was trying to show about Jesus. Which picture do you think Christians might be most likely to use in worship?

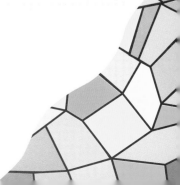

11 *Early Church history*

Persecution

For the two to three hundred years after it began, Christianity's most important task was to survive. The Romans considered Christians to be a threat. This was because Christians said their first duty was to God, not the state, and they refused to take part in Emperor-worship. This led to horrific persecutions. Although the persecutions were supposed to put an end to Christianity, they had the opposite effect. People were inspired by the bravery and willingness with which many of the **martyrs** died. Many more people became believers. The persecution also meant that the beliefs of the new religion became clearer.

Disagreements

For several hundred years, there were many disagreements as Christian leaders tried to thrash out the beliefs of the Church. Councils of bishops were held, where they drew up **creeds** and statements of beliefs. The leaders were trying to make sense of some of the most complicated teachings of Christianity, and express them clearly:

- There is only one God.
- This God can be seen as God the Father, God the Son and God the Holy Spirit.
- Jesus of Nazareth was both completely human and completely God.

Beliefs like these were totally new. It is not surprising that the Church leaders found the task difficult!

The problems

One of the problems with trying to reach agreement in all the discussions was that everyone believed the ideas were desperately important. Everyone taking part believed that if the right answer was not agreed, it could make the whole teaching of Christianity wrong. Since Christianity is about being saved from sin, this would affect people not only in this life, but also after death. People had strong views and many were not prepared to change their minds. Another problem was that the leaders came from many different places and spoke many different languages. Even when they were using the same words, they did not always mean the same thing. (As a modern example, a Big Mac *could* mean a large raincoat!) Misunderstandings, disagreements and strong words were almost inevitable.

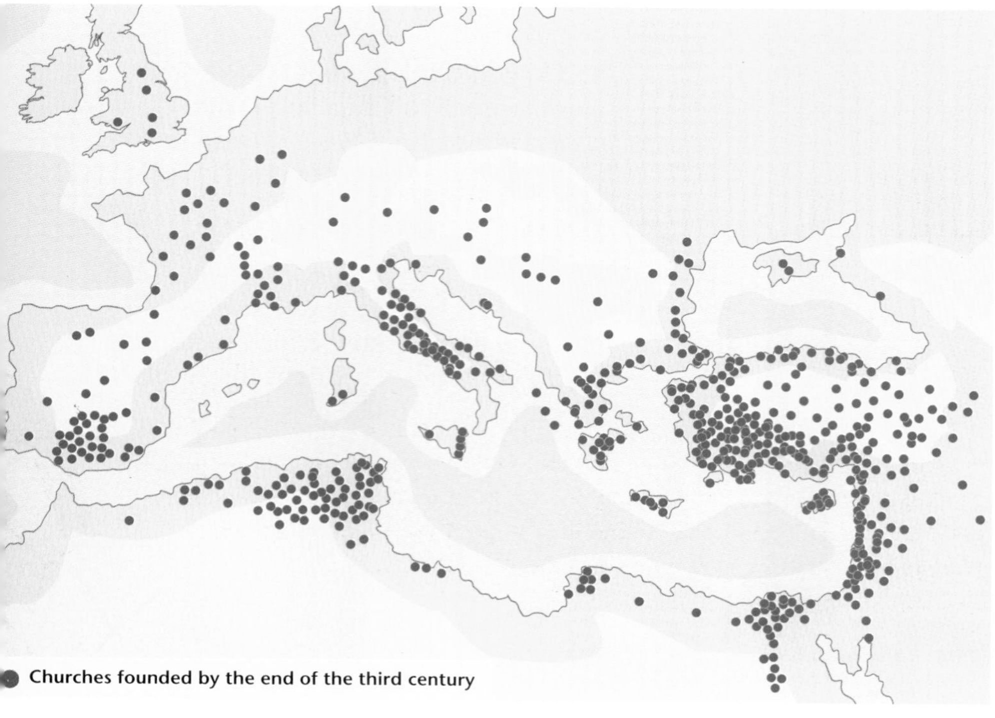

The spread of Christianity by the third century CE

The cathedral at Canterbury, one of the first places in England where Christianity was established

Gradually, the leaders became divided into two groups. One group followed the **Pope**, the leader of the Church in Rome. The other group followed the **Patriarch**, the leader in Constantinople. The two groups produced very different answers to the questions they were discussing. It became more and more difficult to find any agreement. At last, in 1054CE, the leaders of the two groups exchanged letters. In these letters, each refused to accept the authority of the other. This was very serious because it meant a complete split in the Church. It is called the Great **Schism**, which comes from a Greek word which means 'to split apart'.

The Church in Rome became the **Catholic** Church. Catholic means entire or universal. The group based in Constantinople became the Orthodox Church. Orthodox means 'right belief' or 'right worship'. Both groups claimed that theirs was the 'true' Church. These two groups were the beginnings of the Western and Eastern Churches which still exist today.

Other developments

The arguments over **doctrine** were obviously not the only things that happened in the first thousand years of Christianity. The religion spread from country to country. Everywhere it went, churches and cathedrals were built for worship. Many buildings today use the same sites, and sometimes parts of the original buildings can still be seen.

Summing up

Christian beliefs needed explaining, so that the religion could grow and develop.

Activities

A

1. Why did the early Church leaders find it so hard to agree about the ideas they were discussing?
2. What does schism mean? Why is this part of church history called the Great Schism?

B

3. Why did the fact that they spoke different languages cause problems in the meetings of the early Church leaders? How are things different today when leaders from different countries meet?
4. An early Christian writer said, 'The blood of the martyrs is the seed of the Church.' Explain in your own words what he meant.

C

5. Why do you think the same sites might have been used for Christian worship for hundreds of years? Why do you think many churches were built in places which had been used for worship of other gods in the days before Christianity?

12 *The Reformation*

For about 500 years after the Great Schism in 1054, there was only one Church in the Western world. It became enormously powerful. The Popes, the leaders of the Church, were often as powerful as kings and emperors. Sometimes they were even more powerful! The Church gained enormous amounts of money. Sometimes the Popes seemed to be more concerned with keeping the money and their power than they did with leading the Church and looking after the spiritual life of the people.

One way of raising money was the sale of **indulgences**. An indulgence was a certificate which promised that the person buying it (or someone they bought it for) would have their sins forgiven, and so could go to heaven. In those days people believed that it was possible to buy forgiveness in this way, so selling the certificates raised a great deal of money.

By the beginning of the sixteenth century, the world was beginning to change. Printing had been invented and books, though still very expensive, were becoming more common. People were being better educated and some were able to read the Bible for themselves for the first time. Some people began to think that the teachings of the Church did not agree with the teachings of the Bible. They felt that the Church needed to change.

Erasmus

An important leader of the new thinking was a man called Erasmus. He was a **monk** and a serious Bible scholar, but he also wrote many little books which criticized the Church in clever and witty ways. These books were very popular and they affected the way many people thought. People thought that the Church needed to be re-formed, so the changes are called the **Reformation**. The Reformation happened in slightly different ways at almost the same time in several different countries. This unit concentrates on one of the most important leaders, a German called Martin Luther.

Martin Luther

Martin Luther

Martin Luther was a monk and a professor at the University of Wittenberg. He had been troubled for years about the sale of indulgences. On 31 October 1517, he nailed a paper to the church door in Wittenberg. It contained 95 Theses (ideas) about why the sale of indulgences was wrong. This began a chain of events which led to a turning point in the history of Christianity.

The north door of the church in Wittenburg (altered in the nineteenth century to commemorate Luther)

In 1517 and 1521 Luther was brought in front of church courts called 'Diets'. He was expected to give up his ideas. He refused. This made it inevitable that he would be **excommunicated** (thrown out of the Church). This was a very serious punishment. In those days the Church was the centre of people's lives, and following its teaching was thought to be the only way to get to heaven. Luther's life was in danger. For his own protection, he was kidnapped by a local prince who supported him. Whilst he was a prisoner Luther spent his time translating the New Testament into German, so that ordinary people could read it for the first time.

Luther's ideas

Luther did not just disagree with the sale of indulgences. As his ideas developed, he disagreed with many of the teachings of the Catholic Church. The Church taught that priests are the link between the people and God. Luther came to believe that each person can reach God themselves, and the link between God and human beings is through the Bible. He disagreed with the idea that human beings have to struggle to be good enough to reach God. He said that, according to the Gospels, God had come to human beings in Jesus. He published books so that ordinary people could read his ideas. More and more people began to agree with him. In 1529 a group of princes who supported Luther delivered a protest against attempts to stop him preaching. After this the new group was given the name **Protestant**, and it split away from the Catholic Church. All over Europe, changes were beginning.

Summing up

The Reformation was a movement for change in several European countries. Martin Luther was one of its most important leaders.

Activities

A

1 Why did the invention of printing affect the Reformation?

2 Explain why being excommunicated was such a serious punishment in the time of Martin Luther.

B

3 A famous historian wrote, 'Erasmus laid the egg that Luther hatched.' What do you think he meant?

4 Do you think people today would buy indulgences? What reasons can you give for your answer?

C

5 Martin Luther wrote his protest and nailed it to the church door. What methods might people use today if they wanted to protest about things they feel are wrong?

13 The Reformation in England

The background

King Henry VIII had succeeded to the English throne in 1509. He was not the sort of king who wanted to share his power, and Popes at that time had a great deal of power. Things came to a head over the problem of the King's marriage. The story is quite complicated, but Henry VIII wanted to divorce his queen, Catherine of Aragon. He needed special permission from the Pope to do this – permission which the Pope refused to give. Henry was furious. He was desperate for a son to succeed him as king and Catherine had had only daughters. He was also in love with Ann Boleyn, an attractive young lady-in-waiting at court, and wanted to marry her. So he decided that if the Pope would not allow him a divorce, he would organize matters himself. In those days, the monarch had some control over Parliament, and Henry organized changes in the law. Between 1532 and 1536, Acts passed by the English Parliament made Henry head of the Church of England, and took away all the Pope's authority in England.

Henry VIII

Fountains Abbey was dissolved in 1539

Dissolution of the monasteries

There were hundreds of **monasteries** in England. Almost all of them belonged to **Orders** based in other countries. Once Henry was head of the Church, the monasteries that were ruled from abroad were declared to be illegal. This is one reason why they were dissolved (destroyed). The other reasons were simpler. Henry's government was desperately short of money. Many of the monasteries were very rich. When they were dissolved, the King and the government took over their land and possessions. Henry then used some of the money and monastery lands as presents for people he wanted to get on his side. The income from what was left doubled the amount of money the King received every year. Between 1536 and 1538, all 560 monasteries in England were dissolved.

What effect did Henry have on the Church of England?

Henry did not intend to make the Church of England Protestant. He believed in Catholicism without the Pope. But the changes that happened during Henry's reign were very important. The Bible was published in English for the first time. Service books were produced with parts of the service in English instead of all in Latin. Now people could understand more of the services.

The Reformation under Edward VI

In the reign of Henry's son Edward, England became Protestant. Edward was only ten years old when he became king, and adults helped him rule. They carried on the changes that Henry had begun. In 1549, a new service book, the Book of Common Prayer, was introduced. This had to be used, by law. A new statement of belief called the Forty-Two Articles was produced in 1553. All the clergy in England were expected to say that they agreed with this.

Edward died when he was sixteen, and his half-sister Mary became queen. She was a Catholic. In the five years that she was queen, she tried to make the country Catholic again. In the long reign of her sister Elizabeth (1558–1603), it became Protestant again. Things began to settle down. The Church of England became the official (Established) Church and in 1563 a shorter statement of belief called the Thirty-Nine Articles was agreed. This is still an important statement for the Anglican Churches today. Although she was more tolerant than many rulers, Elizabeth did not allow religious freedom, and everyone was expected to be a member of the Church of England. Roman Catholics and **Puritans** (extreme Protestants) were persecuted during Elizabeth's reign.

Elizabeth I

Summing up

The sixteenth century was a time of great changes in England's religious life.

Activities

A

1 What reasons did Henry have for dissolving the monasteries? Which do you think was the most important reason? Why?

2 The Pope in Italy was head of the Catholic Church. What difficulties do you think this caused rulers in other countries?

B

3 What effect do you think it had on people when they could understand more of the Bible and more of the services in church?

4 What do you think ordinary people would have noticed in the changes that took place in England in the sixteenth century? How do you think they would have felt?

C

5 Elizabeth I is once supposed to have said, 'There is only one Jesus Christ, and all the rest is dispute over trifles.' What do you think this means? Do you think many Christians would agree with her?

14 Monks and nuns

Benedictine monks today

The word monk comes from a word which means 'one who lives alone' and this is what the first monks did. They were **hermits** who lived alone away from other people. They concentrated on prayer and study. These holy men were very respected and people who wanted to live in the same way went to join them. This was how communities of monks, called monasteries, began. Communities for women began, too, and these were called **convents**.

St Benedict

St Benedict was born in Italy in about 480CE. As a young man he was a hermit, but he became sure that the best way of living a Christian life was with other people. He set up a community and wrote a 'guidebook' for how the monks should live, called the Rule. His rule was based on two things – work and prayer. Benedict said, 'we shall not make the rules too strict and heavy', but the Rule was detailed:

> *At the brothers' mealtimes there should always be a reading. There shall be complete silence at table, and no whispering or any voice except the reader's should be heard. The brethren should pass to each other in turn whatever food is needed so that no one needs to ask for anything.*

Benedict's Rule became the standard on which other Orders were based. In 1209 St Francis of Assisi formed the Franciscan Order, often called the Greyfriars because of the grey tunics they wore. (A **friar** is similar to a monk.)

The early Franciscans lived lives of extreme poverty, travelling from place to place, preaching and teaching. Other Orders followed. One of the best known Orders of monks is the Society of Jesus, also called the Jesuits. This was founded by Ignatius Loyola in 1534, to defend Catholicism against the Reformation.

Orders

Today there are thousands of Christian monks and **nuns**, living all over the world. Most belong to the Roman Catholic or Orthodox Churches. They are people who have felt that they should live in a special way, dedicating their lives to God. Most monks and nuns are members of Orders, which means they live together in communities where everyone follows the same rules. When they join an Order, monks and nuns take **vows**. These are solemn promises about how they will live for the rest of their lives. The three most common vows are poverty, **chastity** and obedience.

- Poverty: the nun or monk will own nothing of their own. Everything necessary for their life is provided by the Order.
- Chastity: they promise not to marry, and not to have sexual relationships.
- Obedience: they promise to obey the head of their Order.

Taking these vows means that the person does not have to be concerned about all the things that normally occupy a lot of people's attention – where to live, earning money, etc. They can concentrate instead on serving God.

Different types of Order

There are two main types of Order. Some are 'enclosed', which means the nuns and monks do not have any contact with the outside world in their day-to-day lives. Other Orders work 'in the world', usually with their members working in professions such as teaching or nursing.

Nuns and monks work in many different ways

Summing up

Christian men and women can dedicate their lives to worshipping God by becoming monks or nuns.

Activities

A

1 Explain the three vows taken by monks and nuns. Why do they take them?

2 What are the two types of religious Order? What are the differences between them?

B

3 Why do you think St Benedict instructed his monks to eat in silence, listening to a reader? How does this compare with dinners in your school? Which would you prefer?

4 Why did Ignatius Loyola begin the Jesuits? Why might a new Order of monks have been appropriate at this time?

C

5 Find out more about an Order of monks or nuns. Write an article about the founder of the Order, how the monks or nuns live and work today. If you choose an open Order, it may be possible to invite one of their members into school to talk to you about their life.

15 God called me …

This unit has articles by two people who have devoted their lives to God.

Father Francis

As a boy of nine, I met a Capuchin friar whose kind and friendly manner impressed me and inspired me to follow in his footsteps. My parents were saintly and encouraged my ***vocation****. From the age of eleven I attended a Franciscan school and grew to love the Franciscan way of life. Gradually I became aware that I wanted to spend the rest of my life as a Franciscan friar and priest. Our work is very varied and we are available anywhere that the Church needs us. This may include parish work, foreign and home* ***mission****, working with the homeless, writing, preaching, teaching, broadcasting and giving* ***retreats****.*

Life in a friary revolves around our spiritual schedule. We have prayers three times a day, **Divine Office** *and daily Mass. We share three formal meals. We have our individual jobs – parish priest, bursar, hospital chaplain – and household chores to be shared as well. We are kept busy dealing with telephone calls and visitors to the friary. In our friary we provide facilities for Alcoholics Anonymous meetings, and a soup kitchen and clothes distribution for the homeless.*

Personally my day varies. I usually spend the morning preparing my sermons, writing articles and answering numerous letters. In the afternoon I like to have a little nap – after all, I get up at 6.00 a.m! – then more desk work. In the evening I do my parish visiting. We end each day with recreation, enjoying a chat and some television. One day a week I sing in shopping centres to raise money for the starving, and give an evening concert to help local charities. I have recorded 31 tapes and CDs and in recognition received a gold disc. Through my charity work I was honoured in 1997 with the MBE. Being a friar is a great life, in which people can use their skills and talents and find enormous job satisfaction.

Father Francis Maple

Father Francis is a Capuchin Franciscan friar based in Chester.

Sister Marion Campbell

Sister Marion is a **novice** nun in an enclosed Benedictine Order at Tyburn Covent in London.

Very simply, God called me. A vocation is not an easy thing to understand even for the person who has been given one. I had come closer to God in the ***Eucharist****, and the Church I'd known as a child, but it wasn't enough. Daily Mass wasn't enough. I found myself lingering after Mass, going into the church at other times in the day when no one was there. I was being gradually withdrawn from the world. Activities I'd once enjoyed seemed empty. I saw a difference between my friends and myself. I could see the lack of God, and couldn't see what was driving them or the world. You can feel torn between family, friends and the way he's calling you, but if you love him and respond, then he gives you the strength to say 'Yes'. He had given me a thirst that could only be quenched by giving myself wholly to him in religious life.*

Community life is family life. You don't choose the members of your family but you accept each other 'warts and all'. You love each other for what they are. Here, everything points to God, unlike the world where God is sometimes ignored. You make God the centre of your day, and not ME. I got a shock when I first came, because I come from a small family and suddenly I was living with over 20 nuns! But lack of privacy soon doesn't bother you. When you settle down the routine seems like the most natural way of life. You find a peace in your innermost being where there is just you and God, and 20 nuns buzzing around you can't disturb that peace. Whatever your task, you learn to find God in it. Our life is very structured. We all assemble in chapel seven times a day for Mass and Divine Office. In between we have work time (two hours), study (two hours), ***adoration*** *(two half-hours in the day, one hour at night), meals together (two half-hours), recreation (one hour). Community life helps us serve God, and serve him in each other.*

Sister Marion

Summing up

Some people feel called to dedicate their whole lives to serving God.

Activities

A

1 For friars, what sort of areas might be 'where the Church needs us'?

2 In what ways do the nuns 'make God the centre of the day'?

B

3 Outline the similarities and differences between life in the convent and life in the friary. What reasons can you give to explain them?

4 If you asked both writers how they serve God, what do you think they would say?

C

5 Nuns and monks in enclosed Orders believe that they can help the world by praying for it. Work in a group to put together a prayer list that such a group could use.

16 *The Taizé Community*

This unit and the next one are about two different sorts of Christian community.

The Taizé (pronounced te-zay) Community takes its name from a small village in eastern France. In 1940, a young Swiss man bought a house there. It was the middle of World War II and France was partly occupied by the Nazis, but Brother Roger, as he is known, had a dream of forming a Christian community. He wanted it to be a place for **reconciliation** in the midst of war. At first, he gave shelter to people, especially Jews, who were escaping from the Nazis. In the years that followed, other young men came to join him. In 1949, the first group of brothers took vows of commitment to a life of great simplicity, chastity and living together as a community. Today there are almost 100 brothers, who come from 25 different countries and many different branches of Christianity. Not all of them live in France. Small groups of brothers work in poor areas in Asia, Africa and North and South America.

Life at Taizé

The community at Taizé is based on three things – prayer, work and welcoming people to the community. There are three prayer times every day, with other activities fitted around them. The prayers include a lot of singing and silent reflection; the style has become famous all round the world. It is used in many churches and even in other monasteries. The brothers at Taizé do not accept any gifts or money for themselves and they support themselves by their own work. They believe that their simple lifestyle can be a way of showing the teachings of Jesus.

Taizé and young people

The enormous number of visitors to Taizé is one of the things which makes it different from any other religious community. Every year, tens of thousands of young people are welcomed there. They are mainly between the ages of 17 and 30, and most spend a week camping in the fields around the community. During the summer months, in any one week there may be up to 6000 people in Taizé from up to 35 countries.

The young people share the prayer times with the brothers and have Bible studies, times of silence and meditation. There are also 'sharing-groups' where small numbers of people can get to know each other. They discuss what it means to be a Christian and how their Christian beliefs affect their lives.

Worship in the church at Taizé

The small discussion groups are an important part of staying at Taizé

Everyone is encouraged to go home to their own community and use what they have learned. Many of the people who go to Taizé say that the experience has changed their lives for ever.

Pilgrimage of trust on earth

To try to help the young people continue with what they have learned after they go home, the community at Taizé began its 'pilgrimage of trust on earth'. At the end of each year, there is a meeting of up to 100,000 young people in a major city in Europe.

In 1998, the 20th annual meeting was held in Vienna. Similar meetings have also been held all over the world, in cities as far apart as Johannesburg, Dayton USA, Manila and Madras, India. The people stay in churches and with families in the city, and spend five days praying and sharing together.

Summing up

Many of Taizé's visitors find that their lives are changed by the experience of staying there.

Activities

A

1 Why might Brother Roger have felt so strongly about establishing a community for reconciliation in 1940?

2 Look at the picture of a service at Taizé. What does it tell you about the way people worship at Taizé? Describe what you think the people in the picture might be feeling.

B

3 Why do you think the brothers who work in countries other than France choose the poorest areas?

4 Think of as many reasons as you can why the brothers thought it was a good idea to set up regular meetings for people who had been to Taizé. What do you think 'pilgrimage of trust on earth' means?

C

5 Work in pairs. Discuss why so many young people go to Taizé, and what you think they gain from the experience. Write up your conclusions.

17 The Corrymeela community

Corrymeela is in Northern Ireland, where bombs, shootings and hatred have been a part of life for many people during the last 30 years. This has become known as 'the troubles'. The causes of the conflict are complicated, but they are focused around the divisions between Roman Catholics and Protestants. Corrymeela works to try to heal those divisions.

Corrymeela began in 1965 when a group of Christians led by Rev Ray Davey bought a house to use as a centre for a new Christian community. The house was called Corrymeela, which means 'the hill of harmony', and this was adopted as the name of the group. The aim of the Corrymeela community is reconciliation. Reconciliation means bringing people back together – it comes from a word which literally means 'to make friendly'. The idea is to bring together Roman Catholics and Protestants who would normally never have any contact with each other. One of its first achievements was in 1966, when it organized a joint Roman Catholic and Protestant conference on the future of Northern Ireland, the first time that this had ever been done.

Corrymeela's work

Corrymeela provides a place where people can meet and talk without fear. Much of its work involves young people from schools in Northern Ireland, but it also works with many other groups. Around 8000 people a year visit Corrymeela, staying from two days to a week. They may be families in difficulty, people whose relatives have been killed, who are unemployed or who live in areas where life is hard, etc. The community also has refuges for people who have had to leave their homes because of threats or violence. Since 1995 it has run special support groups for children who have been bereaved, as well as play schemes and school projects. In the words of its leader, Trevor Williams, 'We have a hope to share, when many are gripped by despair.'

'The troubles' have been part of everyday life in Northern Ireland

A summer holiday programme at Corrymeela

Seed groups

One of Corrymeela's main areas of work is in its 'seed groups'. These are groups of young people aged from 18 to 21, who come from different backgrounds. They meet at weekends over a period of six months. For many of them it is the first time they have met together with people from the 'other side'. Northern Ireland has separate schools for Roman Catholics and Protestants, and the two communities do not normally have any contact. The young people can discuss their differences, and what they have in common. The idea is that by allowing people to get to know each other, the barriers will be broken down and bridges will be built instead. One young man who had been a member of a residential group at Corrymeela said afterwards,

I think that everybody wanted to make friends with the other group. At the start it was really difficult because you didn't want to be the first one to be shunned. As time went by the barriers broke down.

Summing up

The Corrymeela community's work for peace has influenced many thousands of people, not just in Northern Ireland, but all over the world.

Activities

A

1. Why was Corrymeela a good name for the house bought by the group?
2. Why do you think the groups of young people are called 'seed groups'?

B

3. Write down as many reasons as you can to explain why a lot of Corrymeela's work concentrates on young people.
4. Do you think Corrymeela will still be needed if the troubles in Northern Ireland come to an end? Why?

C

5. Imagine that you are a young person about to go on a weekend at Corrymeela. Write about your feelings. Then write another article about how you might feel when you return home.

18 Tell the world!

In the story of the Ascension in the Acts of the Apostles, Jesus tells his disciples to,

> *be witnesses for me in Jerusalem, in all Judea and Samaria, and to the ends of the earth.*
>
> (Acts 1, 8)

From the beginning, Christians have felt that it was their duty to spread the message of Christianity as far as they could. Someone who travels to tell other people about their religion is a **missionary**. The earliest Christian missionaries were the **apostles**. The greatest was probably St Paul, who spent most of his life travelling to teach people about Christianity. However, he was not the only one. There is a strong tradition that St Peter travelled to Rome, and some people believe that St Thomas went to India. There were certainly Christians there by the third century CE. Of course, there must have been many other Christians who are not remembered, who also acted as missionaries as they went about their normal lives as traders or travellers.

Spreading the word

In its first thousand years, Christianity spread widely. Many of the new religious Orders of monks and friars devoted a lot of their time to missionary work. St Francis himself, for example, travelled to Egypt and preached to the Sultan. Along with other groups, Franciscans set up centres in Eastern Europe, Asia and India, and they followed the Spanish and Portuguese explorers to South America. The Society of Jesus (the Jesuit Order) was begun by St Ignatius Loyola in 1534. One of the first Jesuits was St Francis Xavier, who baptized thousands of people in India, Sri Lanka, Malaysia and Japan.

The Reformation brought great changes to Christianity but missionary work continued, both by Protestants and Roman Catholics. In eighteenth-century England, the Church of England was failing to reach many ordinary people. John Wesley (1703–91) began preaching in market places and fields. Although his meetings were frequently interrupted by riots, thousands of people were **converted**. In his life, Wesley rode 250,000 miles (over 400,000 km) on horseback, and preached more than 40,000 sermons. He went to America and Ireland, crossing the Irish Sea 42 times! The support system which he set up for the people who had been converted through his preaching became the Methodist Church. At the same time, missionary societies were being set up in many countries. The London Missionary Society was set up in 1795 and sent workers all over the world.

Early missionaries felt they should teach and educate

Missionaries today work with people in practical ways

In the eighteenth and nineteenth centuries the interest in building empires, especially in Africa and Asia, meant an increase in missionary work in those countries. One of the best-known missionaries in Africa was David Livingstone (1813–73). He was also an explorer and spent much of his life in areas where no European had ever been before. He walked right across southern Africa, from west to east.

Modern missionary movements

In the 20th century, the focus of missionary work has changed. More emphasis is now put on helping people in practical ways, rather than just going to teach about Christianity. Christians who go to work in other countries today go mainly because they have skills which they can offer, for example as doctors, teachers or engineers. Teaching people about Christianity is being seen more and more as the job of Churches which are based in a country, rather than missionaries who are visiting it.

Summing up

Telling other people about what they believe has been important to Christians ever since the time of Jesus.

Activities

A

1 Explorers and missionaries tended to work in the same places. What does this tell you about attitudes at the time to the people who were being 'discovered'?

2 Why did John Wesley spend almost all his life preaching out of doors? What advantages and disadvantages were there in his methods?

B

3 Jesus told his followers to 'be witnesses for me'. What do you think he meant? In how many ways can a Christian be a witness for Jesus?

4 Explain how and why the role of the missionary has changed in the last hundred years.

C

5 Some missionary groups today (for example, Mother Teresa's Missionaries of Charity) are forbidden by their Rule to preach or baptize. In groups, discuss why you think this was decided, and what difference it makes to them and to the people they work with.

19 A world Church

For just over a thousand years there was only one Church. Everyone who was a follower of Jesus belonged to it. However, as the Church got bigger, disagreements became greater and, in 1054, the Great Schism split the two main groups in the Church (see unit 11). In both Orthodox and Western Churches, other splits occurred in later years (see unit 12). Jesus taught his followers to care for other people, but many of them seem to have forgotten this! Disagreements and squabbles between Churches continued, in some cases for hundreds of years. It was not until the 20th century that people seriously began to try to bring the different parts of the Church back together.

The Ecumenical movement

Ecumenical comes from the Greek word *oikoumene*, which means 'inhabited' – that is, the world. The Ecumenical Movement really began at a meeting in Edinburgh in 1910. Its aim was to help different Churches to work together. At first, this was to help missionary work. Missionaries who were taking Christianity to other countries found that people were confused by the differences between the Churches. No one in the Ecumenical movement wanted to get rid of the differences and make all Christians the same. Each **denomination** has its own way of doing things, and is special to its own members. However, it seemed sensible for different denominations to work together more and try to understand more about other groups. At that time, this did not often happen.

The World Council of Churches

The World Council of Churches (WCC) began in 1948. More than 300 different Churches are members, from Orthodox and Protestant backgrounds. The Council does not include the Roman Catholic Church and some Evangelical Churches. Although not members, in the last 30 years Roman Catholics have worked quite closely with the WCC.

The WCC claims to represent 400 million Christians all over the world. It does not aim to make one big Church. It is a fellowship of Churches working together so that everyone benefits. The co-operation between Churches which has been achieved would have been impossible even 50 years ago. Many Churches now work together at a local level, and it is not uncommon for different Churches to share services. Every year, there are special services when Churches join together in the Week of Prayer for Christian Unity.

The logo of the World Council of Churches

Talking to people of other faiths

In the last 50 years or so, the attitude of many Christians to other religions has changed. Once, most Christians felt that their religion was 'the right one' and other people should be persuaded to join it. Today, many Christians feel that things are not so simple. They feel that people of different faiths can learn from each other and that other people's beliefs must be respected.

Different denominations now share services

It has been possible for representatives of other faiths to be invited to be guests at important Christian events, for example when Dr Carey was made Archbishop of Canterbury in 1991. Special events are sometimes organized where people from different faiths can pray together about things that affect everyone – for example, concern about refugees or the homeless or the environment. Every year since 1974, many different faith groups have joined together during a week in October, called the 'Week of Prayer for World Peace'. In Britain, one of the organizations which tries to encourage contact between people of different faiths is the Inter-Faith Network. This was set up in 1987, and links nearly 70 organizations.

Summing up

Many Christians now feel that working more closely with other Christians and with members of other religions can have benefits for everyone.

Activities

A **1** Why do you think that it was missionaries who first saw a need for Churches to work more closely together?

2 Why does the World Council of Churches not want to see one huge Church?

B **3** Make a list of the benefits of different Churches working together. What disadvantages can you think of?

4 'Religion is a mountain, and many paths lead to the summit.' What do you think this means? Why might it be a useful statement for an inter-faith group to use?

C **5** Write a prayer or a poem which would be suitable to use at a worship meeting in your area for the Week of Prayer for World Peace.

20 Where did the Bible come from?

The Bible is a collection of 66 books. They were written over such a long period that no one really knows how long it took. It may have been up to 2000 years. Christians call the first part of the Bible the Old Testament. These are the books that were the holy books of the Jews for hundreds of years before Christians began using them, too. They had been collected together by the second century BCE. The New Testament is a collection of books about Jesus and the early days of Christianity. These books were written down during about the first hundred years after the time of Jesus.

What is in the Bible?

The books which are included in the Bible are called the **canon.** This comes from a Greek word for a ruler used for measuring. The canon is a collection of books which were accepted as being genuine. There were many other manuscripts that could have been included in both the Old Testament and the New Testament. John's Gospel ends with the words:

> *Now there are many other things that Jesus did. If they were all written down one by one, I suppose that the whole world could not hold the books that would be written.*
>
> (John 21, 25)

The books chosen to be included were those that were thought to be the best and most accurate. We know that by 200CE, 20 of the 27 books in the New Testament were agreed to be the most important. We also know that the canon as it is today was agreed by 367CE. It is listed in a letter which was sent by Athanasius, bishop of Alexandria, to all the churches of which he was in charge.

Other documents

There are several other sources which add to the information in the Bible. For example, the Gospel of Thomas was found in 1946 at a place called Nag Hammadi in Egypt. It has been dated back to the second century CE. It begins with the words 'These are the secret sayings which the living Jesus spoke and which Didymos Judas Thomas wrote down.' There are 114 sayings of Jesus. Some are the same as sayings recorded in the Bible, some are different. The different sayings show influence from a group known as the Gnostics, who believed in special knowledge. Another tiny piece of manuscript which is very similar to the Gospels is called the Egerton Papyrus 2. This is kept in the British Museum and has been dated to about 150CE. Apart from texts in the Bible, this is probably the oldest surviving text to mention Jesus.

The Egerton Papyrus

Biblical criticism

Study of the Bible is called 'Biblical criticism'. Used this way, the word criticism does not mean finding fault, it means looking at the Bible text carefully, and analyzing it. When they are looking at the Bible, scholars examine the differences between different manuscript versions and try to work out what is genuine and what might have been added later. One of the simplest methods of criticism is looking at passages which tell the same story in the different Gospels. The way in which the writers choose to tell the story can tell scholars a lot about their interests and what they wanted their readers to understand.

Why do Christians believe this is so important?

Not all Christians agree about whether everything in the Bible is literally true, but all would agree that it was inspired by God. For many Christians, learning more about how and why it was written helps them to understand more about the lessons that it teaches.

Reading the Bible is important for Christians

Summing up

The Bible is one of the most important books that has ever been written. It has influenced many people, non-Christians as well as Christians.

Activities

A

1 What do people mean when they talk about Biblical criticism? How is this different from the way we usually use the word criticism?

2 What might a Christian say if they were asked why they wanted to learn more about the background of the Bible?

B

3 What clues does the original meaning of the word canon give you about how (or why) the books of the Bible were chosen?

4 What do you think Christians can learn about the Bible by studying texts which were not included in it?

C

5 In a Bible, look up Matthew 28, 1–4, Mark 16, 2–5 and Luke 24, 1–4. Draw up a chart of similarities and differences between the three accounts. Then write a paragraph explaining what you have found and what this tells you about the interests of the writers of the Gospels.

21 The Old Testament and Jesus

The first part of the Christian Bible – 39 of its 66 books – are also the holy books of **Judaism**. Christians call them the Old Testament. Jews and Christians look at the books in different ways. Jews believe that they show how the Jewish people gradually learned more and more about what God is like, and how they should live. Christians agree with this, but they also believe that the Old Testament looks forward to the coming of Jesus. This is because Christians believe that in the life of Jesus, God finally showed what he was really like. Jews do not accept this.

Jesus and the writers of the New Testament were all Jews. They knew and loved the Jewish Scriptures. Jesus used quotations from the Scriptures when he was teaching and in the titles which he used (see unit 9). The Gospel writers and especially St Paul used many other quotations from them. There are almost 250 quotations from the Old Testament in the New Testament. This unit looks at two examples of where Christians believe that the Old Testament looks forward to Jesus.

Matthew's Gospel

Matthew's Gospel was written for Jewish readers, and so there are many references in it to the Jewish Scriptures. The readers of the Gospel would have known them, so it would have helped them understand the message of Christianity. There are several passages which begin with words like 'This happened to make what the Lord said through the prophet come true'. For example, in chapter 2, Matthew tells how Mary and Joseph and Jesus went to Egypt to escape King Herod. He says that this is to make come true what God said through the prophet Hosea: 'I called my Son out of Egypt.' (Hosea 11, 1). The readers of the Gospel would have known the passage from Hosea, so this would have made sense to them.

There are also places where Matthew shows how well Jesus knew the Jewish Scriptures. For example, in chapter 15, Matthew tells how religious leaders of the Jews came to talk to Jesus. They accused him of not obeying the **Torah**, the rules for living which are an important part of the Jewish faith. Jesus quoted the Torah back to them and even accused them of being hypocrites who were more concerned about following their own rules than obeying the Torah itself. Another example is during the crucifixion, where Matthew records that Jesus cried, 'My God, my God, why did you abandon me?' This is a quotation from Psalm 22, which begins with this cry of despair but ends with a hymn of praise to God. Matthew obviously expected his readers to understand that there was a deeper meaning behind Jesus' words.

Golgatha (Edvard Munch, 20th century)

Important manuscripts were found in the caves at Qumr'an

The suffering servant

There is a passage in the book of the prophet Isaiah which describes a suffering servant of God. Christians believe that it shows clearly their belief that Jesus' death was because of the sin of human beings. Christians say that sin puts up barriers between people and God. They teach that because of Jesus' death, these barriers were removed.

> *He endured the suffering that should have been ours, the pain that we should have borne …*
> *because of our sins he was wounded, beaten because of the evil we did.*
> *We are healed by the punishment he suffered, made whole by the blows he received.*
>
> (Isaiah 53, 5–6)

Summing up

Christians believe that knowing the teachings of the Old Testament helps them to understand more about the life of Jesus.

Activities

A

1 Why do the Jewish Scriptures form part of the Christian Bible?

2 Why do you think the person described in Isaiah 53 is called a suffering servant?

B

3 Explain the reasons why Matthew used so many quotations from the Old Testament in his Gospel. Why might this cause difficulties to modern readers of the Gospel?

4 Look up Psalm 22. Write a paragraph explaining how the writer of the psalm changes his mind as he prays. What difference would knowing this psalm have made to the first readers of the Gospel?

C

5 Look up the story of Jesus' meeting with the Jewish leaders in Matthew 15. Write two reports describing what happened. Write one from the side of the Jewish leaders, showing why they held their opinions. In the other, take Jesus' side.

22 *John's Gospel*

The first three Gospels, called the Synoptics, all look at Jesus' life and teaching in more or less the same way. Ever since Biblical criticism began, people have realized that John's Gospel is quite different.

Why is John's Gospel different?

John obviously believed that his readers already knew the facts about Jesus' life which are written in the other Gospels. His purpose in writing the Gospel seems to have been to draw out the meaning of things that happened to Jesus. He does not include many of the stories of Jesus' miracles which are in the Synoptics. The ones he does use, he calls '**signs**'. Jesus' preaching is also mainly collected together in **discourses**. The discourses are usually connected to the signs.

Who wrote John's Gospel?

This question has been argued about for years. Unless a new manuscript turns up providing an answer, no one will ever know for certain. Many early Christians thought that it was written by the disciple John, the brother of James. However, there are good reasons for doubting this.

- Most scholars believe that the Gospel was not written until about 110CE. John was an adult around 30CE when he became a disciple, and so would have been at least 98–100 years old by 110CE. This is not impossible, but very unlikely.
- Where John is mentioned in the Gospel, he is called 'the disciple whom Jesus loved'. This seems rather a conceited way for someone to refer to himself.
- Many people doubt that a fisherman from Galilee would have had the education to be able to use the Greek language as well as it is used in this Gospel.

However, it is clear from the Gospel that the words come from someone who was present at the events it describes, and some of them could only have been known to very few people. Many Christians believe that the most likely explanation is that the original words came from John the disciple, but they were written down by a younger friend or follower.

A thirteenth century painting of John writing his Gospel, guided by an angel

Logos and reason

John's Gospel is much more 'Greek' than the Synoptics. It was written for people used to thinking in a Greek way. This can be shown in the way John uses the word **logos**. Logos is a Greek word which means 'word' or 'reason'.

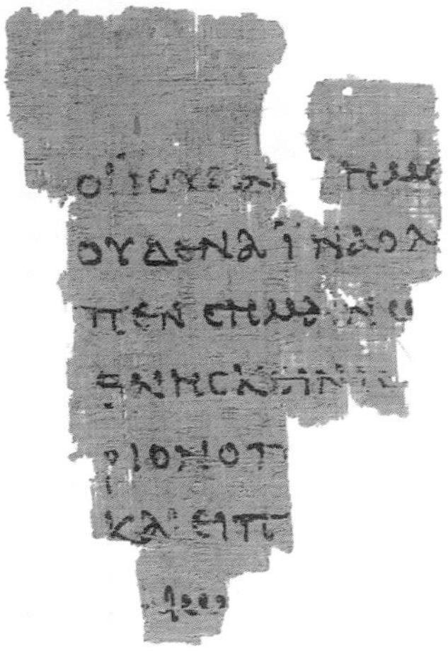

A papyrus fragment of John's Gospel

Greeks at the time believed that the whole idea of order in the universe (night and day, the seasons, etc.) all came from the logos of God. John developed this idea to say that the logos had come to earth in the form of a man, so that people could see what the mind of God is really like. This explains one of the most difficult passages in John's Gospel, the opening section. Christians often read this in church at Christmas. It is summed up in the words,

> *The Word became a human being and, full of grace and truth, lived among us. We saw his glory, the glory which he received as the Father's only Son.*
>
> (John 1, 14)

The signs

There are seven signs in John's Gospel. John shows them not just as miracles which happened, but as 'windows' which allow people to see through to God, and to Jesus as God. This is why they are connected to the discourses, which explain them. For example, John tells the story that Jesus fed 5000 people, but this is connected with the teaching that Jesus is the Bread of Life. The story that he once healed a man who was blind is connected to the belief that Jesus is the Light of the World.

Summing up

Many Christians find John's Gospel the most difficult to understand, but they believe it adds to the picture from the Synoptic Gospels.

Activities

A

1. Why are the miracles used in John's Gospel called 'signs'?
2. How can we tell that John's Gospel was written for people who were used to thinking in a Greek way?

B

3. Explain why 'the disciple whom Jesus loved' would probably not be a title someone would use about themselves. Why could it be used by a friend of theirs?
4. Look up the first chapter of John's Gospel. Explain what you think John was saying. Why do you think Christians use it as a reading in church at Christmas?

C

5. Find out more about the titles which John uses for Jesus. (Unit 9 will help.) Write a paragraph for each one, explaining why you think he used this description. You could illustrate it if you wish.

23 The Epistles

There are 27 books in the New Testament, and 21 of them are letters. The correct name for these letters is the **Epistles**, which comes from the Greek word for letter. About half of the letters were written by St Paul, and they are the best known of the Epistles. They are mainly addressed to friends in towns and cities where Paul had preached. The other letters are known as the 'general letters' because it is not possible to work out exactly whom they were written to. They are I and II Peter, I, II and III John, James and Jude. There is good evidence that they were written by – or at least contain teaching that came from – the apostles. All the Epistles are an important source of information about early Christian preaching, and about how Christian beliefs developed.

The Basilica of St John in Ephesus (I, II and III John were probably written to Christians in Ephesus)

The teaching of the Epistles

The Epistles do not contain much new information about the life and teaching of Jesus. They were written for people who were already Christians and who needed more detailed instructions about Christianity. In some cases this involved making particular beliefs clear. In other cases it involved giving advice about how Christians should live in particular situations. There were two reasons why this was necessary.

- Some new Christians still lived among friends and neighbours who did not share or understand their beliefs. They needed to be advised about how to keep themselves apart from people who still lived in the 'old ways'. In the second letter to the Corinthians, Paul says,

> *Do not try to work together as equals with unbelievers, for it cannot be done. How can right and wrong be partners? How can light and darkness live together? How can Christ and the Devil agree? What does a believer have in common with an unbeliever?*
>
> (II Corinthians 6, 14–16)

- As Christianity sorted out its beliefs, there were 'false teachings' which influenced some Christians. For example, in his letter to the Galatians, Paul bitterly attacks the people who have been 'fooled' by teachings that they still have to obey the Jewish Law. Paul had taught them the Christian teaching that their sins could be forgiven because of Jesus' death.

> *You foolish Galatians! Who put a spell on you? Before your very eyes you had a clear description of the death of Jesus Christ on the cross! Tell me this one thing: did you receive God's Spirit by doing what the Law requires or by hearing the gospel and believing it? How can you be so foolish!*
>
> (Galatians 3, 1–3)

Elsewhere in the letters, there are instructions for general Christian behaviour. For example, in his letter, James emphasizes how important it is to treat everyone alike.

> *My brothers and sisters, as believers in our Lord Jesus Christ, the Lord of glory, you must never treat people in different ways according to their outward appearance. Suppose a rich man wearing a gold ring and fine clothes comes to your meeting, and a poor man in ragged clothes also comes. If you show more respect to the well-dressed man and say to him, 'Have this best seat here,' but say to the poor man, 'Stand over there, or sit here on the floor by my feet,' then you are guilty of creating distinctions among yourselves and of making judgements based on evil motives.*
>
> (James 2, 1–4)

Readings from the Epistles are often used in church services, because Christians believe that the teachings they contain are still valuable today.

A Crisis shelter in London – Christians believe it is important to help people less fortunate

Summing up

The Epistles contain many different sorts of teaching, which is why they have been valued by Christians through the years.

Activities

A

1. Explain why the Epistles were written.
2. Write a paragraph explaining the difference between an epistle and an apostle.

B

3. What impression of Paul do you gain from the part of his letter to the Galatians in this unit? How would you describe his attitude to them?
4. Put together a list of reasons why new Christians might find it difficult to live among non-believers. At the time when the Epistles were written, Christianity itself was a new religion – do you think this would have made it easier or harder?

C

5. Work in a small group. Put together two short plays about the ways in which people from different backgrounds could be treated when they come to church. Use one to show what should not happen, and one to show the way James advises.

24 The Book of Revelation

The Book of Revelation is the last book in the Bible. It was probably written during the reign of the Roman Emperor Domitian (81–96CE). During this time, a serious persecution of Christians took place. Revelation was written to encourage the people who were being persecuted, and to persuade them that everything they were suffering would be worthwhile when God's kingdom began.

Who wrote Revelation?

The writer identifies himself as John, and for many years Christians believed that it must have been written by the John who had been Jesus' disciple. It was certainly not written by the same person who wrote John's Gospel, because the style of writing is quite different. Like many of the books in the Bible, no one will ever be sure who the author was. Most Christians today would say that the question of who wrote the words is less important than what they say.

The message of Revelation

Revelation is a difficult book to understand. It was written at a time of persecution, so a lot of its message is in a sort of code. The symbols it contains would have been obvious to the people it was written for, but it was evidently intended to be difficult for the authorities to understand if they got hold of it. Nearly 2000 years later, even for Christians, the symbols are not always clear. Many Christians today respect Revelation for the beauty of its language and its imagery rather than trying to understand every part of it.

The writer says that he was told by a loud voice that sounded like a trumpet to write down what he saw. The voice belonged to a figure who,

looked like a human being, wearing a robe that reached to his feet, and a gold belt round his chest. His hair was white as wool, or as snow, and his eyes blazed like fire; his feet shone like brass that has been refined and polished, and his voice sounded like a roaring waterfall. He held seven stars in his right hand, and a sharp two-edged sword came out of his mouth. His face was as bright as the midday sun. When I saw him, I fell down at his feet like a dead man.

(Revelation 1, 12–17)

The figure gave him messages to each of the seven churches for which the book was written. Then John saw a series of visions about the destruction of the earth. The visions are full of fantastic images of angels, beasts and other creatures, and they tell how the earth was destroyed, with the faithful (Christians) being rescued.

An illustration for the Book of Revelation in Martin Luther's German Bible (1541)

The New Jerusalem (nineteenth century)

After all the visions of destruction comes another vision, about the new heaven and new earth which John saw. This is probably the passage from Revelation which Christians use most often.

The book ends with a description of the new Jerusalem and what it is like.

Then I saw a new heaven, and a new earth. The first heaven and the first earth disappeared, and the sea vanished. And I saw the Holy City, the new Jerusalem, coming down out of heaven from God, prepared and ready, like a bride dressed to meet her husband. I heard a loud voice speaking from the throne: 'Now God's home is with human beings! He will live with them, and they shall be his people. God himself will be with them, and he will be their God. He will wipe away all tears from their eyes. There will be no more death, no more grief or crying or pain. The old things have disappeared.'

(Revelation 21, 1–4)

Summing up

Although its message is sometimes difficult, Christians believe the Book of Revelation is important, and its imagery has inspired many writers and artists through the centuries.

Activities

A

1 What advantages were there in writing the Book of Revelation in code? What are the disadvantages?

2 Why do you think many Christian writers and artists have used the Book of Revelation in their work?

B

3 Looking at the quotations, why do you think a book like this might have inspired Christians who were being persecuted?

4 Many early Christians believed that God spoke to people in visions. Why do you think they believed this? What is your opinion of visions like this?

C

5 Revelation ends with a description of a perfect land. Write your own description of a place where nothing goes wrong. What would it look like? Who would be there? What would life be like?

25 Marriage and divorce

In the UK about 350,000 couples marry each year. About half of these weddings take place in church. Christians believe that marriage was given to human beings by God. In the story of Creation in the Book of Genesis, God creates man first, then woman, and it says,

> *a man leaves his father and mother and is united with his wife, and they become one.*
>
> (Genesis 2, 24)

Victoria and Kenneth

Today, marriage is a legal ceremony, and it does not have to have a religious content. However, most Christians want to marry in church, and feel that making their vows in God's presence is important. This is how one Christian couple, Victoria and Kenneth, felt about it:

> *When we became engaged and fixed our wedding date, it never occurred to us, as Christians, that we would marry anywhere other than in church. We look on marriage as a life-long commitment, so it was important to us that we made our promises to each other, not only in front of all our friends and family, but most importantly of all, in front of God. The prayers and the service helped us to develop our relationship as Christians and gave an extra dimension to a special day.*

By law, marriage must take place in a licensed building, certain sentences must be included, and the couple and at least two witnesses as well as the vicar or minister must sign a register. Otherwise, the marriage is not legal. In a Western church wedding, the marriage begins with member of the clergy saying something like, 'We have come together in the presence of God to witness the marriage of (the couple's names).' The couple promise that they do not know any reason why they should not marry each other, and they promise to live together and love each other and no one else until one of them dies. As a sign of the promises they have made, the bridegroom gives the bride a ring. The bride may give the bridegroom a ring, too. After prayers and blessings, the service ends with the signing of the register. In many Churches, the marriage includes the service of the Eucharist.

A Russian Orthodox wedding

The service in Orthodox Churches is similar, and it also has to include the words which are required by law. In the second part of the service, after they have exchanged rings, the couple are given crowns to wear. These are a symbol of God's blessing. At the end of the service they share a cup of wine which is a symbol of the life they will share together.

The end of a marriage

Christianity teaches that a marriage should last until death, but this does not always happen. If a marriage breaks down, the attitude of the Churches is different. The Roman Catholic Church accepts separation, where the couple no longer live together, but it does not accept divorce. The Orthodox Churches have a different service for people who are marrying for the second time, but they do allow divorcees to marry in church. The Anglican Churches do not normally allow divorced people to remarry in church, although some of their members do not agree with this. **Free Churches** generally allow remarriage of people who have been divorced if the minister who is performing the service really believes that the couple are serious about making the marriage work.

Summing up

Most Christians wish to make their beliefs an important part of their marriage. If the marriage does not work out, all Churches agree that forgiveness is important.

Activities

A

1 What are the legal requirements for a marriage? Why do you think these were decided on?

2 Rings and crowns are symbols used in some weddings. Make a list of other symbols which are part of a church wedding service, and say why they are used.

B

3 The majority of couples who marry in church do not normally attend worship there. What reasons can you think of why they choose a church wedding? Do you think it is right for people who are not Christians to marry in church?

4 In the last few years, some vicars have hit the headlines by agreeing to hold a special service for people who have just been divorced. What do you think about this?

C

5 Find out more about what the Churches teach about divorce. Then organize a class debate about whether divorced people should be allowed to remarry in church.

26 Death and beyond

For many people today, including some Christians, death is a difficult subject. They try to avoid talking about it, and are embarrassed by the word. Passed away, at rest, gone, lost, are all ways of avoiding saying that someone has died. Phrases such as 'kicked the bucket' and 'bought it' are ways of making a joke out of it. Although we know that everyone must die one day, most people find it easier to pretend that it won't happen to them.

Leaving flowers can be a sign of grief

Funerals

The service held when someone has died is called a **funeral**. A Christian funeral is partly a sad occasion, because the relatives and friends are going to miss the person who is no longer with them. It is usual for people to wear black or dark clothes. Prayers are said for the person who has died, entrusting their soul to God, and asking God to bless the people who are left behind. The funeral service also emphasizes that Christians believe in life after death. This means death is not only a time of sadness, but also a time of hope and even joy. A passage from John's Gospel is often read, where Jesus tells his disciples,

> *Do not be worried and upset. Believe in God and believe also in me. There are many rooms in my Father's house, and I am going to prepare a place for you. I would not tell you this if it were not so.*
>
> (John 14, 1–2)

After the service, the body is either buried in a cemetery, or **cremated**. Cremation, where bodies are burned in special ovens at a crematorium, is becoming more common.

After cremation the ashes that are left may be buried, or scattered in the grounds of the crematorium or somewhere that was important to the person. The place of burial is usually marked with a stone or plaque with the person's name and other details on it.

After death

Much of the 'unmentionable' attitude to death comes about because of fear of the unknown. Being afraid of what you do not know is natural, and even Christians, who believe in life after death, do not know what that life will really be like. They believe that the most important thing is that it will be life with God. There is a story which Christians use to illustrate this: A man went to visit a friend. He left his dog outside, but before long, it began scratching and whining at the closed door, wanting to be let in. The dog knew nothing about what else was in the room, but it knew its master was inside, and it wanted to be with him.

Christians say that the lesson of the story is that the details of life after death do not matter, just as the inside of the room did not matter to the dog. What is important is that 'the master' – God – will be there. They believe that the love of God means that he cares for human beings whom he created, but his love is mixed with justice.

Most Churches teach that everyone will have to account for the things that they have done in this life and will be judged accordingly. In olden days, the teaching was simple: good people went to heaven, a place of light and peace, and bad people went to **hell**, a place of burning fire and torture.

Today, many people find it quite difficult to think of a loving God sending people to burn in hell for ever. Modern teaching usually says more vaguely that heaven is a state of being with God, hell is a state of being away from God.

'The jaws of Hell' (twelfth century)

Summing up

For Christians, death is a new beginning in their eternal life with God.

Activities

A **1** Why is a Christian funeral a time of hope as well as of sadness?

2 Death has only become 'unmentionable' in the last hundred years or so. Write down as many reasons as you can think of to explain why this happened.

B **3** Do you think believing in life after death affects the way someone lives? What sort of differences could it make?

4 'What the caterpillar calls the end of the world, the master calls a butterfly' (Richard Bach). Explain what you think this means. How does it fit with Christian teaching about death?

C **5** Write an article on 'What I believe happens after death'. Include illustrations if you wish!

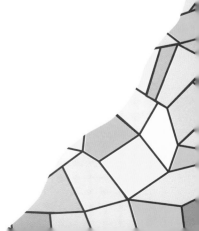

27 Christian stewardship I

A steward is someone who looks after something on behalf of someone else. The idea of Christian stewardship is that everything human beings have, including themselves, was given by God. So everything must be looked after so that it can be returned to God.

Stewardship of the body

The Christian attitude to the body is summed up in the words of St Paul when he was writing to his friends in Corinth.

> *Surely you know that you are God's temple and that God's Spirit lives in you! So if anyone destroys God's temple, God will destroy him. For God's temple is holy, and you yourselves are his temple.*
>
> (I Corinthians 3, 16–7)

Later on in the same letter, Paul adds,

> *Don't you know that your body is the temple of the Holy Spirit, who lives in you and who was given to you by God? You do not belong to yourselves but to God; he bought you for a price. So use your bodies for God's glory.*
>
> (I Corinthians 6, 19–20)

This affects the way in which Christians view their bodies, and the many ways in which their bodies can be damaged or abused. This unit looks at three of the most common ways in which people today can abuse their bodies.

Alcohol

People drink alcohol for pleasure in celebrations and parties. It can relax people so that they feel able to enjoy themselves more. However, alcohol is a poison. Drinking alcohol causes hundreds of deaths every year, some directly, many brought about through people who drink and drive. The attitude of the Churches reflects this 'use and abuse'. Some Churches say that their members should never drink alcohol. This is especially true of the Salvation Army, whose members often work with people with alcohol problems. An information statement from the Salvation Army includes the fact that,

> *The Salvation Army operates more alcoholism centres than any other organization in the world, including more than 200 specialized units in English-speaking countries alone … Salvationists prove by personal example that alcohol is not an essential part of a fulfilled life.*

Most other Churches are not so strict, though all would suggest that a responsible attitude to drinking is necessary.

Salvation Army members work with people who have alcohol-related problems

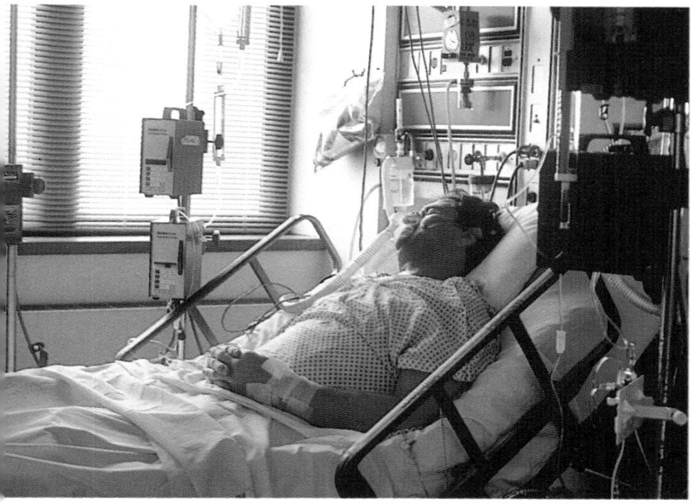

'Smoking can damage your health'

Smoking

The arguments about smoking are similar to those about alcohol. Smoking harms the body and is therefore something which Christians should avoid. In recent years, some scientists have suggested that passive smoking is dangerous, too. Passive smoking means inhaling the smoke from someone else's cigarette. Jesus taught his followers to care about other people, so causing illness to others, even accidentally, would go against Christian teaching.

Drug abuse

Drugs can affect the mind as well as the body, and drug abuse is closely linked with crime. From a Christian point of view, even 'soft' drugs should be avoided. Some people believe that they are not particularly harmful themselves, and they are certainly no more harmful than alcohol or tobacco. However, the fact that many drugs are illegal relates to Biblical teaching about Christians obeying the law. All drugs change the way your body works. Christians believe that life should be lived relying on God. Using non-medical drugs as a way of facing problems or improving your attitude to life does not fit with this.

Summing up

The Bible's teaching about respecting the body and treating it well means that Christians should avoid anything which harms it.

Activities

A

1 What do you think Paul means by 'he bought you for a price'?

2 What is a temple? What do Christians mean when they call the body the temple of the spirit?

B

3 The Salvation Army works with people who have alcohol problems. Why do you think they are so strict about their members not drinking alcohol?

4 Some people might look at the information in this unit and say that Christians obviously never have any fun. What do you think a Christian would answer?

C

5 Working in groups, do some research on the problems caused by teenagers becoming involved with one of the areas mentioned in this unit. Put together an information pack which could be used by a leader working with a Church youth group.

28 Christian stewardship II

Then God said, 'And now we will make human beings; they will be like us and resemble us. They will have power over the fish, the birds, and all the animals, domestic and wild, large and small.' God looked at everything he had made, and he was very pleased.

(Genesis 1, 26, 31)

'A gift from God given to us to share and develop ... '

Whether or not they believe that the story of Creation in the Bible is literally true, Christians believe that human beings should have a responsible attitude to the environment. This section looks at Christian attitudes to stewardship of the planet we live on.

Individual Christians

It is very easy for anyone – Christian or not – to say that what they do as an individual does not really matter. What one person does usually has little effect on the world at large. However, Christian teaching says that God cares about every individual, and the idea that everyone is important works both ways. It is becoming clear that the world cannot go on as it is, and many Christians are becoming concerned about the impact they have on the world they live in. Christians in the developed world may be especially worried about this. The standard of living in Western countries means that people who live in poorer countries suffer. For example, one-quarter of the world's population uses four-fifths of the world's energy. There are simply not enough resources in the world for everyone to have the same standard of living as people in rich countries, or for life in those countries to go on as it is.

Of course, all Christians are individuals and the way they act on this knowledge varies. It ranges from doing very little to devoting their whole life to trying to change things. In between are people who try to 'do their bit' by recycling, saving energy and supporting groups who work to improve things.

The Churches

It is only in the last few years that most Churches – like governments – have woken up to the dangers of the way we live. Most Churches now have policies on environmental issues, and in the last ten years concerns have grown. For example, a statement from Pope John Paul in 1988 described the earth as 'a gift from God given to us to share and develop'. In 1991, a statement from the Methodist Church said, 'Christians must support those working for conservation, and the development of more appropriate, sustainable lifestyles.'

Other groups

There are also several groups which work with Churches of different denominations, trying to increase knowledge and awareness of environmental issues. An example is Christian Ecology Link, which was set up in 1981. It publishes a magazine called Green Christians and runs conferences and other meetings where people can learn more about environmental issues. Another organization is Earthcare Action which began work in 1991. It gives advice to businesses and churches so that they can look at their impact on the environment, and aims to 'enable responsible stewardship'.

Pollution affects everyone

Christians' concern about issues like this is more than just because it is a nice idea. All Christian teaching is based on the idea of human beings in partnership not only with each other but with the world around them. If we cannot achieve this, there is a very real threat that the world itself will cease to exist.

Summing up

Concern for the environment is common sense as well as being part of Christian teaching.

Activities

A

1 What does the idea of the earth as 'a gift from God' mean to you?

2 Make a list of the ways individual Christians can do their bit to help the environment.

B

3 A famous hymn written by St Francis refers to 'brother sun and sister moon'. What does this tell you about how St Francis viewed the universe?

4 Christianity includes the belief that God cares equally for every individual. Explain why this means that Christians cannot be happy with the way the world is at the moment.

C

5 Christians celebrate harvest festivals every year, when they thank God for the earth's produce. Write a prayer or a hymn (or a whole assembly!) which could be used at a harvest festival, bringing home the message of the damage human beings are doing to the earth.

29 Christian charities

This unit is about work done by two British-based Christian charities which try to help people who are less fortunate. Both charities work in the UK, but most of their work takes place abroad, in developing countries.

Christian Aid

Christian Aid began in 1945, when a group of churches in Britain and Ireland began raising money to help people in Europe rebuild their lives after World War II. By 1970, Christian Aid was working in more than 40 countries. Today it supports 700 organizations in more than 70 countries, and in 1997 its income was £39 million. Almost a quarter of this came from door-to-door envelope collections during Christian Aid week. It provides funds and workers where there is a crisis, but most of Christian Aid's funds go to local community groups or churches in the countries where it works. It aims to tackle the causes of poverty, as well as trying to put right the problems which are caused by poverty.

Christian Aid does not get involved in party politics but it does campaign on political issues. Much of its work is in countries which are crippled by the debts they owe to developed countries such as Britain. It has been a leader in campaigns to cancel the backlog of these debts. It also works for fair trade. This means paying producers in other countries a fair price for their goods. A Christian Aid campaign in 1998 focused on persuading large supermarkets to pay more attention to fair trade. They encouraged people to send a letter to the managers of their local supermarkets, with a till receipt to show how much money they had spent. The idea was that ordinary people could show that they cared about fair trade and the supermarket managers, who worry about what their customers think, would look at their trade policies.

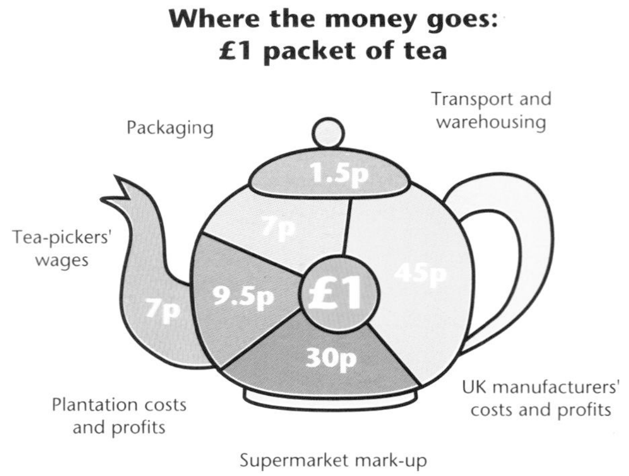

The price of a packet of tea

Christian Aid works to help boys like these

A play-scheme supported by Tearfund

Tearfund

Tearfund began in 1968. It grew out of a fund begun by a Christian organization called the Evangelical Alliance. 'Tear' stands for The Evangelical Alliance Relief fund. Tearfund took as a sort of motto the words of Jesus that he had come to 'bring good news to the poor'. In its first year, Tearfund's income was just £34,000. In 1996–97 it had an income of over £23 million and was working in over 90 countries all over the world.

How does Tearfund work?

Most of Tearfund's work is done through partners, organizations based in the countries where it is working. Except in cases of emergency or disaster, Tearfund does not set up projects or manage them. It aims to build up and support local churches and other Christian groups. They can then go out and work with the people in their town or neighbourhood, whatever religion or race they are. Tearfund gives advice, money and sometimes volunteers to work with local people to over 400 partner groups around the world. Its Disaster Response Team helps in emergencies where there is no local organization.

Summing up

Christian-based charities work all over the world, trying to follow the teachings of Jesus about caring for other people.

Activities

A

1 Why do you think both Christian Aid and Tearfund work mainly with people in the local communities? What could happen if they didn't?

2 How do you think Tearfund brings 'good news to the poor'?

B

3 Each person in the UK drinks an average of 1314 cups of tea a year! Look at the diagram of a teapot, and write an article explaining why Christian Aid campaigns for fair trade.

4 Using a Bible to help you, write a paragraph about why Christians believe that working to help other people is important.

C

5 Find out more about the work of Christian Aid or Tearfund, or another Christian charity (for example, CAFOD, World Vision UK, Operation Christmas Child). Work in groups to put together a wall display, showing how the charity started, where and how it works, how it raises money, etc. Don't forget to include pictures.

Important places in Christianity

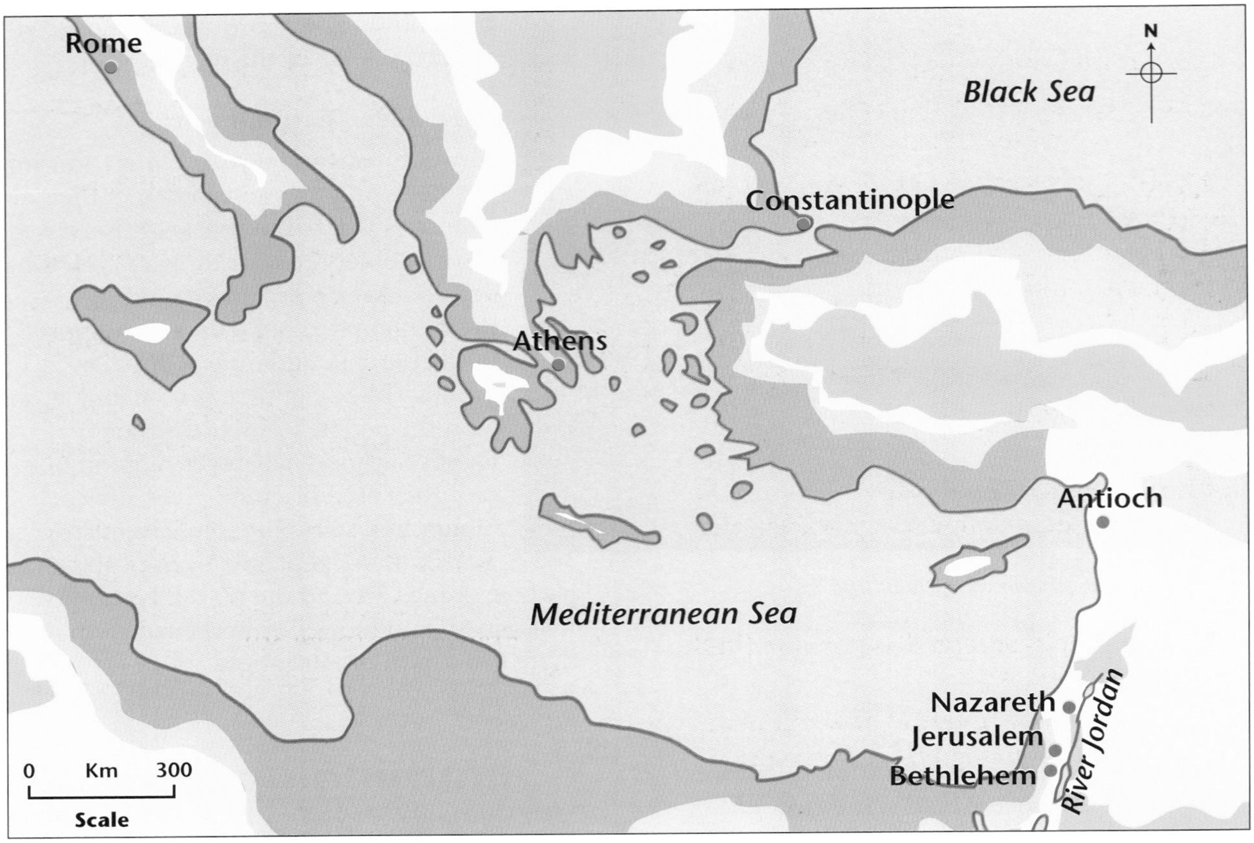
Rome
Black Sea
N
Constantinople
Athens
Antioch
Mediterranean Sea
Nazareth
Jerusalem
Bethlehem
River Jordan
0 Km 300
Scale

Time chart

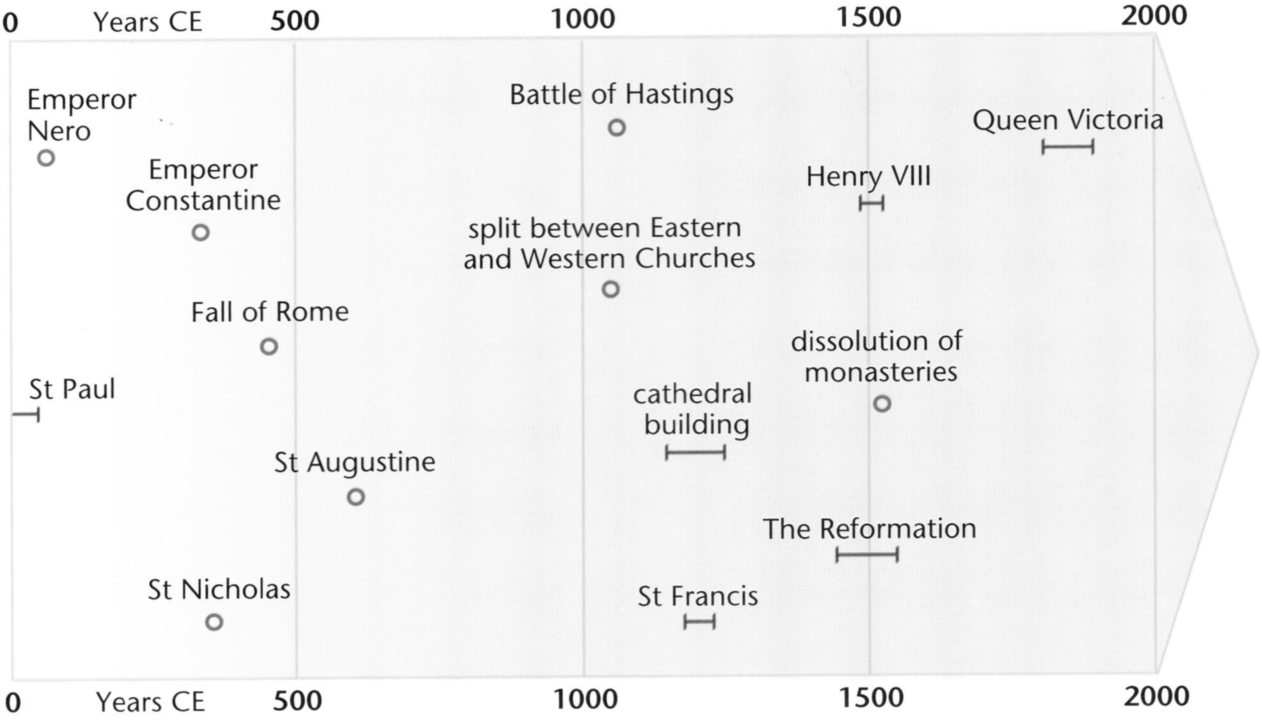
0 Years CE 500 1000 1500 2000
Emperor Nero
Emperor Constantine
Fall of Rome
St Paul
St Augustine
St Nicholas
Battle of Hastings
split between Eastern and Western Churches
cathedral building
St Francis
Henry VIII
dissolution of monasteries
The Reformation
Queen Victoria
0 Years CE 500 1000 1500 2000

Glossary

Adoration special time of prayer (page 33)

Agnostic someone who says it is impossible to know if God exists (page 6)

Anoint to pour oil over, or rub with oil (page 20)

Apostle 'one who is sent out' – name given to some of the first followers of Jesus (page 38)

Atheist someone who says that there is no God (page 6)

Big-bang theory idea that the universe began with an enormous explosion (page 6)

Canon books accepted as genuine (in the Bible) (page 42)

Carbon-dating method of working out the age of once-living things based on changes to the carbon molecules they contain (page 22)

Catholic universal (page 25)

Chastity not taking part in sexual relationships (page 30)

Convent place where nuns live (page 30)

Convert 'to change' – become a member of a religion (page 38)

Creed a statement of belief (page 24)

Cremate burn a person's body after their death (page 54)

Denomination a branch of Christianity (page 40)

Discourses long passages or collections of Jesus' teachings (John's Gospel) (page 46)

Divine Office particular prayers recited every day by priests etc. (page 32)

Doctrine official teachings of religion (page 46)

Ecumenical 'worldwide' – a movement to try to bring different denominations together (page 40)

Epistle letter in the new Testament (page 48)

Eternal without beginning or end (page 4)

Eucharist service of Holy Communion, in which Christians eat bread and drink wine (page 33)

Excommunicate to ban someone from being a member of the Church (page 27)

Free Churches Protestant Churches in the UK which are not Anglican (page 53)

Friar member of a religious order, e.g. Franciscans (page 30)

Funeral service held when someone dies (page 54)

Heaven state of being with God (page 4)

Hebrew language of the Jews (page 20)

Hell state of being away from God (page 55)

Hermit one who lives alone (page 30)

Indulgences promise of forgiveness of sins (page 26)

Judaism the religion of the Jews (page 44)

Logos 'word' or 'reason' – John's term for Jesus (page 46)

Martyr someone who dies rather than give up their faith (page 24)

Messiah one sent by God to free the Jews (page 18)

Miracle an event which cannot be explained, but which shows God's power (page 6)

Mission working on behalf of God, with people who are not necessarily Christians (page 32)

Missionary someone who travels to preach about what they believe, or their religion (page 38)

Monastery building where monks live (page 28)

Monk man who has chosen to dedicate his life to God (page 26)

Mystery play medieval play based on Bible stories (page 12)

Novice 'trainee' monk or nun who has not taken final vows (page 32)

Nun woman who has chosen to dedicate her life to God (page 30)

Order group of monks or nuns who live by the same rules (page 28)

Orthodox 'right belief'; name of Eastern Churches, mainly based in Greece or Russia (page 22)

Patriarch leader of the Orthodox Church (page 25)

Pope head of the Roman Catholic Church (page 25)

Prophet messenger from God (page 18)

Protestant Christians who are neither Roman Catholic nor Orthodox (page 27)

Puritan member of an extreme Protestant group (page 29)

Reconciliation establishing friendship between enemies (page 34)

Reformation movement for change to the Church in the sixteenth century, causing the split between the Roman Catholic and Protestant Churches in Europe (page 26)

Resurrection the Christian belief that Jesus rose from the dead (page 21)

Retreat a time when people can withdraw from ordinary life and think about their faith (page 32)

Sacrifice killing something so that its life can be offered to God (page 21)

Schism 'split' (the split between Rome and Constantinople in 1054 CE) (page 25)

Scriptures holy books (page 19)

Shroud length of cloth in which a dead body is wrapped (page 22)

Sign technical term for the way John presents the miracles of Jesus in the Fourth Gospel (page 46)

Sin wrong-doing which separates people from God (page 21)

Soul the part of a person believed to survive death, sometimes called the spirit (page 12)

Symbol something that stands for something else (page 18)

Synoptic 'Same view' – name given to the first three Gospels (page 18)

Temple the most important building in the Jewish religion (page 12)

Torah Books of teaching (first part of the Jewish scriptures) (page 44)

Transfiguration changing appearance (page 18)

Vocation a 'calling' – an urge to live in a particular way (page 32)

Vows solemn promises (page 30)

It's another Quality Book from CGP

This book is for anyone doing GCSE Double Science Physics.

It contains lots of tricky questions designed to make you sweat — because that's the only way you'll get any better.

It's also got some daft bits in to try and make the whole experience at least vaguely entertaining for you.

What CGP is all about

Our sole aim here at CGP is to produce the highest quality books — carefully written, immaculately presented and dangerously close to being funny.

Then we work our socks off to get them out to you — at the cheapest possible prices.

Contents

Contributors:
Chris Dennett
Dominic Hall
Lindsay Jordan
Tim Major
Isaac Newton
Claire Thompson
Tim Wakeling
James Paul Wallis
Suzanne Worthington

Published by Coordination Group Publications Ltd.
ISBN 1 84146 404 X
Groovy website: www.cgpbooks.co.uk
Jolly bits of clipart from CorelDRAW
Printed by Elanders Hindson, Newcastle upon Tyne.
With thanks to Colin Wells for the proof-reading

Doing Formula Questions

Physics is famed for being hard but once you can do one formula, you can do them all.
OK, they change the letters, but all these formula questions are really asking the same thing.

It doesn't matter what the letters are

a=bc P=IV F=ma

1) Those three formulas look totally different.
2) But when you get given b and c and have to work out a, it's exactly the same as if you're given I and V and have to work out P.
3) Nearly all formula questions are exactly the same, just with different letters.

It's all multiplying or dividing

1) When you're given a=bc, there are three things they could ask — "what is a", "what is b" or "what is c".
2) But two of those are exactly the same — you work out b in exactly the same way as you work out c.
3) So there's really only two things they can ask you to work out: two things multiplied or one thing divided by another.
4) And that's all these questions are, just dividing or multiplying.

They're all the same as these examples

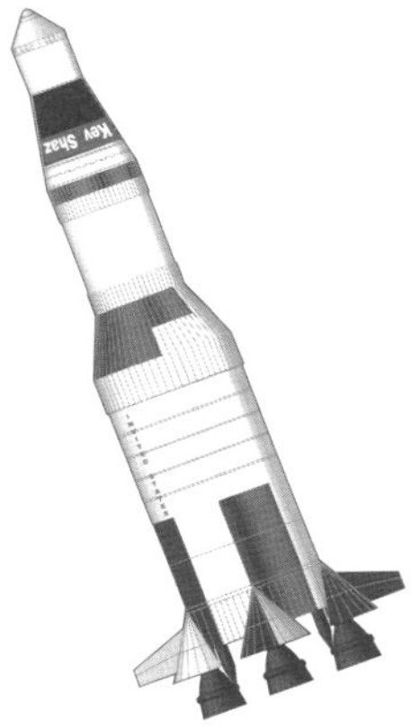

EXAMPLE QUESTION A toy rocket of mass 0.3 kg has an acceleration of 5 m/s². What is the resultant force on it?

ANSWER:
1) The quantities are mass, force and acceleration.
2) The formula with those in is F=ma (you can look it up in the table on the inside front cover, but you're going to have to learn it sometime).
3) So put 0.3 in place of m and put 5 in place of a.
4) F=0.3×5=1.5 N

EXAMPLE QUESTION A resultant force of 4.7 N acts on a tiny 1 kg dog. What is its acceleration?

ANSWER:
1) The quantities are mass, force and acceleration.
2) The formula with those in is F=ma, but this time you want to work out a, not F.
3) Rearrange it to get a=F÷m.
4) Stick 4.7 in for F and 1 in for m.
5) a=4.7÷1=4.7 m/s²

Check your answers aren't ridiculous

1) If you had a question about the height of a person, and your answer was 3000 m, chances are you've screwed up.
2) You might have multiplied instead of dividing, or got your units wrong somewhere.
3) If you get something like 3000 m or 0.0000012 as an answer, check it again.
4) You'd have to be pretty confident to leave something like that as your final answer.

The opposite of juggling — looks hard, but it's easy...

Blimey — so it's actually easy, then. Seems like a con — physics is supposed to be hard. That's what I thought anyway. But once you know what formula you've got to use, you just stick the numbers in instead of the letters, and either multiply or divide. After you realise that, it's easy.

See the "Using Formulas" pages of our Physics Revision Guides

The Secret of Formula Triangles

Remembering formulas is easy as long as you bother to learn them — and multiplying and dividing are a push-over, so the only bit left is rearranging the formulas. And this page makes that easy too.

Use a formula triangle if you want to get it right

Formula triangles make doing formula question about 137 times easier.
And practically every formula in Physics goes into one.

1) If the formula is "A=B×C" then A goes on the top and B×C goes on the bottom.
2) If the formula is "A=B/C" then B must go on top (because it's the only way you can get B divided by something), so A and C go on the bottom.

EXAMPLES

V=I×R becomes:

F=ma becomes:

F=W/d becomes:

Using Formula Triangles — Three Steps

1) Write down the thing you want, and put '=' after it.
2) In the triangle, cover up the thing you want to find, and write down what's left showing.
3) You've now got the formula — stick the numbers in and you're done.

EXAMPLES

1) To find W from the 3rd triangle, cover up W and you get F×d. So W=F×d.

2) To find m from the 2nd one, cover up m, and write down the rest: F/a. So m=F/a.

...so I used the formula triangle and proved 1 + 1 = 2!

EXAMPLE QUESTION

A bulb is connected to a 15 V battery. The bulb has resistance of 30 W. What current flows through it?

ANSWER:

1) You've got voltage and resistance, and you want current. So the formula you need is V=IR.
2) Put it into a formula triangle (V on top):

3) Cover up what you're after (I) and write down what you get: I=V/R

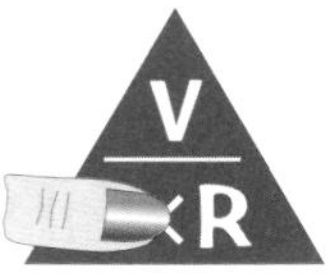

4) Stick the numbers in and there you go: I=15/30=0.5 A
5) Check it's sensible — it's not 50 000 A or 0.00000765436 A.

That's it — easy once you've learnt it.

Take 2 equations into the exam? Not me, I just rearrange and go...

2 short pages, one big message — it's nowhere near as hard as it's cracked up to be. There are 3 things you've got to do: remember all these formula questions are the same thing, learn how to use a formula triangle, and do the hard grind of learning the formulas. Then you'll get them all right.

See the "Using Formulas" pages of our Physics Revision Guides

The Secrets of Units and Formulas

Checking units is a real pain in the neck. But the alternative is getting the answer wrong, which is even worse. It's one of life's little niggles that you have to put up with.

Check your units before you start the sums

1) Make sure the units you put into the formula are standard (SI) units.
2) If the question gives you mass in grams, change it to kg before you use it.
3) If you don't put standard units in, there's no way you can get standard units out.
4) And if your answer isn't in standard units, it'll be wrong, plain and simple.
5) Unless they specifically ask for it in some other unit, in which case you pretty obviously have to use the one they ask for.

Give your answer in the right units

1) In the exam, they normally give you the units.
2) But you still need to check them.
3) Make sure the units you've used are the same as the ones they want.
4) Don't put time in minutes if they have it in hours. Or length in cm if they use metres.

The 'Units Trick' for Speed and Electricity Used

1) This is a great trick that works for s=d/t, P=F/A and E=Pt (electricity used=power×time).
2) If they give you the units, you can work out the formula.
3) Just write down the most complicated unit (ie the one that's got several bits).
4) Replace each bit of the unit with what that bit would measure. (Eg: in N/m^2, N measures force, m^2 measures area.)
5) Bingo. What you've written down is the formula.

That sounds a bit confusing, but look at this example and it'll all become clear:
QUESTION: What's the formula for speed, distance and time?
ANSWER:

1) The units are m/s, m and s.
2) So write down the unit made up of several bits: speed = m/s
3) Change m to distance (because metres measure distance) and change s to time (because seconds measure time).
4) You get speed = distance/time or s=d/t.
5) Voilà, that's the formula.

You can do the same thing with the formula for pressure, force and area (remember pressure is measured in N/m^2, which is the same as Pascals) and for the formula for Electricity used, power and time.

For some reason I expected to see two politicians on page 3...

Watch out for those units. The golden rule is ALWAYS USE STANDARD UNITS. That way you can't end up with it all getting mixed up. I know I'm going on about it, but it is blummin' important. If you don't bother to get basic stuff like this right, you're going to have real problems later on.

See the "Using Formulas" pages of our Physics Revision Guides

Electrical Power

Electrical power is measured in Watts (W) or Kilowatts (kW).

$$P = V \times I$$

Power Voltage Current

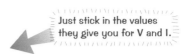

Just stick in the values they give you for V and I.

EG:
Find P if V=230V and I=12A

$$P = 230 \times 12 = 2880\ W$$

Q1 Find the power from circuits with these voltages and currents.

a) Voltage 6 V, current 3 A
b) Voltage 8 V, current 2 A
c) V = 9 V, I = 3 A
d) Voltage 3 V, current 3 A
e) V = 12 V, I = 0.2 A
f) Voltage 12 V, current 1.4 A
g) Voltage 9 V, current 2.5 A
h) V = 1.25 V, I = 4 A
i) Voltage 5.13 V, current 10 A

You need to rearrange the formula for the next questions. Have a look at page 2 for the easy way to do it. Then just stick the numbers in.

Q2 Find the voltage of appliances with these power values and currents.

You need the power in Watts, not Kilowatts.

a) P = 10 W, I = 2 A
b) P = 5 W, I = 2 A
c) P = 17 kW, I = 850 A
d) P = 8 kW, I = 16 A
e) P = 9 W, I = 4 A
f) P = 10 kW, I = 200 A
g) P = 5 kW, I = 4 A
h) P = 10 kW, I = 16 A
i) P = 225 W, I = 6 A

Rearrange the formula again and stick in the numbers.

Q3 Find the current flowing through appliances with these power and voltage values.

a) Power 10 kW, voltage 200 V
b) P = 14 kW, V = 7 V
c) Voltage 12 V, power 24 kW
d) P = 15 kW, V = 250 V
e) Power 9 kW, voltage 2 V
f) P = 25 W, V = 2 V
g) Voltage 0.5 V, power 55 W
h) P = 2 kW, V = 2.5 V
i) V = 75 V, P = 30 kW

With wordy ones like this you have to read through it to find the letters, then stick it into the formula.

Q4 Francis is using a hairdryer plugged into the mains. It has 230 V across it.

a) Work out the power from the hairdryer if 6 A flows through the circuit.

Most electrical appliances have their power and operating voltage written on them.

b) Work out the power of the hairdryer if 4.6 A flows through the circuit.

c) Work out the current that flows through a hairdryer with 30 V across it, if it gives 300 W.

d) Francis has another hairdryer rated at 120 V, 1.4 kW. Find the fuse needed for the circuit.

Hint — the fuse should be a round number, slightly higher than the normal current.

Electrical power — you can't lick it...

Better get used to this formula, it's like all the ones in this book — easy to remember, but not the most fascinating thing in the world. The Electrical Power formula is one of the easiest — make sure you've got it stuffed into your brain, or you won't have much chance with all the others.

See the "Work Done, Energy and Power" pages of our Physics Revision Guides

Electrical Power

Electrical power questions crop up all the time in exams. There's only three things they can ask you — find P, find I or find V. It's only easy if you know the formula...

Q1 A treadmill has a power output of 1.5 kW.

a) If a current of 10 A flows, what is the voltage rating of the treadmill?

b) What voltage would be across the treadmill if the current was 12 A?

c) What voltage would be across the treadmill if the current was 6 A?

Remember to use a fuse with a value above the normal current in the circuit.

d) What kind of fuse would be needed if the voltage rating of the treadmill was 600 V?

Q2 A computer running off the mains has 230 V across it.

a) What's the power of the computer if 5.2 A flows through it?

b) If 6.1 A flows through the computer, how much power is there?

c) What value of fuse should be used if the power from the computer is 500 W?

d) What fuse would be needed if the power from the computer was 2.15 kW?

e) If the computer is run from a cyclo-generator, which gives 200 V, and the current flowing is 4 A, what would the power be?

f) If the computer's still being driven by the cyclo-generator, and the power is 500 W, what current would be flowing?

Q3 An electric piano has a power value of 600 W.

a) The voltage of mains electricity is 230 V. What current flows through the piano at this voltage?

b) If a current of 5 A flows, what's the voltage across the piano?

c) Would you use a 20 A or a 30 A fuse if the voltage across the piano was 24 V?

d) Would you use a 35 A or a 40 A fuse if the voltage across the piano was 16 V?

I'm an electrifying cook — my current buns are to die for...

Sometimes you'll get a question about $P=I^2R$. It looks complicated, but it's just what you get when you combine $P=IV$ and $R=V/I$. Work out V by using $R=V/I$ (see p.6) and then stick it into $P=IV$, that's my advice. Saves you learning another formula. So don't panic if you see $P=I^2R$.

See the "Work Done, Energy and Power" pages of our Physics Revision Guides (that's just in case you haven't read page 4...)

Resistance

$$R = \frac{V}{I}$$

R = Resistance, V = Voltage, I = Current

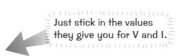

Just stick in the values they give you for V and I.

EG:
Find R if V = 230 V and I = 15 A

$$R = 230 \div 15 = 16\ \Omega$$

Q1 Work out the resistance of bulbs with these voltages and currents.

Resistance tells you how much current a component allows to flow through it.

a) V = 6 V, I = 3 A
b) V = 8 V, I = 2 A
c) V = 9 V, I = 3 A
d) V = 3 V, I = 3 A
e) V = 12 V, I = 2 A
f) V = 12 V, I = 4 A
g) V = 9 V, I = 2 A
h) V = 1 V, I = 4 A
i) V = 5 V, I = 10 A

Q2 Work out the voltage across resistors with these resistances and currents.

You'll have to swap the formula around: voltage = current × resistance

Resistance is measured in Ohms, written as Ω.

a) R = 3 Ω, I = 2 A
b) R = 2 Ω, I = 5 A
c) R = 4 Ω, I = 4 A
d) R = 6 Ω, I = 3 A
e) R = 4 Ω, I = 0.5 A
f) R = 18 Ω, I = 0.5 A
g) R = 9 Ω, I = 0.5 A
h) R = 12 Ω, I = 0.25 A
i) R = 1.2 Ω, I = 10 A

Q3 Work out the current through wires with these resistances and voltages.

You'll need to swap the formula round again.

a) R = 2 Ω, V = 4 V
b) R = 2 Ω, V = 6 V
c) R = 3 Ω, V = 9 V
d) R = 6 Ω, V = 12 V
e) R = 4 Ω, V = 12 V
f) R = 4 Ω, V = 4 V
g) R = 8 Ω, V = 4 V
h) R = 8 Ω, V = 2 V
i) R = 10 Ω, V = 6 V

Q4 A Physics teacher has wired his talking bear up to a circuit. There are 30 V across it, and the current is 6 A.

a) What is the resistance of the bear?
b) The teacher puts a 12 V battery in the circuit instead of the old one. What's the current now?

Q5 Now the Physics teacher has wired the bear into the mains.

a) What is the current through the bear if its resistance stays the same?
b) What would the current be if he used a 120 V adaptor?

You need to know that mains voltage is 230 V for this question.

Resistance isn't futile, it's very, very useful...

© Prof Davros

I bet you love it when you can make one formula into three different ones just by swapping the terms around. Well maybe not — but it means you only need to remember the formula once and then work out the others. And making formulas easy to learn is what makes the world go round.

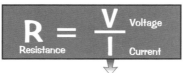

See the "Current, Voltage and Resistance" pages of our Physics Revision Guides

Resistance

There isn't much to exam questions about resistance. If you slog through all these practice questions, you'll be able to do them in your sleep.

Q1 A special edition belly-dancing stereo has 120 V across it.

a) What is the resistance of the stereo if there is a current of 5 A through it?

b) If the current through the stereo increases to 8 A, what must the new resistance be?

c) Bruce powers the stereo from a 6 V battery. If the resistance is now 1.2 Ω, what is the current?

Q2 A circuit has 3 components in series with resistances of 4 Ω, 6 Ω and 2 Ω.

a) What is the total resistance in the circuit?

b) If the circuit is connected to a 24 V battery, what is the current in the circuit?

Use the TOTAL resistance to work this out.

c) What battery voltage is being used if a current of 0.5 A flows through the circuit?

d) What current (to 1 d.p.) flows through the circuit if it is connected to the mains voltage of 230 V?

Q3 A new lawnmower motor has 18 Ω resistance.

a) What current (to 1 d.p.) flows through the motor if it runs off 230 V mains electricity?

b) If the lawnmower is unplugged from the mains and is run off a 30 V battery instead, what current will flow? (1 d.p.)

c) What battery voltage would allow a 1.5 A current to flow?

1000 mA=1 A.

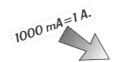

d) Another lawnmower runs off the mains and allows a current of 6500 mA to flow. What is its resistance to 1 decimal place?

What makes batteries work in Warsaw? — Pole volts...

Questions on resistance in exams are usually pretty easy, just like the ones on this page. As long as you don't get the formula the wrong way round, you're laughing. It'll help if you remember that mains electricity is at 230 V — and don't forget to keep values in the right units.

See the "Current, Voltage and Resistance" pages of our Physics Revision Guides

Energy in Kilowatt-hours

$$E = P \times t$$

Energy — Power — Time

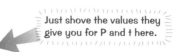

Just shove the values they give you for P and t here.

EG:
Find E if P=6 kW and t=2 hours

$$E = 6 \times 2 = 12 \text{ kWh}$$

An electricity meter counts the number of units used. Another name for a unit is a kilowatt-hour (kWh or kW-h).

Q1 Work out how much energy (in kWh) is used for each of these periods of time for a 2 kW appliance.

a) 3 hours
b) 6 hours
c) 12 hours
d) 2.5 hours
e) 1.5 hours
f) 7.5 hours
g) a day
h) 10 minutes
i) 6 minutes

You'll need the time in hours.

Q2 Work out the power output of appliances that transfer these amounts of energy in 4 hours.

a) 8 kWh
b) 12 kWh
c) 32 kWh
d) 2 kWh
e) 6 kWh
f) 3 kWh
g) 46 kWh
h) 90 kWh
i) 4.8 kWh

Q3 These appliances of different powers used 6 kWh of energy each. Work out the number of hours that they were used for.

a) 6 kW
b) 2 kW
c) 1 kW
d) 12 kW
e) 24 kW
f) 8 kW
g) 3000 W
h) 500 W
i) 100 kW

Don't forget to change the power to kW for each calculation.

Q4 A cyclist is pedalling an exercise bike to power a huge light bulb. He has a power output of 30 kW.

a) How much energy will he have used in 3.5 hours?

b) How much energy will he have used in 15 minutes?

c) How long can he power the bulb for, if he uses 20 kWh of energy?

d) The cyclist powers the bulb from a battery because he's tired out. It uses 1152 kWh of energy in two days. What was its power output?

Give me NRG in kWh ASAP SVP...

The important thing to remember on this page is that a kilowatt-hour is an amount of energy, not a unit of power. And the best way of figuring out the formula is by remembering the unit — energy is measured in kWh, which means kW×h. So that's one formula you'll have sussed in the exam.

See the "Cost of Domestic Electricity" pages of our Physics Revision Guides

Cost of Electricity

cost (of electricity) **= units** (of electricity) **× price** (per unit)

Stick in the values they give you for units and price.

EG:
Find the cost in £ if 100 units are used and a unit costs 8 p

cost = 100 × 0.08 = £8

Q1 Work out the cost (in £) of these amounts of energy if the price of one unit is 7.5 p.

1 kWh = 1 unit.

a) 100 kWh
b) 1000 kWh
c) 90 kWh
d) 150 kWh
e) 500 kWh
f) 1600 kWh
g) 516 kWh
h) 998 kWh
i) 34 612 kWh

Q2 Work out the number of units you could pay for with these amounts of money if the price of one unit is 8 p.

Watch it — don't mix up £ and p in questions like this.

a) 80 p
b) £1.60
c) £16.00
d) £80.00
e) £45.00
f) £500.00
g) £750.00
h) £51.80
i) £757.20

Q3 Work out what the cost of one unit of energy was (to the nearest tenth of a penny) if £70.00 bought this number of units.

a) 1000 units
b) 500 units
c) 700 units
d) 750 units
e) 650 units
f) 550 units
g) 825 units
h) 574 units
i) 631 units

Q4 Sherlock is inspecting his electricity meter. The last time he checked, its counter read 564 215.4 units. Now it reads 565 897.5 units.

a) How many units has he used since the last time he checked?

b) One unit costs 8 p. How much will his electricity bill be?

c) Last month, Sherlock paid £210. How many units did he use?

d) Ten years ago, electricity was cheaper. One month, Sherlock paid £130 for 2000 units. How much did one unit cost?

What do electric companies and herons have in common?...

You've got to learn this, and it's useful too, because now you can check your own electricity meter — which is nice. Always make sure you've got both the price per unit and the cost in either pounds or pence before you plug them into the formula, or you'll end up with an answer that's utter rubbish.

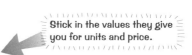

Energy and Cost

Questions in exams often lump different formulas together into one question — so you've got to be able to work out amounts of energy used, and then how much it all costs.

Q1 A hand buzzer has a power output of 3.5 kW from the battery.

a) For how long had the buzzer been buzzing by the time 14 kWh of energy had been used?

b) The battery will run out after 7.5 hours of buzzing. How much energy will it have used by then?

c) A different battery gives 31.5 kWh of energy before it runs out. How many extra hours of buzzing does this battery provide?

Q2 Cliff's washing machine has a power output of 4.5 kW.

a) How much energy does the washing machine use in 3 hours?

b) If the washing machine has used 15.75 kWh of energy, how long has the washing machine been in use?

c) Last time he paid a bill, Cliff's electricity meter read 3546237 units. It now reads 3551243 units. If Cliff's bill this time comes to £300.36, how much is one unit?

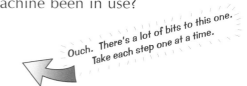

Ouch. There's a lot of bits to this one. Take each step one at a time.

Q3 Harold's illuminated jacket has a power output of 2.5 kW.

a) If 3.125 kWh of energy has been used, for how many minutes has Harold been using the jacket?

b) Harold's plugged his jacket into the mains. How much energy is used by the jacket in two hours?

c) How much has Harold added to his electricity bill in two hours, if the price of one unit is 9 p?
Use the answer to another question to work this out, and remember Cost=Units×Price.

d) Harold plugs three jackets into the mains — each with a power rating of 2.5 kW. How much will he add to his electricity bill in 3 hours, if the price of one unit is 9 p?

Lots of parts to this one — just work it out a bit at a time.

...they can both stick their bills...

Always remember to have <u>energy in kW</u> and <u>time in hours</u> for these questions. If there's lots of steps to a question, just figure out what you <u>do</u> know and then work out the rest. And you shouldn't have too much trouble remembering the formulas — they're pretty obvious, really.

See the "Cost of Domestic Electricity" pages of our Physics Revision Guides

Force and Motion

$$F = m \times a$$

Force · Mass · Acceleration

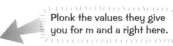

Plonk the values they give you for m and a right here.

EG:
Find F if m = 5 kg and a = 2 m/s²

$$F = 5 \times 2 = 10\ \text{N}$$

Give answers on this page to 1 decimal place where needed.

Q1 Find the force acting on an object with a mass of:

a) 10 kg at 5 m/s²
b) 5 kg at 7 m/s²
c) 94 kg at 4 m/s²
d) 0.75 kg at 3 m/s²
e) 1.26 kg at 1.7 m/s²
f) 38 kg at 5.8 m/s²
g) 58.9 kg at 4.3 m/s²
h) 1237 kg at 6.8 m/s²
i) 0.56 kg at 9.42 m/s²

Q2 What is the acceleration of these masses if the resultant force on them is:

a) 100 N, mass 5 kg
b) 35 N, mass 7 kg
c) 84 N, mass 6 kg
d) 20.4 N, mass 3.2 kg
e) 12.5 N, mass 37.5 kg
f) 4 N, mass 0.64 kg
g) 56 N, mass 2 kg
h) 193 N, mass 49 kg
i) 7.1 N, mass 238 g

Q3 What is the mass of an object if the acceleration and resultant force are:

a) 4 m/s², 40 N
b) 8 m/s², 64 N
c) 2.4 m/s², 92 N
d) 5.2 m/s², 13 N
e) 9.81 m/s², 56 N
f) 2.34 m/s², 43 N
g) 1.2 m/s², 78 N
h) 3.5 m/s², 20.5 N
i) 7.25 m/s², 109 N

Q4 What is the resultant force on these objects?

Use 2 d.p. for parts e, f and g.

a) A car of mass 1200 kg accelerating at 3 m/s².
b) A 14 kg dog running with an acceleration of 1.8 m/s².
c) A scooter and rider with a total mass of 270 kg accelerating at 3.4 m/s².
d) A 200 kg jetski and the 68 kg rider accelerating at 1.2 m/s².
e) A feather of 3 g falling with an acceleration of 7.2 m/s².
f) A 183 kg motorised oven containing a 2.7 kg cake accelerating at 2.56 m/s².
g) A 76 kg skyboarder with his 5 kg board falling with an acceleration of 9.81 m/s².

Force calculations complete them well you must mmmmm.

Force and Motion — what can I say... Learn it.

The resultant force F is the overall unbalanced force. If the forces are balanced then the object moves at constant speed. You need to understand this so it all becomes obvious, then you'll wonder how you got through life without the genius of Newton. (Aaaah — ignorance is bliss...)

See the "Three Laws of Motion" pages of our Physics Revision Guides

Force and Motion

The best way to get formulas into your head is to do practice question after practice question. That's why, kind soul that I am, I've given you so many.

Q1 Which object has the biggest force acting on it?

Give your answers to 1 d.p.

a) A 5 kg rock accelerating at 3 m/s^2 or a 7 kg boulder accelerating at 2 m/s^2.

b) A 800 kg Mini accelerating at 4 m/s^2 or a 5000 kg van accelerating at 0.5 m/s^2.

c) A 78 kg skier accelerating at 1.6 m/s^2 or a 83 kg snowboarder accelerating at 1.4 m/s^2.

d) A 250 kg motorbike accelerating at 0.75 m/s^2 or a 20 kg bicycle accelerating at 8 m/s^2.

e) A 59 kg skydiver accelerating at 9.81 m/s^2 or a 63 kg parachutist decelerating at 9 m/s^2.

f) A 100 g sparrow accelerating at 1.8 m/s^2 or a 700 g magpie accelerating at 0.5 m/s^2.

g) A 500 kg horse decelerating at 5.5 m/s^2 or a 180 kg motorbike decelerating at 12 m/s^2.

Q2 What is the change in acceleration if the force changes from:

Work out the acceleration for both forces, then find the difference.

a) 10 N to 20 N on a 2 kg mass

b) 32 N to 64 N on an 8 kg mass

c) 89 N to 104 N on a 3 kg mass

d) 26 N to 24 N on a 0.25 kg mass

e) 40.5 N to 57 N on a 29 kg mass

f) 114 N to 138 N on a 52 kg mass

g) 2.7 N to 4.9 N on a 520 g mass

h) 429 N to 786 N on a 780 kg mass

Q3 a) What resultant force does a 30 kg mass need to accelerate at 2.45 m/s^2?

b) A car has a forward thrust of 680 N and a drag of 49 N acts in the opposite direction. What is the resultant force in the forward direction?

c) A child on a skateboard is accelerating at 2.95 m/s^2 with a resultant force of 138 N. What is the child's weight to the nearest kilogram if the skateboard has a mass of 1.4 kg?

d) In a cheese-rolling competition the heaviest cheese is 14 kg. The cheese accelerates at 4.2 m/s^2. What is the resultant force on it at this acceleration?

e) The maximum resultant force a fish can generate when swimming is 38 N. What will its acceleration be if the fish weighs 7 kg?

f) A thief is pulling a woman's bag with a force of 29 N. The woman is trying to get her bag back with a pull of 18.5 N. How heavy is the bag if the acceleration is 1.6 m/s^2? Is the bag accelerating towards the woman or the thief?

I'm fed up of these puns — they're all too forced...

F=ma is absolutely fundamental to Physics. It's as famous as $E=mc^2$ but with one huge difference — you have to learn F=ma and know how to use it. If you don't get it into your brain, you may as well wave goodbye to several tasty marks. That'd be a shame — it's dead easy really.

See the "Three Laws of Motion" pages of our Physics Revision Guides

Force and Motion

F = ma doesn't usually get a whole question all to itself. The examiners could chuck in speed, power, energy and anything else that takes their fancy.

Q1 A young farm-hand's tractor won't start so she pushes it along the road to a garage. The tractor has a mass of 340 kg.

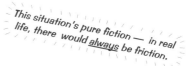

For these questions, give answers to one decimal place.

a) If she pushes the tractor with a resultant force of 860 N, what acceleration will it have?

b) There are several things she can do to decrease the acceleration. Write down two things.

c) The farmer's sheepdog thought it might be fun to sit on the tractor while she pushes. If he has a mass of 17 kg, how much harder will she have to push to get the same acceleration?

d) Would the tractor stop if the girl stopped pushing it and there was no friction at all?

This situation's pure fiction — in real life, there would always be friction.

Q2 A supermarket trolley has a mass of 32 kg. If it's fully loaded, it has a mass of 275 kg.

a) At the start of a trolley dash, what force must an empty trolley be pushed with for it to accelerate at 3 m/s^2?

b) If the trolley is full, what force would the trolley have to be pushed with to get the same acceleration?

c) The woman can push the trolley with a maximum force of 800 N. To the nearest kg, what is the maximum mass that the trolley can have if she is to accelerate at 3 m/s^2?

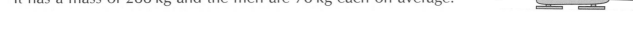

Q3 Four men use a snowmobile to travel across ice and snow. It has a mass of 288 kg and the men are 78 kg each on average.

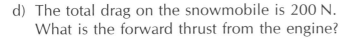

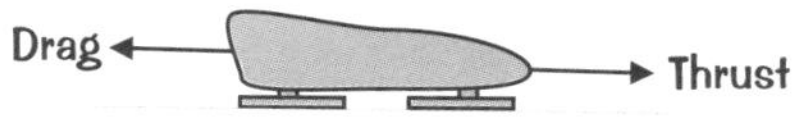

a) What force does the full snowmobile exert on the ice when it's standing still?

b) What force does the ice exert on the full snowmobile when it's not moving?

c) The snowmobile moves on the ice with an acceleration of 4.7 m/s^2. What is the resultant force on the snowmobile and what direction is it in?

There's no acceleration in the up/down direction...

d) The total drag on the snowmobile is 200 N. What is the forward thrust from the engine?

e) The men add a 22 kg jet-pack to the snowmobile. If this adds another 55 N to the forward thrust, what would the new resultant force be if the drag stays the same? What is the new acceleration to one d.p.?

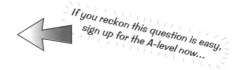

If you reckon this question is easy, sign up for the A-level now...

Just think — if Newton had died at birth, these 3 pages wouldn't exist...

Questions using F=ma crop up all over the place in Physics. Just when you think you're done with using that formula it will pop up again. That's why it's absolutely essential that you know it off by heart. You've got to know how to use it as well — it'd be pretty useless otherwise...

See the "Three Laws of Motion" pages of our Physics Revision Guides

Mass and Weight

$$W = m \times g$$

Weight — Mass — Pull of Gravity

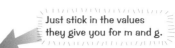

Just stick in the values they give you for m and g.

EG:
Find W if m = 70 kg and g = 10 N/kg

$$W = 70 \times 10 = 700\ \text{N}$$

Q1 Work out the weights of these masses on the Earth (where g = 10 N/kg):

a) 5 kg
b) 10 kg
c) 227 kg
d) 32.5 kg
e) 0.5 kg
f) 3.5 kg
g) 0.3 kg
h) 231.5 kg
i) 0.25 kg

Q2 Work out the masses of these weights on the Earth:

Sometimes you need the formula the other way round: mass = weight ÷ g

a) 6 N
b) 8 N
c) 143 N
d) 50 N
e) 320 N
f) 2 N
g) 34 N
h) 254 N
i) 0.5 N

Q3 Work out what these masses would weigh on the Moon, where g = 1.6 N/kg:

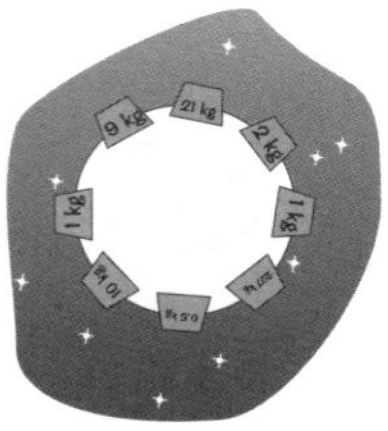

a) 5 kg
b) 10 kg
c) 227 kg
d) 32.5 kg
e) 0.5 kg
f) 3.5 kg
g) 0.3 kg
h) 231.5 kg
i) 0.25 kg

OK, so g is different on the Moon. You still need to think about which way round the formula should be.

Q4 Bob weighs an object with a mass of 12 kg. It weighs 19.2 N.

a) Is he on the Earth or the Moon? How can you tell?

b) Bob (naked) has a mass of 65 kg. How much does he weigh: i) on Earth, ii) on the Moon?

c) When Bob puts his thick coat on, he has a mass of 80 kg.
How much does he weigh now: i) on Earth, ii) on the Moon?

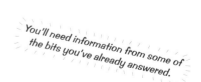

You'll need information from some of the bits you've already answered.

d) One of Bob's shoes weighs 8 N on the Moon. What is its mass?

e) What is Bob's weight on Earth if wears the coat and a pair of shoes?

Weighty Mass — A heavy-going church sermon...

Don't go thinking MASS and WEIGHT are the same thing — mass is the amount of matter in something (measured in kg), weight is the force (measured in Newtons) on it from the pull of gravity. It's yet another formula you can put into a formula triangle, so it's nice 'n' easy.

See the "Gravity, Weight and Moments" pages of our Physics Revision Guides

Mass and Weight

Exam questions about mass and weight are often in bits of questions about something else. But not always.

Q1 A parachutist has a mass of 70 kg. His parachute has a mass of 10 kg.

a) What is their combined weight?

Watch out: don't think all you have to do is add up 70 and 10. It's weight you're after, not mass...

b) At the time this picture was taken, the force upwards due to air resistance was 670 N. What was the resultant force downwards?

c) What was the parachutist's acceleration at that point in time?

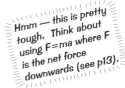

Hmm — this is pretty tough. Think about using F=ma where F is the net force downwards (see p13).

Q2 Victor and his dog weigh 1176 N together. Victor has a mass of 63 kg.

Watch out — you've got a mixture of kg and N.

a) What is the mass of Victor's dog?

b) Victor, his dog and his saxophone are standing on a box. Victor's saxophone has a mass of 2 kg and the box weighs 30 N. What is the total weight of them all?

c) Victor's dog jumps off the box. About half way to the ground, his acceleration is 8 m/s². What is the upward force on the dog, due to air resistance, at that point?

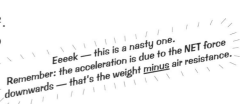

Eeeek — this is a nasty one. Remember: the acceleration is due to the NET force downwards — that's the weight minus air resistance.

Q3 Paddy O'Paddle and his boat have a mass of 125 kg together. The boat weighs 417 N.

a) What is the mass of the boat?

b) What is the combined weight of Paddy and his boat?

c) What is Paddy's weight?

d) As he goes over a waterfall in the boat, Paddy's acceleration is 6.5 m/s². What is the upward force on Paddy and his boat due to air resistance as they fall?

Damon Hill's rubbish at Physics — he only knows one formula...

Don't get fazed when you get 2 formulas in the same question. It's just as easy as doing them separately. You work out the answer to one formula, then bung that answer in the next formula. No clever tricks, no conspiracy theory — just do one bit, then do the other bit. Cheesy peas.

See the "Gravity, Weight and Moments" pages of our Physics Revision Guides

Speed and Velocity

$$\text{speed} = \frac{d}{t}$$ d = Distance, t = Time

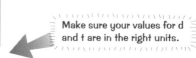

Make sure your values for d and t are in the right units.

EG:
Find speed if d=40 m and t=6 s

Speed = 40 ÷ 6 = 6.7 m/s

Give answers on this page to 1 d.p.

Q1 Work out the speed of a car travelling on a straight track for:

a) 100 m in 10 s
b) 300 m in 20 s
c) 700 m in 35 s
d) 1000 m in 200 s
e) 1500 m in 180 s
f) 450 m in 22 s
g) 320 m in 16 s
h) 50 m in 4 s
i) 500 m in 60 s

Q2 How far does a lorry move if it's travelling at:

Watch out for tricky units.

a) 10 m/s for 30 s
b) 20 m/s for 20 s
c) 2 m/s for 100 s
d) 15 m/s for 28 s
e) 12 m/s for 180 s
f) 5 m/s for 70 s
g) 15 m/s for 20 mins
h) 100 km/h for 300 s
i) 180 km/h for 20 mins

Q3 How long does it take a car to travel:

a) 10 m at 20 m/s
b) 50 m at 10 m/s
c) 200 m at 8 m/s
d) 180 m at 6 m/s
e) 40 m at 12 m/s
f) 1100 m at 14 m/s
g) 50 km at 100 km/h
h) 55.5 km at 80 km/h
i) 2 km at 16 m/s

Q4 What's the speed of:

a) A postman walking his route of 1 km in 900 s?
b) A snail crawling 10 cm in 60 s?
c) A cyclist on a track covering 200 m in 15 s?
d) Herbie the Beetle racing at 1 km in 1 minute?
e) A triple jumper bouncing 17 m in 8 s?
f) A boyracer driving 2 km in 75 s?
g) A giraffe strolling 120 m in 200 s?
h) A streaker running 100 m in 15 s?
i) A satellite travelling 4 km in 2 s?

Having tried everything else, the only option for pole position was go-faster stripes.

What's Damon Hill's favourite physics topic — radioactivity...

Working out speed gets you <u>easy marks</u> in the exam. It might be hidden among other things but it's a cast-iron <u>guarantee</u> that you'll get a question on it. You've got to learn that formula — by the time the exams come round, you'll be keeping the neighbours awake by shouting it in your sleep.

See the "Speed, Velocity and Acceleration" pages of our Physics Revision Guides

Speed and Velocity

$$v = \frac{d}{t}$$

v = Velocity, d = Displacement, t = Time

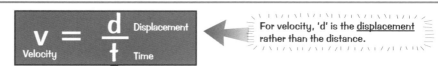

For velocity, 'd' is the displacement rather than the distance.

EG:
Find velocity if d=40 m and t=6 s

Velocity = 40 ÷ 6 = 6.7 m/s

Q1 A bike racer is riding on his new bike at Silverstone. The track is 4 km long.

For this page, give all answers to one d.p.

a) What is his average speed in km/h if he does a lap in 2 mins 10 s?

b) What is his velocity after one lap?

Watch out for this one, it's dead sneaky — after a lap he's back where he started.

c) How long will it take to complete the lap while racing at 100 km/h?

d) The superbike racer completes his final lap in 1 min 20 s. Work out his average speed for the last lap in km/h.

Velocity has direction because it depends on displacement — the distance and direction from the starting position.

Q2 A jet has a top speed of 1500 km/h.

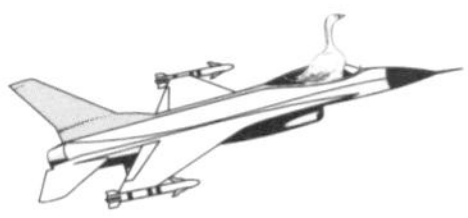

a) The pilot boasts that he can fly at 410 m/s. Is he telling the truth?

1 mile=1.609 km

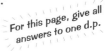

b) Darlington is 470 miles north-east of Farnborough. It takes 40 mins for the pilot to fly to Darlington in a straight line from Farnborough. Work out his velocity in km/h.

c) After re-fuelling, the pilot leaves Darlington and flies south at top speed for 535 km then due west back to Farnborough for 535 km at 1000 km/h. How long does his return journey take?

d) Was the journey to Farnborough faster than the journey to Darlington?

Q3 A team of rowers are training on the Thames. The river's flowing in an easterly direction.

a) The captain gets there early and warms up. It takes him 30 s to row 100 m in the direction of water flow. What is his velocity in m/s?

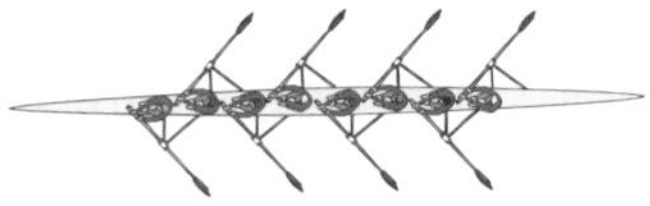

b) The team of eight row 500 m in 180 s. If they keep going at the same speed, how long will it take them to row a full 2 km?

c) The world record for an 8-man team is 2 km in 6 minutes. How long would it take the record-holders to row 500 m at the same speed? How does this compare to the speed of the team on the Thames?

d) The captain decides to show the team how it's done. He rows 2 km in 7 mins. What's his speed in m/s?

e) The captain realises he's gone a bit too far so he hitches a lift back on a passing speedboat. Its speedo says 55 km/h. How long does it take for him to get back to the team?

Faster than a velociting bullet...

Speed's pretty straightforward, but don't forget that velocity must have a direction. If a car's been driven East at a speed of 10 m/s, its velocity was 10 m/s E or 10 m/s 090°. You'll be throwing marks away if you mix up speed and velocity. Grit your teeth and practise 'til it hurts.

See the "Speed, Velocity and Acceleration" pages of our Physics Revision Guides

Acceleration

$$a = \frac{(v-u)}{t}$$

a = Acceleration; (v−u) = Change in velocity; t = Time taken

Just stick in the values they give you for v, u and t.

EG:
Find a if u=2 m/s, v=4 m/s and t=1 s

$$a = 2 \div 1 = 2\,\text{m/s}^2$$

'u' is the initial velocity, and 'v' is the final velocity.

Q1 Find the acceleration if the velocity changes from:

Acceleration is the change in metres per second per second. So stick another 's' in the units to get m/s².

a) 2 m/s to 4 m/s in 4 s
b) 5 m/s to 10 m/s in 2 s
c) 100 m/s to 120 m/s in 5 s
d) 86 m/s to 94 m/s in 4 s
e) 21 m/s to 35 m/s in 18 s
f) 2 m/s to 36 m/s in 4 s
g) 0 m/s to 12 m/s in 9 s
h) 40 m/s to 42 m/s in 8 s
i) 11 m/s to 67 m/s in 3 s
j) 124 m/s to 345 m/s in 12 s

Answers on this page to 1 d.p. again.

So this is what they mean by 0 to 60 in 4 seconds...

Q2 How long does it take a car to change from:

a) 6 m/s to 10 m/s at 2 m/s²
b) 30 m/s to 60 m/s at 5 m/s²
c) 2 m/s to 74 m/s at 8 m/s²
d) 18 m/s to 50 m/s at 5 m/s²
e) 12 m/s to 38 m/s at 6 m/s²
f) 1.5 m/s to 7 m/s at 1.1 m/s²
g) 35 m/s to 42 m/s at 7.2 m/s²
h) 12.4 m/s to 18.6 m/s at 4 m/s²
i) 0 km/h to 160 km/h at 20 m/s²
j) 152 km/h to 168 km/h at 30 m/s²

Oooh — time to convert some units, methinks.

Q3 What's the acceleration of:

0 m/s is just another way of saying 'standing still'.

a) A moonwalking astronaut going from 1 m/s to 3 m/s in 40 s?
b) A hare going from sitting still to hopping at 2 m/s in 0.5 s?
c) A cyclist moving off from stationary to 15 m/s in 5 mins?
d) A jet flying at 52 m/s increasing its velocity to 125 m/s in 12 s?
e) How long does it take a truck to go from 5 m/s to 28 m/s if its acceleration is 4.5 m/s²?
f) If a juggernaut decelerates at 9 m/s², how long will it take him to stop from 45 m/s?
g) A firework accelerates at 5 m/s². How long does it take to go from 2 m/s to 30 m/s?
h) A car does an emergency stop from 120 km/h in 3 s. What was its deceleration?
i) (For bonus marks...) What was the car's average velocity and what was the stopping distance?

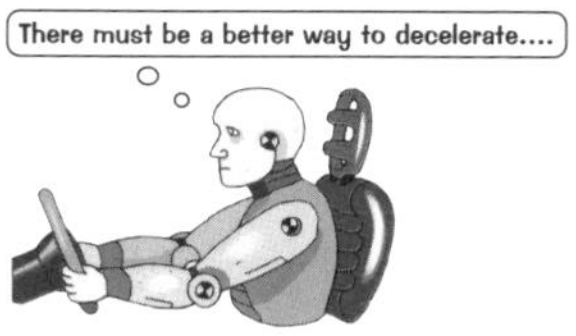
There must be a better way to decelerate....

Easy questions can come wrapped up in tricky wording.

Accelerate your learning — throw your teacher off a cliff...

Anyone thinking that acceleration and velocity are the same thing needs whacking over the head with a weighty Physics textbook. Velocity means <u>how fast</u>, acceleration means how quickly the velocity is <u>changing</u>. Think about cars — foot on accelerator makes you <u>change speed</u>.

See the "Speed, Velocity and Acceleration" pages of our Physics Revision Guides

Velocity and Acceleration

This page has some whopping great questions on it. Take a deep breath and give 'em your best shot. Give all answers to one decimal place.

Q1 A team of pilots are testing a prototype of a new kind of rocket.

Don't let all these units give you brainache. These are easy marks in the exam.

a) It's 20 000 kilometres from Manchester to Sydney, Australia. The rocket does the journey in 4 hours. What was the average speed for the trip in m/s?

b) If the rocket could go straight through the centre of the Earth, the distance is only 12 740 km. If the rocket travelled at the same speed, how long would it take to get to Sydney?

c) From lift-off, the team can get the rocket up to 2 km/s in 14 seconds. What's the acceleration of the rocket in m/s^2?

Q2 It's 70 miles by road from Birmingham to Oxford. The journey usually takes me 1 hour and 10 minutes on the motorway.

1 mile=1.609 km

a) How far is the journey in kilometres?

b) What's my average speed during the journey in mph and km/h?

c) I could get to Oxford in 45 minutes if I went faster. How fast would I have to go and would this be legal? (The motorway speed limit is 70 mph.)

d) Yesterday I overtook a caravan that was doing 80 km/h. The velocity of my car increased from 80 km/h to 110 km/h in 4 seconds. What was my acceleration, in m/s^2?

Q3 Sound travels at a rather stately 330 m/s in air.

Light travels around 1000 times faster than sound, so assume the lightning is seen the instant it strikes.

a) I looked at my watch the moment I saw a flash of lightning and heard the thunder 12 seconds later. To the nearest kilometre, how far away did the lightning strike?

b) A girl and boy are standing under a tree. The boy starts running, accelerating at $0.2\ m/s^2$. What speed is he running at when he reaches the middle of the field 18 seconds later?

c) The middle of the field is 32.4 m away. What was the boy's average speed?

d) If the girl yells at the boy from under the tree, how long will it take her voice to reach him?

e) The next flash of lightning lights up the sky. It takes 18 s this time before I hear the rumble of thunder. How far away is it now? Is is getting closer or further away?

Velocity and Acceleration — that famous comedy duo...

Physics — it's all so useful. Handy for all kinds of situations. Driving, athletics, thunderstorms... oh and let's not forget the EXAMS. Those formulas need to be stuffed into your overflowing grey cells, ready to leap onto the paper and make the examiner drop his hobnob in his tea with delight.

See the "Speed, Velocity and Acceleration" pages of our Physics Revision Guides

Waves

$$f = \frac{1}{T}$$

Frequency — Time period

Easy — Just stick in the value of T.

EG:
Find f if T=5 s

$$f = 1 \div 5 = 0.2 \text{ Hz}$$

Q1 Work out the wave frequency for waves with these time periods:

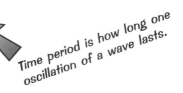

Time period is how long one oscillation of a wave lasts.

a) 10 s	c) 4 s	e) 20 s	g) 0.2 s
b) 5 s	d) 2 s	f) 1 s	h) 0.01 s

Q2 Find the time period for these waves with the following frequencies:

You'll have to re-arrange that formula.

a) 20 Hz	c) 0.1 Hz	e) 250 Hz	g) 0.002 Hz
b) 2 Hz	d) 1000 Hz	f) 4 Hz	h) 125 Hz

$$v = f \times \lambda$$

Velocity — Frequency — Wavelength

Just stick in the values of f and λ.

EG:
Find v if f=10Hz and λ=5m

$$v = 10 \times 5 = 50 \text{ m/s}$$

Q3 These waves all have a wavelength of 12m. Calculate their velocity if they have the following frequencies.

a) 2 Hz	d) 20 Hz	g) 1000 Hz
b) 5 Hz	e) 1 Hz	h) 8 Hz
c) 10 Hz	f) 0.5 Hz	i) 1.2 Hz

Q4 These waves have a frequency of 10 Hz. Find the wavelength if they have these velocities:

a) 3 m/s	d) 0.3 m/s	g) 50 m/s
b) 40 m/s	e) 2500 m/s	h) 20 m/s
c) 100 m/s	f) 0.2 m/s	i) 100 cm/s

Q5 Find the velocity of waves with these time periods and wavelengths:

a) time period: 10 s.
wavelength: 20 m.

b) time period: 5 s.
wavelength: 12 m

c) time period: 1 min.
wavelength: 15 m.

You'll need to use both equations for this one.

Everybody's gone surfing — surfing VFλ...

This stuff's hideously simple — It's just two more triangle formulas. Hertz are just 'waves per second', so don't get in a flap about them. Don't get in a muddle with your units either — just convert everything to metres, seconds and hertz. Then it'll be a piece of cake.

Waves

Here are some longer questions but don't panic — they're pretty much the same thing. Just shove the numbers in the right places in the right formulas.

Q1 Jack threw his annoying little sister Jill in the garden pond. Jill made a large splash and waves rippled across the pond.

a) If each wave has a time period of 2 s, what is their frequency?

b) If the same waves travel across the pond at a speed of 5 m/s, what is their wavelength?

c) Jack wants to see what happens if he throws Jill into different ponds. Finish off his results table.

Pond	Frequency Hz	Wavelength m	Velocity m/s
A	20	0.3	
B	2		7
C	5	1.2	
D		0.4	5

d) On his last throw Jack got so excited he forgot to record the frequency. Luckily he noticed that Jill's shoe had fallen off and bobbed up and down 20 times in 10 seconds. Which pond had he thrown her in?

Q2 In a revenge attack Jill plays her stereo at top volume when Jack is trying to do his physics homework.

Watch your units — 1 kHz is 1000 Hz.

a) The sound waves travel through the wall to Jack's room. The waves have a frequency of 6 kHz and wavelength of 15 cm. What is their velocity?

b) Jack covers his head with a pillow. Through the pillow the sound wave has a frequency of 6 kHz and a velocity of 400 m/s. What is its wavelength in cm?

c) Jack gives up studying and puts on his radio. He listens to his favourite Radio 4 programme on the origins of the universe. Radio 4 transmits radio waves with a wavelength of 1.5 km. They travel at the speed of light. What is their frequency?

Use 3×10^8 m/s as an approximation of the speed of light.

Q3 With this data you can work out and use a more accurate figure for the speed of light. Give answers to 4 s.f.

a) Blue light has a frequency of 7×10^{14}. It has a wavelength of 4.287×10^{-7}. What is its velocity?

b) Red light has a wavelength of 7.49×10^{-7}. It travels with the same velocity as blue light. What is its frequency?

Go dancing with Jonathan Ross — go to a wave...

A tricky thing about waves is the range of sizes they come in. Wavelengths can vary from cm to km. Velocity can be anything from a fraction of a metre per second to the speed of light. It's difficult when some of your answers look ridiculous, but don't be put off. I'm sure you'll get it right...

Moments

$$M = F \times r$$

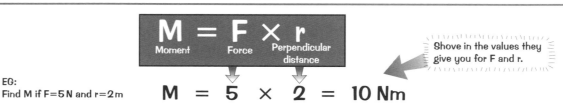

Moment = Force × Perpendicular distance

Shove in the values they give you for F and r.

EG:
Find M if F=5 N and r=2 m

$$M = 5 \times 2 = 10\ \text{Nm}$$

Q1 For each of the pictures, work out the moment and say whether it's clockwise or anticlockwise.

a) 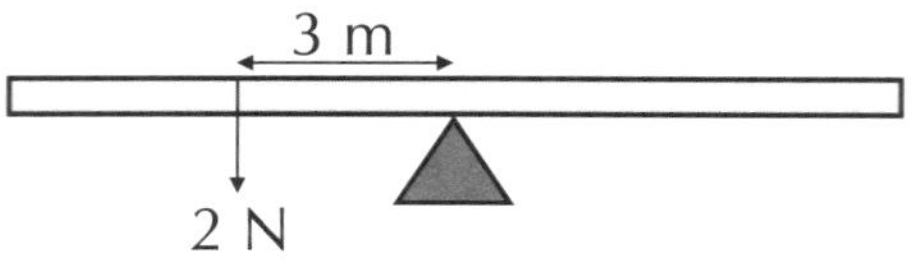

b) 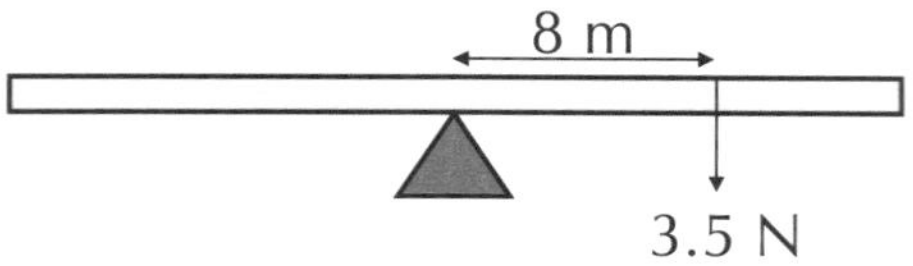

c) 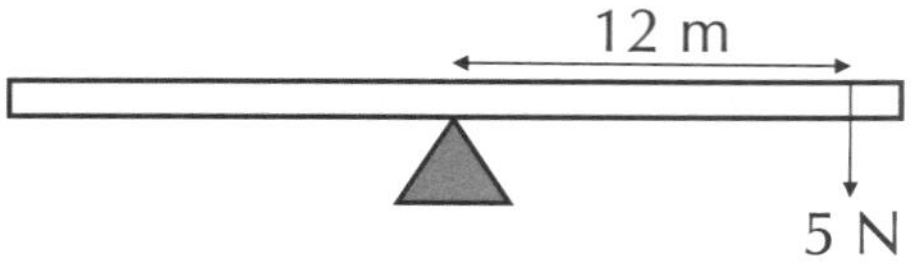

d) 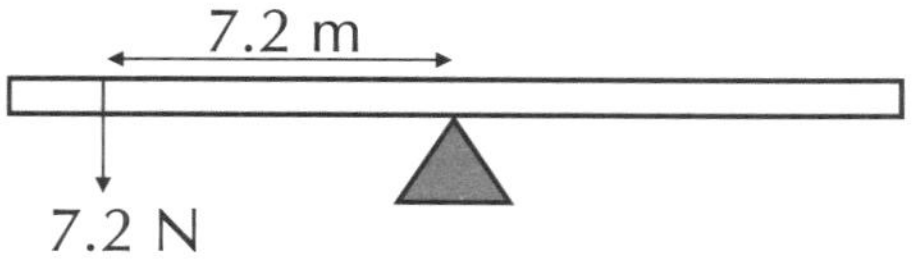

Q2 Find the total clockwise and anticlockwise moments for these seesaws. Which side will tip down — the LEFT or the RIGHT?

a) 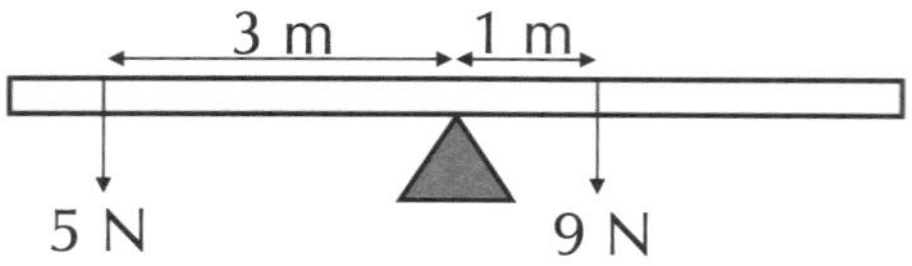

b) 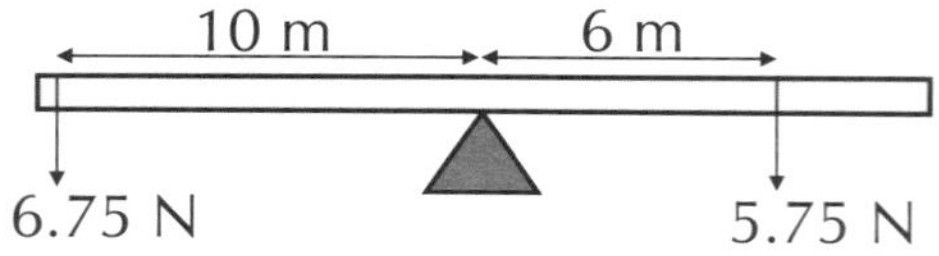

c) 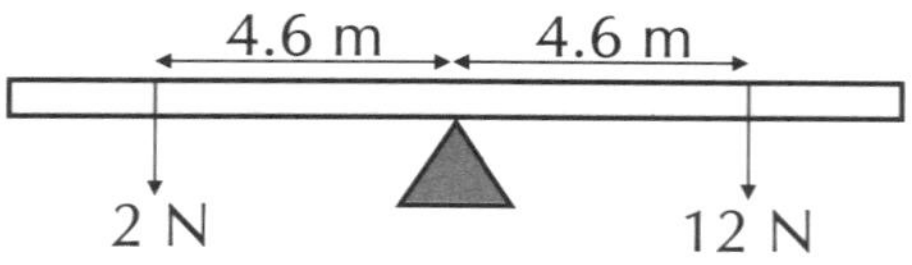

d) 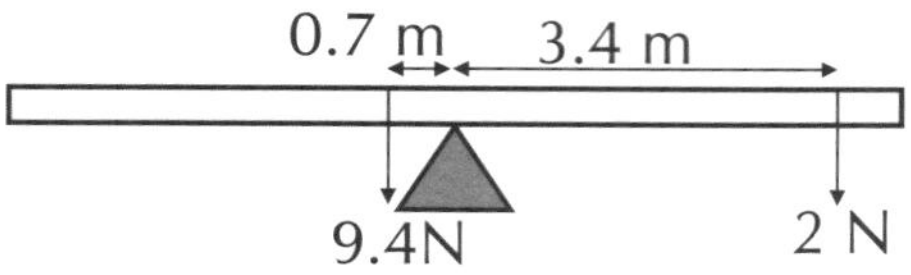

e) 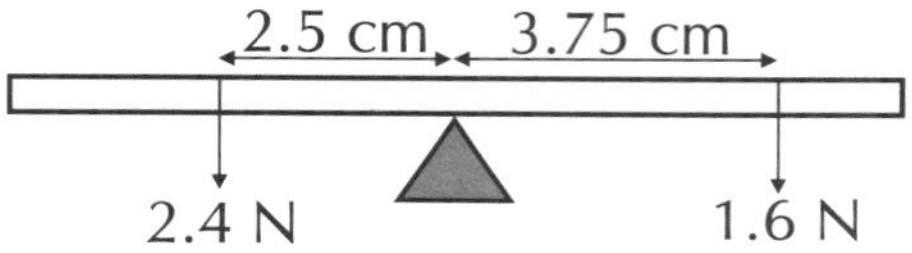

f) 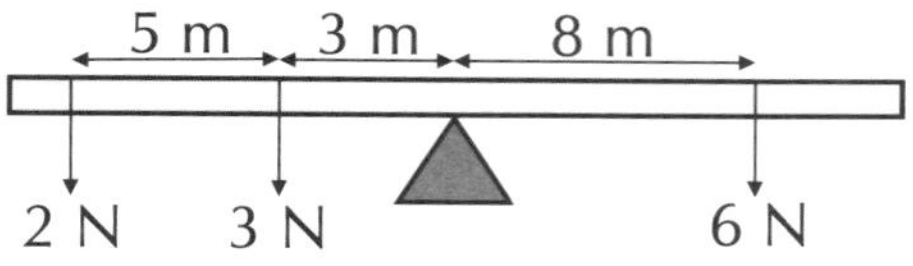

Q3 A 1 kg frog is sitting on a seesaw.

Use g=10 N/kg

a) What is the force on the seesaw, 2 m right of the pivot, due to the frog's mass?

b) What is the moment about the pivot due to this mass? Is this clockwise or anticlockwise?

c) A cat has a mass of 2 kg. What happens if he sits on the other side of the seesaw, 2 m from the pivot?

d) Where does the cat need to sit so that the seesaw is balanced?

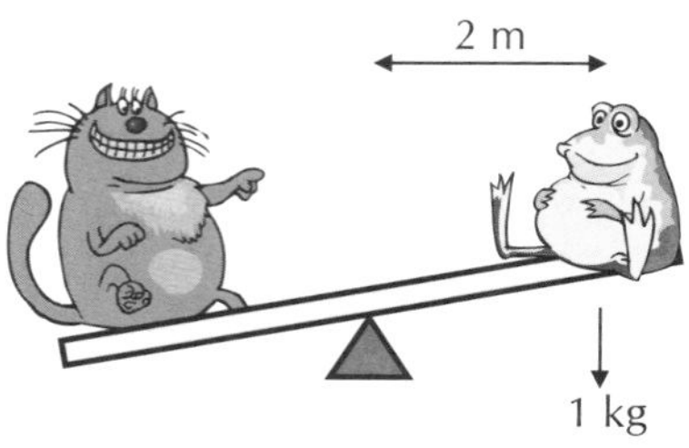

Momentous...

If there's more than one force on one side of the pivot then just add the moments together one by one. If you get muddled by clockwise and anticlockwise, wear an analogue watch in the exam. It's all too easy to get your directions in a pickle, but keep a cool head and it'll be fine.

Moments

Simple, this moment lark. If you haven't been given a diagram, sketch one out. It doesn't take long and it'll make things a lot easier.

Q1 A rabbit is using a fishing line to hook a carrot out of the water.

a) Calculate the moment of the 65 N force about the pivot.

b) The pull exerted by the rabbit is balanced by the pull in the fishing line. Work out the tension in the fishing line.

c) The fishing line will break if the tension becomes more than 60 N. If the pull is in the same direction as before, what's the maximum force the rabbit can use?

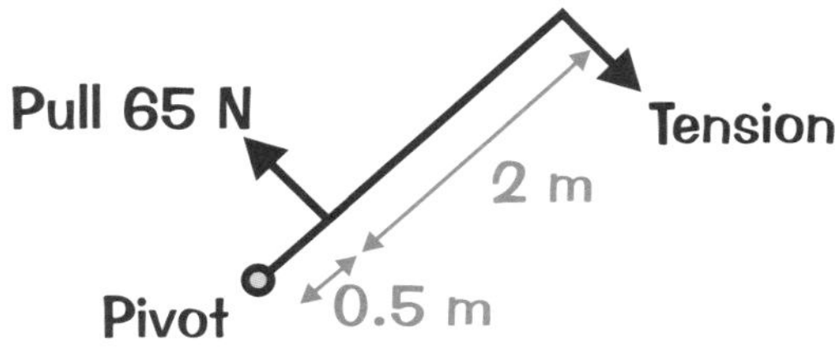

Q2 A 5 m long plank is pivoted at one end. The plank is held up at the other end so that it is horizontal.

Aaaargh...no diagram. Don't panic, draw your own.

a) If a man weighing 500 N stands on the plank, 3 m from the pivot, what upward force is needed to keep the plank horizontal?

b) What force is needed to keep the plank horizontal if the man stands 4 m from the pivot?

c) If the man puts on his thick coat, which weighs 60 N, and stands 2 m from the pivot, how much force will the person holding the end of the plank need to keep the plank level?

d) The plank-holder can push with a maximum force of 550 N upwards. Can she keep the plank level if the man stands 3 m from the pivot wearing the coat and a 200 N hat?

Q3 There are three handles on this door. The hinge needs a moment of 20 Nm to open the door.

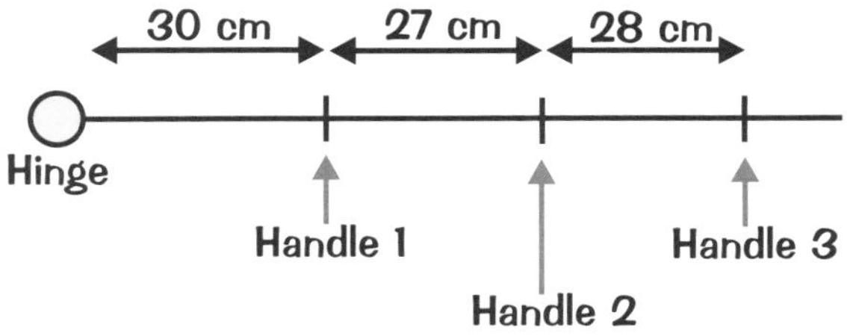

a) If handle 1 is pushed with a force of 10 N, nothing happens. Why won't the door open?

b) What (to 1d.p) is the smallest pushing force needed to open the door with handle 2?

c) What's the minimum force (to 1 d.p.) needed to open the door with handle 3?

d) Why are door handles usually on the opposite side to the hinges?

Moment = Torque = Turning Force... = no fun but you've got to learn it

Moment is a pretty silly name. Think of it as a turning force — that'll help you picture what the force is doing. If the question doesn't give you a diagram, you'll have to draw one for yourself. They don't tell you this of course, oh no. You really need to do it though, it makes it much easier.

See the "Gravity, Weight and Moments" pages of our Physics Revision Guides

Kinetic Energy

$$KE = \frac{1}{2} \times m \times v^2$$
Kinetic Energy — mass — velocity

Stick in m, don't forget to square the v — and that's it.

EG:
Find KE if m=5 kg and v=6 m/s

$$KE = \frac{1}{2} \times 5 \times 6^2 = 90\ J$$

Q1 Find the kinetic energy, to the nearest joule, of a 250 kg horse moving at these velocities:

a) 0.5 m/s
b) 2 m/s
c) 3.5 m/s
d) 5 m/s
e) 180 m/min
f) 1.4 m/s
g) 30 km/h
h) 25 km/h
i) 6 m/s

Remember to change all velocities to metres per second before you use the formula.

Q2 A fleet of motorcycles moves at 3 m/s. Find the kinetic energy, to the nearest joule, of motorcycles with these masses:

a) 150 kg
b) 200 kg
c) 95 kg
d) 350 kg
e) 196 kg
f) 134 kg
g) 208 kg
h) 89 kg
i) 152 kg

Q3 An explosion of gas from a Hawaiian volcano blows a bunch of rocks into the sky. Each has 2000 J of kinetic energy. Find their masses, to the nearest 0.001 kg, if these are their velocities:

a) 15 m/s
b) 20 m/s
c) 8 m/s
d) 1 m/s
e) 32 m/s
f) 16 m/s
g) 2.5 m/s
h) 1 km/s
i) 12 km/h

Q4 Find the kinetic energy in the following situations:

a) A 10 kg dog strolling at 0.5 m/s.
b) A 1250 kg car speeding at 100 km/h.
c) A 3 kg carp swimming at 2 m/s.
d) A 2 kg meteorite hitting my house at 426 m/s.
e) A 63 010 kg meteorite rolling off my roof at 2.4 m/s.
f) A 0.001 kg spec of space dust hitting a satellite at 30 km/s.

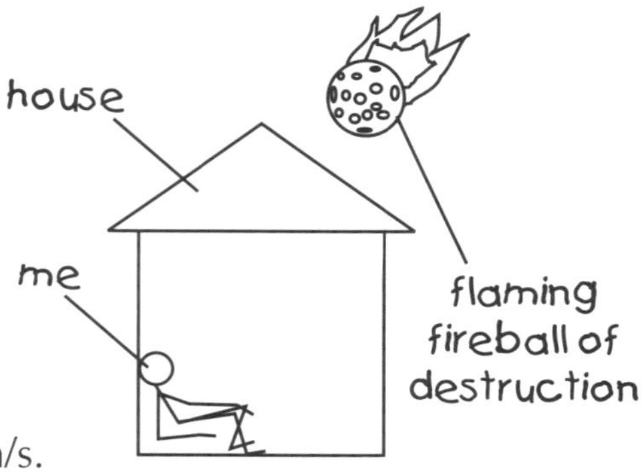

Life on Earth — scream if you want to go faster...

a) The Earth spins to make days, so a point on the equator has to go round about 24 000 miles in 24 hours. That's 444 m/s. If you weigh 65 kg, that makes 6 406 920 J of KE. ***b)*** The Earth orbits the Sun to make years, at about 18 miles per second, that's 28 800 m/s, making 26 956 800 000 J of KE! Grab a sick bag.

See the "Kinetic Energy and Potential Energy" pages of our Physics Revision Guides

Kinetic Energy

...And for some light relief — a graph. Plot the points carefully and join them with a smooth curve. If you feel like you're having fun don't panic — your mind's been fried by p.24...

Q1 A 1200 kg car is crash-tested to see how safe it is. To make sense of the results, the testers need to know how much kinetic energy the car has when driven at different speeds. Fill in this table, and then use it to complete the graph.

Speed (m/s)	Kinetic Energy (joules)
0	0
1	600
2	
4	
	15000
6.5	
7	
	38400
9.5	
	60000

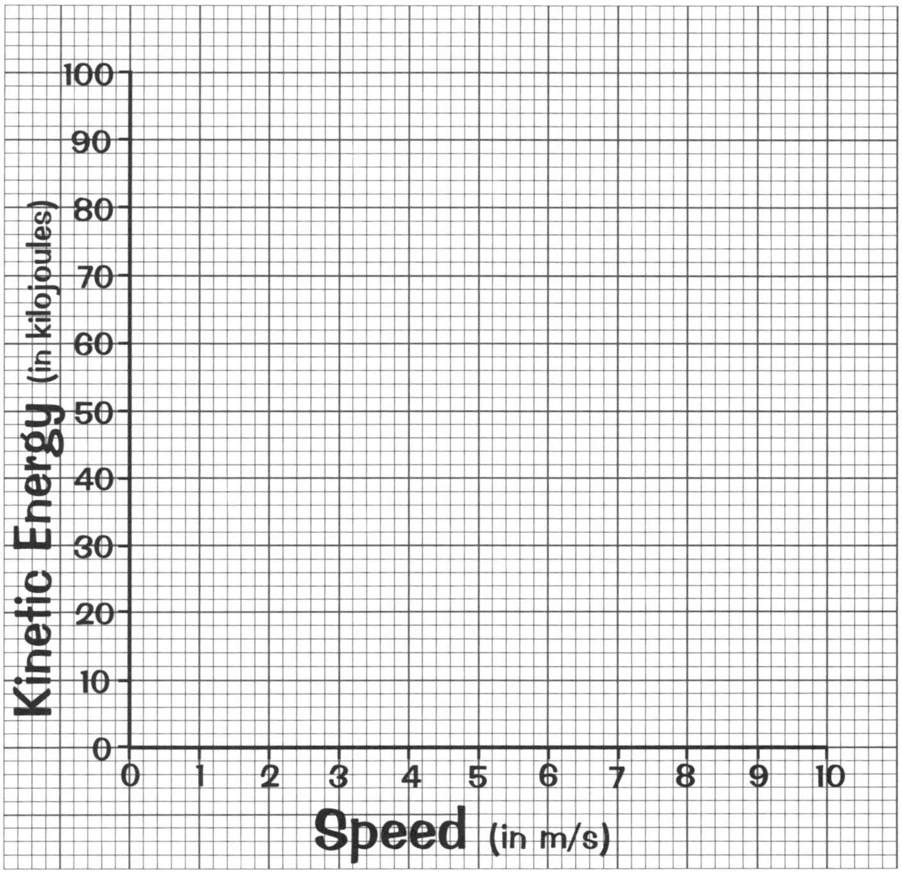

Q2 A school minibus, carrying just the driver, slams on its brakes to avoid driving off a cliff. The brakes do 800 000 J of work.

a) If the minibus and driver were travelling at 20 m/s, what was their combined mass? *(Assume all the minibus's kinetic energy was absorbed by the brakes.)*

b) The minibus picks up 6 cloned teachers weighing exactly 90 kg each. How much energy will the brakes need to absorb to stop from 20 m/s now?

c) The maximum amount of kinetic energy the brakes can absorb without falling to bits is 1 016 000 J. How many cloned teachers can the minibus carry and still be able to stop from 20 m/s?

Kinetic energy — I love it...

The exam questions are usually pretty straight forward, giving you the mass and velocity and asking for the kinetic energy. *But* you never know — the <u>only</u> way to be safe is to learn the formula inside out and back to front. And whenever you draw a speed-KE graph, check it's that nice dish shape.

See the "Kinetic Energy and Potential Energy" pages of our Physics Revision Guides

Gravitational Potential Energy

GPE = m × g × h

GPE: Gravitational Potential Energy; m: mass; g: gravity; h: height

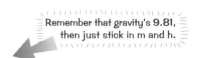

Remember that gravity's 9.81, then just stick in m and h.

EG:
Find GPE if m=40 kg, g=9.81 N/kg and change in height=5 m

$$GPE = 40 \times 9.81 \times 5 = 1692\text{ J}$$

Q1 A 75 kg donkey is lifted by a crane. Assuming g = 10 N/kg, work out the gain in potential energy if the donkey's lifted by these heights:

a) 0 m
b) 5 m
c) 6 m
d) 43 m
e) 2.4 m
f) 67 m
g) 0.49 m
h) 15 m
i) 22 m
j) 2 m
k) 10 m
l) 9 m

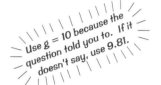

Use g = 10 because the question told you to. If it doesn't say, use 9.81.

Q2 Eight managers run up a mountain as far as they can. Given each manager's mass and how high they climb, work out their gain in gravitational potential energy.

Give your answers to the nearest joule.

a) 120 kg, 20 m
b) 46 kg, 50 m
c) 75 kg, 200 m
d) 62 kg, 35 m
e) 80 kg, 4 m
f) 59 kg, 23 m
g) 70 kg, 32 m
h) 3 kg, 50 m

Q3 Some masses are being raised by these distances. For each pair of masses, work out which one is gaining more gravitational potential energy. Take g = 10 N/kg.

a) 1 kg, 12 m *or* 1.2 kg, 11 m
b) 14.5 kg, 0.75 m *or* 15.5 kg, 0.6 m
c) 3 kg, 4 m *or* 3.5 kg, 3.5 m
d) 8.3 kg, 2 m *or* 4.6 kg, 3.7 m
e) 48 kg, 79 m *or* 37 kg, 105 m
f) 1 kg, 1 m *or* 1000 kg, 10000 m

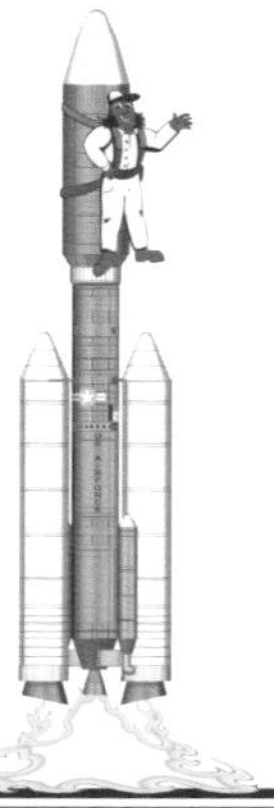

Q4 NASA is firing 154 kg test rockets straight up into the air. Work out how high they'll go, if they can gain this much gravitational potential energy (use g = 9.81 N/kg):

a) 169 kJ
b) 8553 kJ
c) 98 kJ
d) 742 kJ
e) 29 384 kJ
f) 2.5 kJ

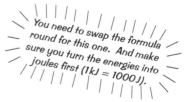

You need to swap the formula round for this one. And make sure you turn the energies into joules first (1kJ = 1000J).

Gravitational Potential Energy — proof hippos don't climb stairs...

Plug the numbers in the formula and away you go. And if you need to rearrange it, use a formula triangle as on page 2. Easy peasy ...as long as you don't start wondering what all this invisible energy actually *is*, and *where* it all goes to, and *how* gravity pulls things together... Beats me.

See the "Kinetic Energy and Potential Energy" pages of our Physics Revision Guides

Gravitational Potential Energy

OK, I admit it. Some of these examples are a bit silly. But behind them all it's just GPE=m×g×h. Work out what bit of the formula it's asking for, and give any energy answers to the nearest joule.

Q1 The 05:30 flight to Malaga takes off with a mass, including fuel, passengers, luggage and crew, of 300 000 kg. The gravitational field strength is 10 N/kg.

a) It climbs to an altitude of 1200 m. If the runway was at an altitude of 220 m, how much gravitational potential energy has it gained (to the nearest kilojoule)?

b) By lunchtime, the plane has used up some fuel and is now 50 000 kg lighter. How much gravitational potential energy has the plane lost? (It's still at 1200 m.)

c) To avoid the in-flight meal, a passenger climbs 2 m up into an overhead luggage locker. He gains 1700 J of gravitational potential energy compared to when he was sat down. How heavy must he be?

d) An air stewardess finds a toupee lying on the floor. When it fell to the floor, it lost 1.25 J of gravitational potential energy. It has a mass of 0.05 kg. Work out if it must have fallen off a man who is sat down, or the man in the overhead locker.

Q2 Answer these questions, using g = 9.81 N/kg.

a) A bucket of pig swill is lifted by 1.5 m to get it over a fence. It's mass is 14 kg. To the nearest joule, how much gravitational potential energy has it gained?

b) Having studied the physics of the bucket, a piglet jumps 1.5 m over the fence, and gains twice as much gravitational potential energy as the bucket did. What must be the piglet's mass?

c) A small cow, with the same mass as the piglet, jumps over the Mune (a local river). At the top of its leap, it has gained the same gravitational potential energy as the bucket did. How high did it jump?

d) A passing research physicist wrongly calculates that a 2.3 kg duck thrown 50.5 m into the air would gain 2206.85 J of gravitational potential energy. What wrong value of g was used?

"What goes up", err, "must have increased gravitational potential energy"..

Blah, blah, blah, ***mass****, blah, blah, blah,* ***change in height****, blah, blah, blah,* ***g = 10 N/kg****.*

That's all this page is — simple formula questions in a long-winded disguise. The trouble is, exam questions are long-winded too, so being able to filter out the details is an important skill I reckon.

See the "Kinetic Energy and Potential Energy" pages of our Physics Revision Guides

Work Done = Force × Distance

Wd = F × d

Work done — Force — Distance

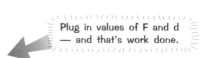

Plug in values of F and d — and that's work done.

EG:
Find Wd if F=20 N and d=5 m

$Wd = 20 \times 5 = 100\ J$

Q1 Find the work done having pushed a shopping trolley with a force of 50 N over the following distances:

Remember to change all measurements to metres before you use the formula.

a) 100 m	d) 430 m	g) 177 m
b) 50 cm	e) 2 km	h) 1355 m
c) 25 m	f) 73 m	i) 986.5 m

Q2 A weightlifter lifts weights 50 cm. Find the work done for each of the following:

a) 10 kg	d) 20 kg	g) 35 kg
b) 60 kg	e) 120 kg	h) 105 kg
c) 55 kg	f) 75 kg	i) 95 kg

Q3 Bricks weighing 1.5 kg are lifted on a platform weighing 3 kg. To the nearest joule, find the work done if the following number of bricks (on the platform) are lifted 5 m:

a) 50	d) 22	g) 19
b) 35	e) 44	h) 53
c) 65	f) 67	i) 71

Q4 Find the work done in the following situations:

a) A stubborn dog being pulled over 5 m of tarmac with a force of 300 N.

b) A car being pushed 1 km with a force of 1600 N.

c) A pram being pushed 2 km with a force of 50 N.

d) A coffee cup of 500 g being raised 40 cm.

e) A rollerblader being pulled 100 m with a force of 100 N.

f) A water-skier being pulled across a harbour 400 m wide with a force of 450 N.

g) A window cleaner of mass 70 kg climbing a ladder 7 m high.

h) A mobile home with a mass of 4000 kg being raised 1 m.

4's 4 U 2 do...

Work done is the same thing as energy transferred, and you can't transfer energy without moving something. Remember that and you're halfway there. What matters is how far you've moved whatever it is, and how much force it took. Work done=Force×distance. Remember it.

See the "Work Done, Energy and Power" pages of our Physics Revision Guides

Work Done = Force × Distance

You've already done some questions with this formula. This page just shows how they might come up in the real world (or an exam). Don't just sit there — get some work done.

Q1 A car has broken down on the isolated, winding Cumbrian roads. There's a garage 2000 metres away, along a flat coastal route.

a) It needs a minimum force of 900 N to push the car along a flat road. What is the minimum energy the driver needs to get the car to the garage?

b) There's another garage 1400 metres away, but it's higher up in the fells along a steep road. The pushing force here would have to be 1700 N. Calculate the total work done if the driver chooses this garage instead.

c) The driver decides he doesn't want to push the car uphill so he chooses the garage on the flat road. Halfway there he notices the road's been resurfaced. It now only takes 700 N to push the car. What is the total energy consumption by the time he gets to the garage?

OK — this is tougher. Work it out for the 1st half and 2nd half separately, then add them together.

Q2 The weightlifter's back in the gym. He's working on loads of different machines this time.

a) The weightlifter lifts 50 kg 40 times. Each time he lifts the load 30 cm. Calculate the work done.

Use g=10 N/kg.

b) This time he does 20 lifts, then bumps the load up to 80 kg and does 10 more. How much work is done this time?

c) The weightlifter moves on to another machine which raises the load 65 cm. How much energy does he use doing 15 lifts of 80 kg?

d) How many lifts of 60 kg (raising the load 65 cm) would use 10 530 J of energy?

Q3 Five secretaries are participating in an annual 'pull the boss' competition.

a) What is the work done by the secretaries together if they move the boss 150 m with a force of 240 N?

b) What is the work done by the secretaries together if they move the boss 1600 m with a force of 130 N?

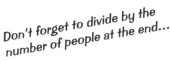

c) How far did they move the boss if they used 6120 J and used a force of 200 N?

Don't forget to divide by the number of people at the end...

d) What was the work done by each of the secretaries if all five of them worked equally, and together they pulled the boss 675 m with a force of 150 N?

I always thought work was boring — I was right...

I always get my brain in a right old twist with this one — it's weird thinking that a man holding a piano above his head isn't doing any work because he's not taking it anywhere. But no-one's saying you have to understand it. You've only got to learn it. Thank goodness for that.

See the "Work Done, Energy and Power" pages of our Physics Revision Guides

Power = Work ÷ Time

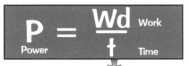

$$P = \frac{Wd}{t}$$

P: Power, Wd: Work, t: Time

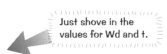

Just shove in the values for Wd and t.

EG:
Find P if Wd=60 J and t=10 s

$$P = 60 \div 10 = 6\,W$$

Q1 Work out the power of these electric fires, to the nearest watt, if they produce 1000 kJ in these amounts of time:

Remember to convert all units of energy to Joules: 1 kJ=1000 J

a) 200 seconds d) 9 mins, 30 s g) 7 mins, 15 s

b) 8 minutes e) 6 mins, 30 s h) 8 mins, 43 s

c) 10 minutes f) 430 seconds i) 5 mins, 29 s

Q2 Work out the power of these toasters, to the nearest watt, if they produce these amounts of heat energy in 3 minutes:

Time values should be converted to seconds.

a) 200 kJ d) 150 kJ g) 316 kJ

b) 400 kJ e) 175 kJ h) 257 kJ

c) 350 kJ f) 225 kJ i) 399 kJ

Q3 A weightlifter's lifting bricks at a building site. He's doing a set of 10 lifts, raising a load of 50 kg by 40 cm. Work out his power, to 3 s.f, if he does the ten lifts in these times:

Watch out for the units, and remember that g=10 N/kg

a) 2 minutes d) 30 seconds g) 27 seconds

b) 40 seconds e) 95 seconds h) 53 seconds

c) 1 minute f) 115 seconds i) 79 seconds

Q4 An electric kettle is rated at 2400 watts. Work out how long it would take, to the nearest second, to supply the water with these amounts of energy:

a) 500 kJ d) 850 kJ g) 1313 kJ

b) 100 kJ e) 955 kJ h) 777 kJ

c) 350 kJ f) 1145 kJ i) 491 kJ

Q5 These wattages are written on the labels of a selection of hairdriers. How much heat energy (in kJ) will each one produce every minute?

a) 1 kW d) 800 W g) 1825 W

b) 1200 W e) 950 W h) 1075 W

c) 1600 W f) 1450 W i) 1375 W

Work divided by time to the people...

Power is a wee bit tricky to get your head round. Don't confuse it with force or energy. Powerful things can transfer a lot of energy in a short space of time. Luckily the formula's easy as pie so all you have to do is remember it and use it, and <u>don't mix up your units</u>.

See the "Work Done, Energy and Power" pages of our Physics Revision Guides

Power = Work ÷ Time

More questions on power. They look wordier, and they are, but once you've found a number for each of the letters in the formula, they're just like the ones on the page before.

Q1 A broken-down car is being pushed to a garage.

a) Work out the driver's power output if he takes 1 hour and 45 minutes to push his car 2 km with a force of 900 N.

Give power to the nearest watt.

b) Work out the total power output if the driver has to stop for a 30 minute kip halfway there.

c) The driver's maximum power output is 500 W. How long would it take him to push the car to the garage at maximum output?

d) If the driver decides to take the uphill route, it would take a force of 1700 N to cover 1400 m in 3 hours. Work out his power output, to the nearest whole number.

e) What percentage of his maximum power output is this?

Q2 The weightlifter's still lifting weights. The pulley he's working with lifts the load 50 cm each time.

a) The weightlifter spends 3 minutes doing 60 lifts of 45 kg. Work out his power output.

b) Work out the weightlifter's total power output if he does 3 sets of 10 lifts with 70 kg in 5 minutes.

Use g=10 N/kg.

c) Over the next 10 minutes, he does 50 lifts of 40 kg, 3 sets of 10 lifts with 75 kg and 2 sets of 15 lifts with 60 kg. Work out his total power output to the nearest whole number.

d) The weightlifter's maximum power output is 100 W. At maximum power, how many times can he lift 80 kg in 4 minutes?

Q3 A team of 8 rowers are training on the Thames.

a) The rowers warm up by rowing with a combined force of 1600 N. They row for 5 minutes and cover a distance of 700 m. Work out the power output of the rowing team.

b) At racing speed, the team row with a combined force of 4000 N. They cover a distance of 3 km in 11 minutes. What is the average power output of the individual rowers?

c) During the cool-down session, the rowers apply a force of 100 N each. The team covers a distance of 400 m in 5 minutes. Work out the power output of the whole team.

d) The most powerful rower on the team is capable of an output of 3000 W, using a force of 4000 N. How long would it take the team to row 3 km, if all the rowers were as good as this?

So much work to do, so little work divided by power...

I know I go on about units a bit, but they're really important. Unless all your distances are in metres, your times are in seconds and your masses are converted to weight in Newtons, you'll end up with a pile of ridiculous answers. Take your time and think carefully — you know it makes sense.

See the "Work Done, Energy and Power" pages of our Physics Revision Guides

Efficiency

$$\text{Efficiency} = \frac{\text{Work done}}{\text{Energy input}}$$

EG:
Find the efficiency if
Wd = 1000 J and
Energy input = 1250 J

Just stick in the values they give you for Wd and Energy.

Efficiency = 1000 ÷ 1250 = 0.8 (80%)

Q1 Work out the efficiency of a machine if it does 1050 J of work with these energy inputs. Write your answer as a decimal, to 2 d.p.

a) 2000 J	d) 3240 J	g) 2001 J
b) 1500 J	e) 10 500 J	h) 1977 J
c) 4000 J	f) 5250 J	i) 1234 J

Efficiency has no units because it's joules divided by joules.

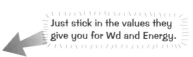

Q2 A machine gets 3500 J of electrical energy. Work out what its efficiency would be as a percentage, to the nearest 1%, if it did these amounts of work:

If you get an answer bigger than 100%, you know you're in trouble.

a) 3000 J	d) 40 J	g) 3105 J
b) 500 J	e) 1400 J	h) 2850 J
c) 3445 J	f) 2500 J	i) 759 J

Q3 A machine must do 5990 J of work. Calculate to the nearest joule the energy that must be supplied if the machine's efficiency is:

a) 0.5	c) 0.25	e) 70%	g) 41%
b) 0.85	d) 0.1	f) 35%	h) 90%

Watch out: you can't just bung the percentage ones into the formula as they are — you need decimals.

Q4 A pulling machine is 6% efficient. How much work can be done for each of these energy inputs:

a) 1000 J	c) 50 000 J	e) 8100 J
b) 2500 J	d) 3400 J	f) 6900 J

Check your answers — the largest energy input should allow the most work to be done.

Q5 A milk float uses 20 000 J to perform each of these tasks. Calculate how much work is done in each task, then calculate the milk float's efficiency to the nearest 1%.

a) driving uphill for 80 m, with a force of 200 N

b) racing downhill for 215 m, with a force of 80 N

c) driving over speed bumps for 90 m, with a force of 100 N

d) pushing a skip for 5 m, with a force of 3150 N

.... (3 marks)

Every few years, some boffin claims they've made a machine with more than 100% efficiency. But if a more than 100% efficient machine exists, I'll eat my cat. So in the exam, remember that and check all your answers are less than 100% efficient. Fluffy's depending on you.

See the "Efficiency of Machines" pages of our Physics Revision Guides

Efficiency

$$\text{Efficiency} = \frac{\text{Useful energy out}}{\text{Total energy in}}$$

It's the same formula —this is just a different way of writing it.

EG:
Find the efficiency if
Useful output = 1000 J
and Total input = 1250 J

Efficiency = 1000 ÷ 1250 = 0.8 (80%)

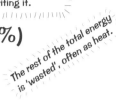

The rest of the total energy is 'wasted', often as heat.

Q1 Work out the efficiency (as a percentage, to nearest 1%) of a speaker that is supplied with 2530 J, and gives out these amounts of sound energy:

a) 1000 J d) 1600 J g) 1490 J

b) 450 J e) 250 J h) 640 J

c) 900 J f) 360 J i) 1810 J

The sound energy is the useful energy here.

Q2 A guitar amp is 35% efficient. Work out the energy input, if the sound energy given out is:

a) 2000 J c) 267 J e) 7503 J

b) 4050 J d) 8900 J f) 10 890 J

Give the answer to the nearest joule.

If these are the input energies, what are the sound output energies?

g) 500 J i) 19 890 J k) 1000 J

h) 3500 J j) 26 080 J l) 64 080 J

Q3 Work out the efficiency of these devices. Each one is given 10 000 J of electrical power.

You've got to decide which is the useful energy out.

a) Lamp: gives out 2100 J light, 7800 J heat.

b) Motor: gives out 6050 J sound, 3950 J kinetic energy.

c) Kettle: gives out 990 J heat to room, 9010 J heat to water.

d) Fridge: gives out 8306 J heat to room, 1694 J sound.

Give the answer to the nearest percent.

Q4 3 scientists are studying Kath's decks.

a) The scientists say the turntables are definitely either 105% or 78% efficient. How efficient must they be? How can you tell?

b) Her headphones are 50% efficient. Listening to ABBA, they waste 1000 J as heat. How much total energy does she need to supply to them?

c) A speaker gives out 50 150 J as sound, and 46 000 J as heat. A garden lamp gives out 48 484 J as heat, and 60 589 J as light. Which is more efficient?

Careful: This one's really tricky. The total energy in will be the same as the total energy out.

Efficiency of a teenager — zero, they don't do anything useful...

Great. This formula's pretty straightforward, but you need to be able to flip it around to work out all the different bits. You've just got to learn it. And watch out if you're not told the Useful Energy Out or the Total Energy In. They don't always hand it to you on a plate. That wouldn't be fun.

See the "Efficiency of Machines" pages of our Physics Revision Guides

Efficiency

You always get Exam questions that mix up topics, so you need more than one formula. It'd only be fair for me to give you a chance to hone your skills by giving you mixed up questions myself.

Q1 A rocket chair is made, which produces energy in 3 ways.

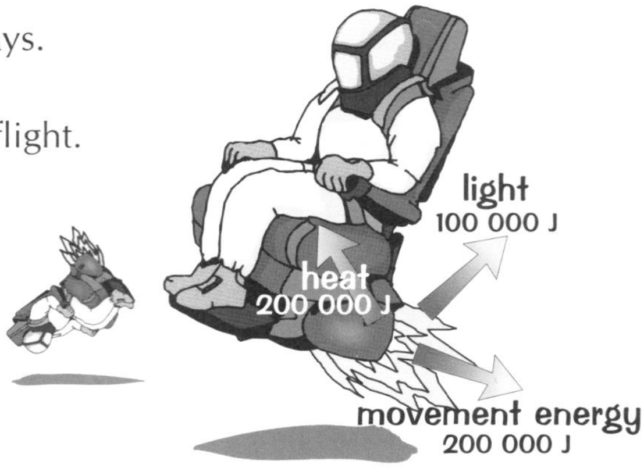

a) The diagram shows all the energy output during a test flight. What must the energy input have been?

b) How much energy is wasted by the chair?

c) What is the chair's efficiency? (to nearest 1%)

Q2 To show 5 minutes of Pets Win Pies, a TV must give out 100 500 J as light from the screen, and 52 500 J as sound from the speaker. Some energy is wasted as heat.

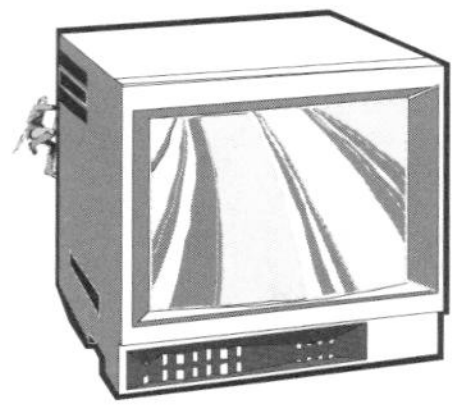

a) The TV is rated at 600 W. Calculate the energy it uses during 5 minutes.

You might want the formula for energy, power and time on page 8.

b) What's the efficiency of the TV?

c) How much energy would it waste if you watched 10 minutes of Who Wants To Be A Milliner?

Q3 A machine has an electric pump and a piston. It applies a pressure of 15 N/m^2 to the piston.

a) The pump operates at 150 W while it makes the piston move 0.1 m. It takes 6 seconds. How much energy is used?

b) The machine is 25% efficient when it moves the piston in this way. How much work is done?

c) What is the area of the piston?

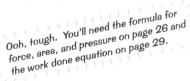

Ooh, tough. You'll need the formula for force, area, and pressure on page 26 and the work done equation on page 29.

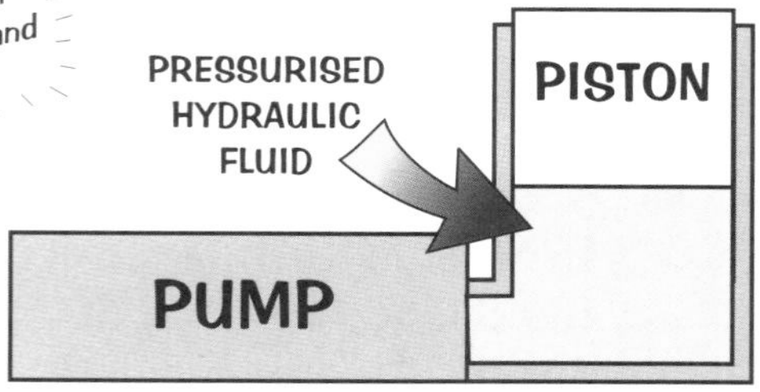

d) To move the piston 0.2 m, the machine uses 2000 J of electrical energy. How efficient is it now?

Inefficient, wasteful, little work done — and that's just me...

One of the nastiest mistakes here is mixing up the useful energy output and the wasted energy. Think what the machine is for — if a heater makes noise that's waste, but if a speaker makes noise that's useful. And watch out for questions that need another formula to work out the energy.

Half-life

Radioactive decay is what happens when radioactive particles or gamma rays are released. One half-life is the time it takes for half of the radioactive atoms to decay. Knowing the half-life of something like carbon-14 can help you to work out the age of a sample.

Q1 The activity of a radio-isotope is 768 cpm. Find its activity after these numbers of half-lives:

a) One
b) Three
c) Five
d) Six
e) Nine
f) Four
g) Eight
h) Two
i) Seven

Activity is measured in counts per minute (cpm). A 'count' is when an atom decays.

Q2 The activity of a radio-isotope is 560 cpm. Two hours later it has fallen to 35 cpm.

a) Work out how many half-lives have passed.

Keep halving the initial activity until you reach the final activity. Count how many times you need to halve the initial activity.

b) Calculate the half-life of the radio-isotope.

This is deceptively simple: you need to divide the time taken by the number of half-lives.

Q3 The activity of a radio-isotope is 7680 cpm. After 6 hours it has fallen to 30 cpm.

a) Work out how many half-lives were taken in 6 hours.

b) Calculate the half-life of the radio-isotope.

Use your working out of Q2 to help you answer this one.

Q4 Work out the half-lives of radio-isotopes with the following activities.

a) 328 cpm originally, falling to 41 cpm in 3 hours.

b) 940 cpm originally, falling to 235 cpm in 36 minutes.

c) 600 cpm originally, falling to 37.5 cpm in 25 hours.

d) 1088 cpm originally, falling to 17 cpm in 1 hour.

e) 128 cpm originally, falling to 8 cpm in 2 hours.

f) 512 cpm originally, falling to 64 cpm in a day.

My cat's radioactive — it's got nine and a half lives...

At first all this half-life business can seem a real pain, but it's really not too bad once you've got to grips with it. As long as you remember that the radioactivity never reaches zero, you're laughing. Repeat after me: half it and then half again and then half again and then half again and...

Half-life

Half-life questions can be tricky. It's remembering which bits to halve each time that's the trick. Remember that half the radioactive atoms decay to non-radioactive ones each half-life.

Q1 Every three minutes, I eat half of the sweets I've got left. I start with a full bag of 128 sweets.

This might sound a bit daft, but it'll really help you get your head round half-lives.

a) What is the 'half-life' of the sweets?

b) How many sweets will I have left after 6 minutes?

c) How many sweets will I have left after 12 minutes?

d) How long will it take for me to have only 2 sweets left?

e) If I'm allowed to divide each sweet up, will I ever finish all my sweets?

Q2 A wooden club is found to contain 1 part in 40 000 000 Carbon-14.

a) Work out how many half-lives it took for this to happen.

You need to know that the C-14 was originally 1 part in 10 000 000.

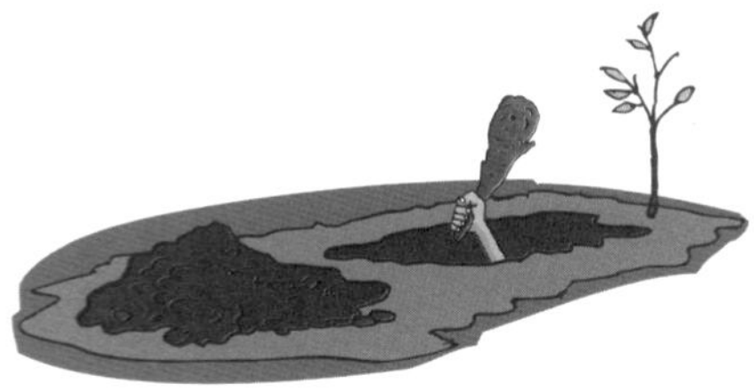

b) Calculate the age of the wooden club.

The half-life of C-14 is 5600 years.

c) How much of the wooden club would be carbon-14 after another 5600 years?

Q3 By using the information on this page about carbon dating, you can work out the age of this organic alien spaceship.

Assume that the amount of radioactive carbon where the spaceship came from is the same as on Earth.

a) Work out how many half-lives have passed if the C-14 in the spaceship is now 1 part in 320 000 000.

b) Calculate the age of the spaceship.

You need to use the original activity and half-life of carbon-14, given above.

c) From now, how long will it take for the C-14 in the spaceship to be 1 part in 1280 000 000?

Carbon dating — is that when you take a pencil to the cinema?...

It's very likely that you'll have to work out how old something is using radio-carbon dating in the exam. Just remember that while the sweets from Question 1 just get eaten, the point of half-lives is that some of the atoms stop being radioactive every half-life — the atoms don't disappear.

See the "Half Life" pages of our Physics Revision Guides

Combining Topics

There's nothing that examiners like better than combining different types of questions. It's really annoying, because it means that you've got to be able to spot when to use different formulas.

Q1 A 15 cm spring stretches to 20 cm when a block of metal with a mass of 4 kg hangs on it.

a) What is the downwards force due to the hanging block?

Use g=10 N/kg.

b) What would the extension of the spring be if a 6 kg mass was hanging on it?

c) The 6 kg block of metal drops off the spring, and the upwards force due to air resistance is 30 N. What acceleration does it have?

Q2 A woman is pushing a pram with a horizontal force of 250 N.

a) Calculate the work done if the pram is pushed a distance of 125 m.

b) Find the woman's efficiency if she uses 50 000 J of energy.

c) Work out her power output if it takes her 50 seconds to push the pram 125 m.

d) Work out the speed of the pram if the woman does not accelerate at all.

e) Now she speeds up to 10.5 m/s in 4 seconds. Work out the acceleration.

Q3 A diver has a mass of 55 kg.

a) How much does the diver weigh?

b) At a certain point, the force upwards due to air resistance is 420 N. What is the net downward force?

c) What was the diver's acceleration at this point?

d) Another diver with the same mass wears a thick swimming costume with a downward force of 100 N. What's the combined mass of the diver and her swimming costume?

e) If the force due to air resistance is the same as before, what is this diver's acceleration at the same point in the air?

Get formulas in the right order — sense it make more will...

Sometimes you know what two formulas you've got to use, but you haven't got a clue what order to use them in. Don't give up and go to the cinema instead — try it each way round. One way it should all fit together nicely, and the other won't. Obviously enough, the one that works is right.

Combining Topics

More questions on combining topics. This stuff trips up hundreds of eager GCSE physics candidates every year. But really it's just doing two straightforward questions, one after the other.

Q1 An amplifier has a resistance of 16 Ω.

a) If the amplifier runs off a 120 V supply, what is the current flowing through it?

b) What value of fuse should be used?

c) What is the power output of the amplifier?

d) Work out the amount of energy transferred by the amplifier in 2 hours.

e) Calculate the efficiency of the amplifier if the power input is 2.25 kW.

Start by working out how much energy is transferred in 2 hours by 2.25 kW.

Q2 The pole-sitting world record holder weighs 700 N and the pole he is sitting on has a mass of 25 kg.

a) What is the combined weight of the pole-sitter and the pole?

b) How much gravitational potential energy does the *pole-sitter* gain if the seat is raised by 3 m?

c) In just 0.25 minutes, the pole can lift the man from a start height of 0.5 m, to a maximum height of 4 m. At what speed does the seat move? (Assume it moves at a constant speed.)

d) If he's moving at that speed, how much kinetic energy does he have?

Q3 A 20 cm long spanner is being used to loosen a nut.

a) Draw a diagram of the forces involved.

b) What is the turning moment if I use 150 N of force to push the spanner?

c) What is the work done by rotating the nut 4 times with a constant force of 150 N?

d) I put 910 J of energy into turning the nut. What was my efficiency?

Take a moment, force yourself, feel the pressure...

There are certain topics that examiners often shove together. Electricity stuff fits nicely into one question. Anything to do with forces can be put into one (including Hooke's Law). Energy and power often turn up hand in hand. And sometimes examiners just put random sections together...

Reading Graphs and Charts

"What on Earth are graphs doing in a book on formulas?" I hear you cry. It seemed like a good idea, given as how they come up in the exam every year.

Q1 Use the bar chart below (calm down statistics freaks, I know it's a beauty) to answer the questions. It shows the time taken for cockroaches to race 10 metres.

a) Which cockroach won the race?

b) Which cockroach was the slowest over 10 m?

c) Which cockroach came second from last?

d) How many seconds faster than Lou was Sue?

e) How many seconds difference were there between the winner and the loser at the end?

f) Which cockroaches were under the Olympic qualifying time of 59 s?

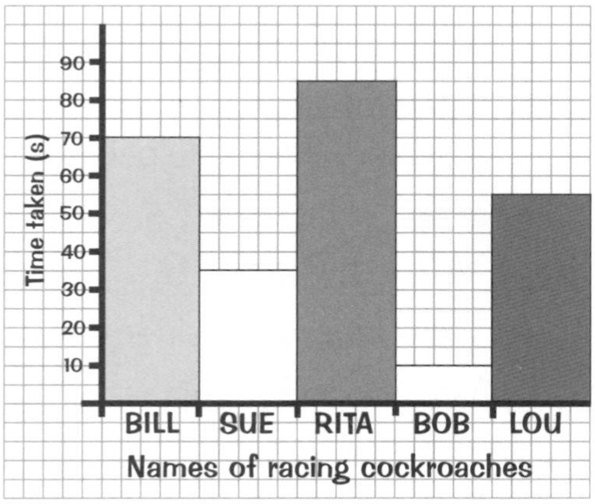

Q2 The line graph below shows the temperature of some soup as it is heated.

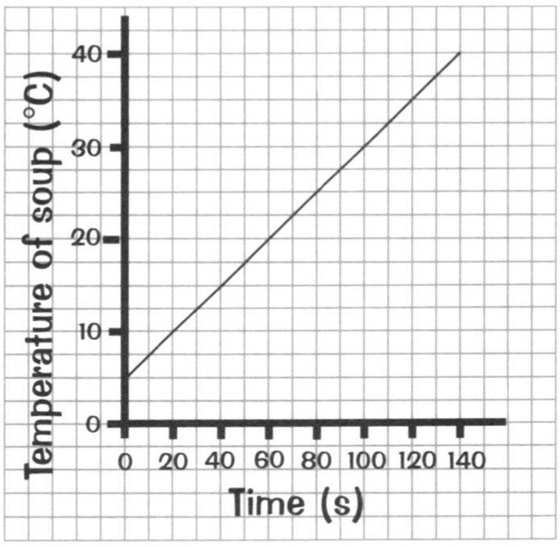

a) How hot was the soup after 20 seconds?

b) How hot was the soup after 1 minute?

c) How long did it take to heat the soup to 30 °C?

d) How long did it take to heat the soup to 40 °C?

e) By how much did the temperature rise every 20 s?

f) Assuming that this temperature rise will remain the same, what is the total time needed to heat it to 60 °C?

Q3 I asked two hundred people what pets they had. My results are displayed in this pie chart.

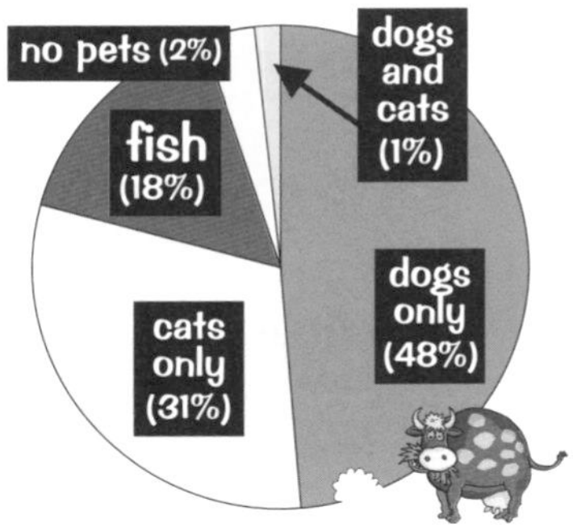

a) What percentage of people had fish?

b) What percentage of people had a dog?

You need to look carefully at all the categories.

c) How many people only had cats?

d) If half of the people with no pets got pet llamas, how many people would have pets that don't live in water?

e) If all the people who had only cats got fish instead, how many fish owners would there be in total?

WARNING: Get ready for a load of terrible graph puns...

Graph questions can be confusing with all that information flying around. Write down all your working — even if you muddle up the answer, you still get marks if the working-out is OK. That's pretty nice of those evil examiners, next they'll be telling you they're actually human. Some chance.

Reading Graphs and Charts

These line graphs are where it all starts getting trickier. It's not just looking and then writing stuff down — this time you've got to work things out with those formulas.

Q1 A skier tucks up and starts to hurtle straight down a slope with strangely even acceleration. This velocity-time graph shows the skier's motion as she shoots down the slope.

a) What's the skier's top speed?

b) How long does it take the skier to reach top speed?

c) What's the skier's acceleration between 0 and 4 s?

d) How far did the skier travel in 4 s?

e) What was the total distance she travelled in 8 s?

f) If she weighs 55 kg what was the resultant force acting on her from i) 0 - 4 s and ii) 4 - 8 s?

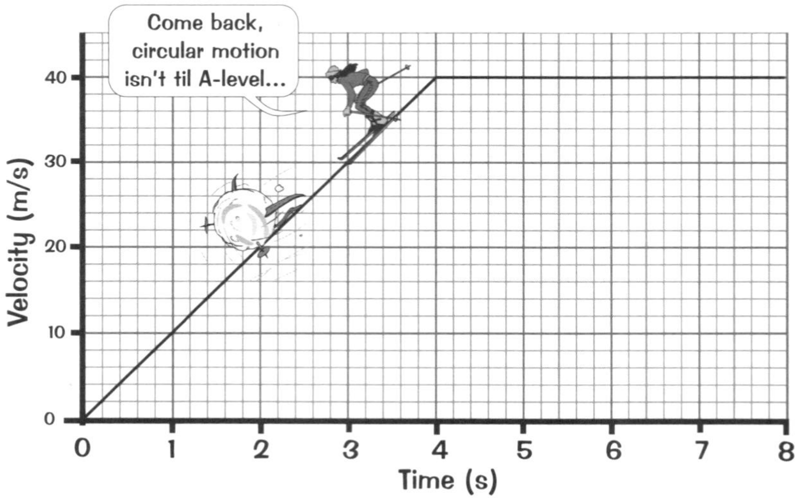

Q2 A truck travelling at 20 m/s started to slow down as it approached a traffic jam. Below is a graph showing the velocity of the truck while it was braking.

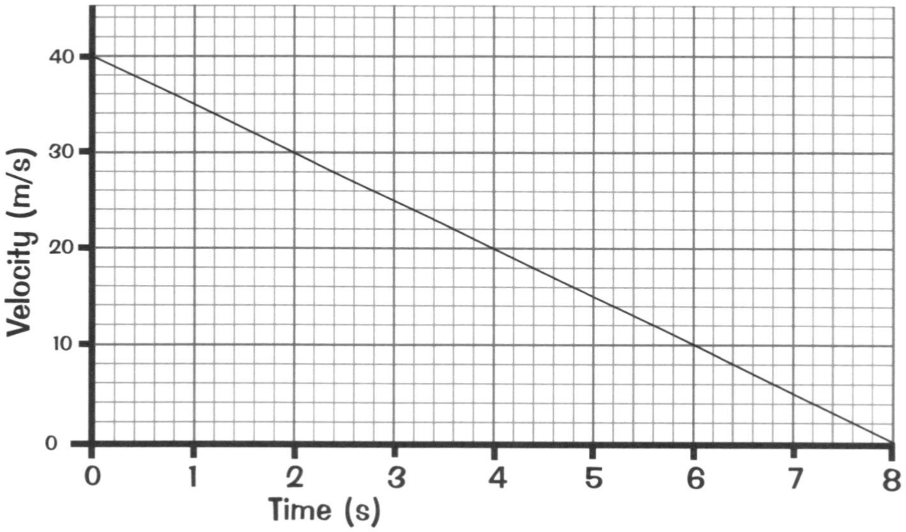

a) What is the truck's deceleration?

b) What is the braking force if the truck's mass is 1400 kg?

c) How far does the truck travel after putting the brakes on before it stops?

You've got to know that trick with the area...

d) After 4 s, if the driver brakes harder to decelerate at 10 m/s^2, how much quicker could the truck stop?

e) What would the truck's stopping distance be if the deceleration was 10 m/s^2 for the whole journey?

You don't have to do this in your head — draw on the graph if it's helpful.

Ban this page — it's too @#?!%&! graphic...

Here's a tip for you, so listen up. You are almost 100 % guaranteed to get one of these beasts in the exam. If you don't, then I'm your uncle's monkey. Figure out graphs — if you don't know your axes from your gradient you'll be heading for trouble.

See the "Distance-Time and Velocity-Time Graphs" pages of our Physics Revision Guides

Completing Graphs and Charts

You could think of these pages as "5 things to do with your favourite graph." If you were sufficiently unusual.

Q1 Complete the bar graphs with the figures from the table and then answer the questions.

	Gargling duration (s)	Spitting distance (m)
JOHN	5	3
SHEILA	8	3.5
MARY	19	1.5
YABBA	9	4
TIM	13	4.5

I know this is gross but it wasn't my idea...

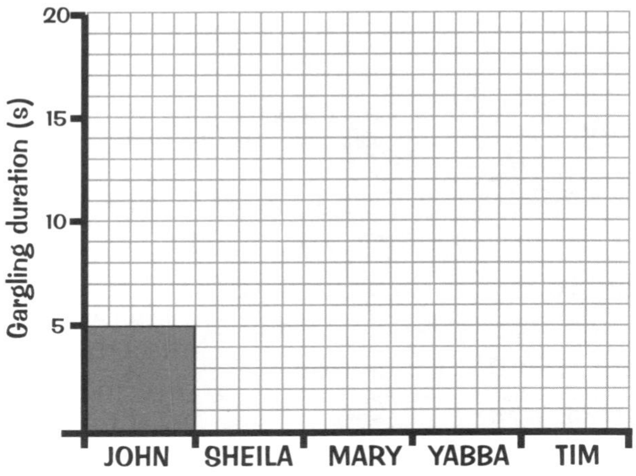

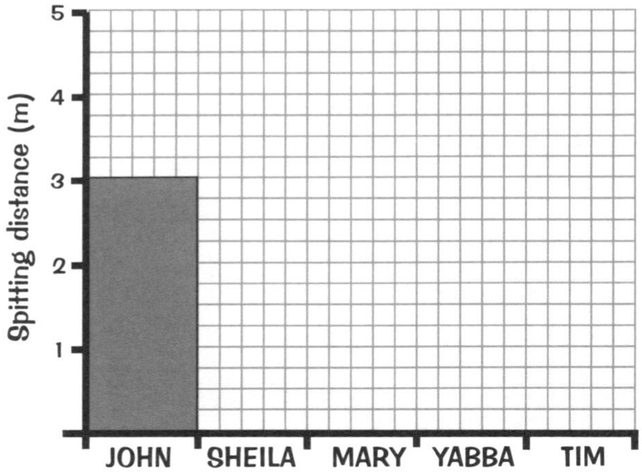

a) Who won the "distance spitting" competition?

b) Who won the "sustained gargling" competition?

c) Who came last in the spitting competition?

d) Who came last in the gargling competition?

e) 10 points were given for coming 1st in either competition, 8 points for coming 2nd, 6 points for 3rd, 4 for 4th and 2 for 5th. Write down the total number of points for each person.

I love graphs — I'm a graphite...

This page is as easy as falling off a log. Graph and chart questions are easy marks. The exam could ask you to stick results into a graph or to look at one and work stuff out. In any case, you need to know what you're doing. You need it for coursework too — you might as well get it right.

Drawing Graphs and Charts

Graphs — you've filled them in, you've finished them off. Now it's time to get your artist's palette out and then put it away again because you don't need it and then get a pencil and a ruler to draw these graphs.

Q1 Complete this pie chart with the information in the table. I'll let you guess what you have to do after that. (Hint: involves a writing implement, your brain and these questions.)

a) What percentage of the sample was graphite?

b) Which type of carbon was least common in this sample?

c) What percentage of the sample was not diamond?

Type of carbon in sample	Percentage
Coal, charcoal or soot	63
Graphite	34
Fullerenes	1
Diamond	2

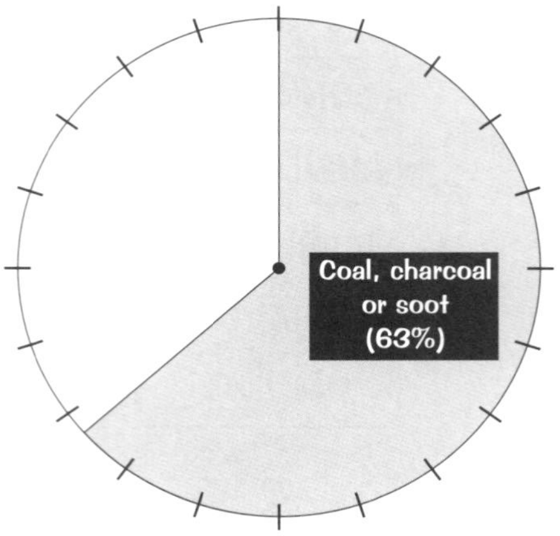

Q2 Draw and label pie charts to show this information.

This is tricky - just take your time.

a) Composition of stars:
Hydrogen 70 %
Helium 28 %
Other elements 2 %

b) Domestic electricity source:
Coal 52 %
Oil and natural gas 16 %
Nuclear 25 %
Wind and Hydroelectric power 5 %
Others 2 %

c) Composition of human body:
Oxygen 65 %
Carbon 18 %
Hydrogen 10 %
Nitrogen 3 %
Calcium 2 %
Others 2 %

Q3 Draw bar graphs or line graphs for the information below. The first two say which type of graph to use. For the third one, choose the best type.

a) Draw a line graph to show this skateboarder's distance with time.

Time (s)	Distance (m)
1	2
2	4
3	6
4	8
5	10

b) Display these weights on a bar graph.

	Weight (kg)
Bobby	80
Sarah	50
Jazza	60
Billwonk	75

c) Show this rollercoaster's speed with time on a graph.

Time (s)	Speed (m/s)
0	0
10	8
20	16
30	24
40	32

These might seem too easy, but you need to practise doing them without making silly mistakes.

Drawing Graphs and Charts

This page is where it all gets hard. You've got to draw precise graphs, remember formulas <u>and</u> work out answers all in the same question. Ick.

Q4 Answer these questions using the information on page 42 and the graphs you drew.

a) What is the speed of the skateboarder?

b) If 50 % of all the carbon in the body is Carbon-14, what percentage of the whole body is Carbon-14?

c) What is the acceleration of the rollercoaster?

d) What percentage of domestic electricity is supplied by coal, oil or natural gas?

e) What is the average weight of the four people in Q3 b)?

f) What distance has the skateboarder travelled in 4.5 s?

g) If the rollercoaster carried on at the same acceleration, what would the speed be after 70 s?

h) If all four people in Q3 b) were on the accelerating rollercoaster, which has a mass of 275 kg, what would be the resultant force on the rollercoaster?

Look back to page 11 if you've not got the formula stuffed into your brain yet...

Q5 A physicist wants to find the half-life of a sample of metal. She records the counts per minute over several hours. The large table shows her results.

a) Plot a graph of her results. Put time on the horizontal axis and draw a smooth curve through the points.

b) What is the half-life of the metal sample (to nearest minute)?

c) Use the table of metal half-lives to identify the sample.

Metal	Half-life
Ag-108	2.4 mins
Ag-110	24.6 secs
In-117	44 mins
Pb-211	36.1 mins
Pb-214	27 mins

Time (mins)	Counts per minute
0	11 000
15	8200
30	5900
45	4450
60	3500
75	2600
90	1900
105	1400
120	1000
135	750
150	550
165	400

You'll get so quick — everyone will want your autograph...

Take extra care drawing graphs in exams. You'll get questions about it so make your life easy — do the job properly. These questions allow you to really show them you know what you're doing. Oh, and whatever you do, don't forget your ruler and pencil. Wibbly biro won't impress anyone.

Drawing Graphs and Charts

Q1 A coach has its speed limited so that it cannot exceed 50 mph.

Time (s)	Velocity (m/s)
0	0
2	5
4	10
6	15
8	20
10	22
12	22
14	22

a) Plot a velocity–time graph for the data in the table.

b) What is the coach's top speed in metres per second? Draw an arrow on your graph to show where the coach reaches this speed.

c) What is the acceleration of the coach from 0 to 8 seconds?

d) If the coach has mass 6500 kg, what resultant force acts on the coach during this time?

e) Estimate how far the coach travelled in the 14 seconds to the nearest 5 metres.

Q2 An electronics engineer has two mystery components. He records current through the components at different voltages.

a) Plot these two sets of data on the same axes.

b) Identify the components and label them on your graph.

c) Which component obeys Ohm's Law? What is its resistance?

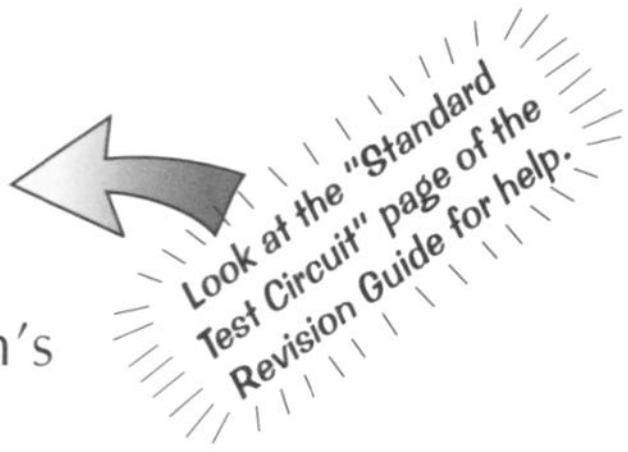
Look at the "Standard
Test Circuit" page of the
Revision Guide for help.

	Component 1	Component 2
Voltage (V)	Current (A)	Current (A)
-4	-2	0
-2	-1	0
0	0	0
2	1	0.3
4	2	1
6	3	2.7
8	4	5
10	5	10

Q3 A rusty old Beetle leaks oil at the rate of one drop every second. The diagram below shows drops of oil on a stretch of road where the car was changing speed. The scale underneath is in metres.

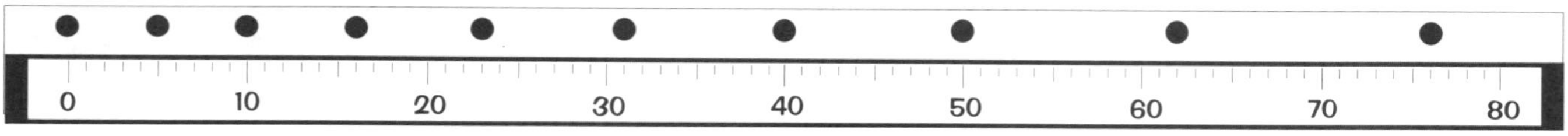

a) How long did the car take to travel the 76 m shown in the picture?

b) How far had the car travelled after four seconds?

c) What was the average velocity over the whole trip (to 1 d.p.)?

d) Draw a blue line on the picture to show where the car had constant speed.

e) What was the maximum acceleration? Draw a red line to show where this occurred.

f) What resultant force acts on the car at this acceleration if it weighs 975 kg?

~~a graph a minute...~~ ~~Graph-t it on...~~ I saw ~~a g-raph in the zoo...~~

Congratulations on surviving to the end of the page. And it's the end of the book as well. Just when you were really starting to enjoy yourself, ahh well. If you're after that good grade, get lots of practice in before the exams. It's up to you now — go forth and multiply (and divide).

Answers

Page 4 Electrical Power
Q1 a) 18 W b) 16 W c) 27 W d) 9 W e) 2.4 W f) 16.8 W g) 22.5 W h) 5 W i) 51.3 W
Q2 a) 5 V b) 2.5 V c) 20 V d) 500 V e) 2.25 V f) 50 V g) 1250 V h) 625 V i) 37.5 V
Q3 a) 50 A b) 2000 A c) 2000 A d) 60 A e) 4500 A f) 12.5 A g) 110 A h) 800 A i) 400 A
Q4 a) 1380 A b) 1058 A c) 10 A d) 13 A

Page 5 Electrical Power
Q1 a) 150 V b) 125 V c) 250 V d) 2.5 A so use a 3 A fuse.
Q2 a) 1196 W b) 1403 W c) 3 A fuse d) 13 A fuse e) 800 W f) 2.5 A
Q3 a) 2.6 A b) 120 V c) 30 A fuse d) 40 A fuse

Page 6 Resistance
Q1 a) 2 Ω b) 4 Ω c) 3 Ω d) 1 Ω e) 6 Ω f) 3 Ω g) 4.5 Ω h) 0.25 Ω i) 0.5 Ω
Q2 a) 6 V b) 10 V c) 16 V d) 18 V e) 2 V f) 9 V g) 4.5 V h) 3 V i) 12 V
Q3 a) 2 A b) 3 A c) 3 A d) 2 A e) 3 A f) 1 A g) 0.5 A h) 0.25 A i) 0.6 A
Q4 a) 5 Ω b) 2.4 A Q5 a) 46 A b) 24 A

Page 7 Resistance
Q1 a) 24 Ω b) 15 Ω c) 5 A
Q2 a) 12 Ω b) 2 A c) 6 V d) 19.1 A
Q3 a) 12.8 A b) 1.7 A c) 27 V d) 35.4 Ω

Page 8 Energy in Kilowatt-hours
Q1 a) 6 kWh b) 12 kWh c) 24 kWh d) 5 kWh e) 3 kWh f) 15 kWh g) 48 kWh h) 0.3 kWh i) 0.2 kWh
Q2 a) 2 kW b) 3 kW c) 8 kW d) 0.5 kW e) 1.5 kW f) 0.75 kW g) 11.5 kW h) 22.5 kW i) 1.2 kW
Q3 a) 1 h b) 3 h c) 6 h d) 0.5 h or 30 mins e) 0.25 h or 15 mins f) 0.75 h or 45 mins g) 2 h h) 12 h i) 0.06 h or 3.6 mins
Q4 a) 105 kWh b) 7.5 kWh c) $^2/_3$ hr or 40 mins d) 24 kW

Page 9 Cost of Electricity
Q1 a) £7.50 b) £75 c) £6.75 d) £11.25 e) £37.50 f) £120 g) £38.70 h) £74.85 i) £2595.90
Q2 a) 10 units b) 20 units c) 200 units d) 1000 units e) 562.5 units f) 6250 units g) 9375 units h) 647.5 units i) 9465 units
Q3 a) 7 p b) 14 p c) 10 p d) 9.3 p e) 10.8 p f) 12.7 p g) 8.5 p h) 12.2 p i) 11.1 p
Q4 a) 1682.1 units b) £134.57 c) 2625 units d) 6.5 p

Page 10 Energy and Cost
Q1 a) 4 h b) 26.25 kWh c) 1½ h extra
Q2 a) 13.5 kWh b) 3.5 h c) 6 p
Q3 a) 75 mins b) 5 kWh c) 45 p d) £2.03

Page 11 Force and Motion
Q1 a) 50 N b) 35 N c) 376 N d) 2.3 N e) 2.1 N f) 220.4 N g) 253.3 N h) 8411.6 N i) 5.3 N
Q2 a) 20 m/s^2 b) 5 m/s^2 c) 14 m/s^2 d) 6.4 m/s^2 e) 0.3 m/s^2 f) 6.3 m/s^2 g) 28 m/s^2 h) 3.9 m/s^2 i) 29.8 m/s^2
Q3 a)10 kg b) 8 kg c) 38.3 kg d) 2.5 kg e) 5.7 kg f) 18.4 kg g) 65 kg h) 5.9 kg i) 15 kg
Q4 a) 3600 N b) 25.2 N c) 918 N d) 321.6 N e) 0.02 N f) 475.39 N g) 794.61 N

Page 12 Force and Motion
Q1 a) Rock b) Mini c) Skier d) Motorbike e) Sky-diver f) Magpie g) Horse
Q2 a) 5 m/s^2 b) 4 m/s^2 c) 5 m/s^2 d) -8 m/s^2 e) 0.6 m/s^2 f) 0.5 m/s^2 g) 4.2 m/s^2 h) 0.5 m/s^2
Q3 a) 73.5 N b) 631 N c) 45 kg d) 58.8 N e) 5.4 m/s^2 f) 6.6 kg, to thief.

Page 13 Force and Motion
Q1 a) 2.5 m/s^2 b) Less push or more weight in tractor. c) 43 N d) No; no forces and so no deceleration.
Q2 a) 96 N b) 825 N c) 267
Q3 a) 6000 N b) 6000 N c) 2820 N in direct. of accel. d) 3020 N e) 2875, 4.6 m/s^2

Page 14 Mass and Weight
Q1 a) 50 N b) 100 N c) 2270 N d) 325 N e) 5 N f) 35 N g) 3 N h) 2315 N i) 2.5 N
Q2 a) 0.6 kg b) 0.8 kg c) 14.3 kg d) 5 kg e) 32 kg f) 0.2 kg g) 3.4 kg h) 25.4 kg i) 0.05 kg
Q3 a) 8 N b) 16 N c) 363.2 N d) 52 N e) 0.8 N f) 5.6 N g) 0.48 N h) 370.4 N i) 0.4 N
Q4 a) Moon — g = 1.6 N/kg b) i) 650 N ii) 104 N c) i) 800 N ii) 128 N d) 5 kg e) 900 N

Page 15 Mass and Weight
Q1 a) 800 N b) 130 N c) 1.625 m/s^2
Q2 a) 54.6 kg b) 1226 N c) 109.2 N
Q3 a) 41.7 kg b) 1250 N c) 833 N d) 437.5 N

Page 16 Speed and Velocity
Q1 a) 10 m/s b) 15 m/s c) 20 m/s d) 5 m/s e) 8.3 m/s f) 20.5 m/s g) 20 m/s h) 12.5 m/s i) 8.3 m/s
Q2 a) 300 m b) 400 m c) 200 m d) 420 m e) 2160 m f) 350 m g) 18000 m h) 8.3 km i) 60 km
Q3 a) 0.5 s b) 5 s c) 25 s d) 30 s e) 3.3 s f) 78.6 s g) 30 mins h) 41.6 mins i) 125 s
Q4 a) 1.1 m/s b) 0.2 cm/s c) 13.3 m/s d) 16.7 m/s e) 2.1 m/s f) 26.7 m/s g) 0.6 m/s h) 6.7 m/s i) 2000 m/s

Page 17 Speed and Velocity
Q1 a) 110.8 km/h b) 0 km/h c) 2 mins 24 s d) 180 km/h
Q2 a) Yes. b) 1134.3 km/h NE c) 53.5 mins d) No.
Q3 a) 3.3 m/s E b) 12 mins c) 90 s (twice as fast) d) 4.8 m/s e) 2.2 mins

Page 18 Acceleration
Q1 a) 0.5 m/s^2 b) 2.5 m/s^2 c) 4 m/s^2 d) 2 m/s^2 e) 0.8 m/s^2 f) 8.5 m/s^2 g) 1.3 m/s^2 h) 0.3 m/s^2 i) 18.7 m/s^2 j) 18.4 m/s^2
Q2 a) 2 s b) 6 s c) 9 s d) 6.4 s e) 4.3 s f) 5 s g) 1.0 s h) 1.6 s i) 2.2 s j) 0.1 s
Q3 a) 0.05 m/s^2 b) 4 m/s^2 c) 0.05 m/s^2 d) 6.1 m/s^2 e) 5.1 s f) 5 s g) 5.6 s h) 11.1 m/s^2 i) 16.7 m/s (or 60 km/h); 50 m

Page 19 Velocity and Acceleration
Q1 a) 1388.9 m/s b) 2.5 h c) 142.9 m/s^2
Q2 a) 112.6 b) 60 mph 96.6 km/h c) 93.3 mph No! d) 2.1 m/s^2
Q3 a) 4 km b) 3.6 m/s c) 6.1 m/s d) 0.1 s e) 5940 m; further.

Page 20 Waves
Q1 a) 0.1 Hz b) 0.2 Hz c) 0.25 Hz d) 0.5 Hz e) 0.05 Hz f) 1 Hz g) 5 Hz h) 100 Hz
Q2 a) 0.05 s b) 0.5 s c) 10 s d) 0.001 s e) 0.004 s f) 0.25 s g) 500 s h) 0.008 s
Q3 a) 24 m/s b) 60 m/s c) 120 m/s d) 240 m/s e) 12 m/s f) 6 m/s g) 12000 m/s h) 96 m/s i) 14.4 m/s
Q4 a) 0.3 m b) 4 m c) 10 m d) 0.03 m e) 250 m f) 0.02 m g) 5 m h) 2 m i) 0.1 m
Q5 a) 2 m/s b) 2.4 m/s c) 0.25 m/s

Page 21 Waves
Q1 a) 0.5 Hz b) 10 m c) 1 m – 6 m/s, 4 m – 3.5m, 3 m – 6 m/s, 2 m – 12.5 Hz d) 4m
Q2 a) 900 m/s b) 6.67 cm c) 200 kHz
Q3 a) 3.001 $\times 10^8$ m/s b) 4.007 $\times 10^{14}$ Hz

Page 22 Moments
Q1 a) 6 Nm Anti-CW b) 28 Nm CW c) 60 Nm CW d) 51.84 Nm Anti-CW
Q2 a) CW 9 Nm, Anti-CW 15 Nm, tip left. b) CW 34.5 Nm, Anti-CW 67.5 Nm, tip left. c) CW 55.2 Nm, Anti-CW 9.2 Nm ,tip right. d) CW 6.8 Nm, Anti-CW 6.58 Nm ,tip right. e) CW 6 Nm, Anti-CW 6 Nm, balance. f) CW 48 Nm, Anti-CW 25 Nm, tip right.
Q3 a) 10 N b) 20 Nm CW c) Cat goes down d) 1 m left of pivot.

Page 23 Moments
Q1 a) 32.5 Nm b) 13 N c) 300 N
Q2 a) 300 N b) 400 N c) 224 N d) Yes
Q3 a) Mom only 3 Nm b) 35.1 N c) 23.5 N d) Max dist; min force.

Page 24 Kinetic Energy
Q1 a) 31 J b) 500 J c) 1531 J d) 3125 J e) 1125 J f) 245 J g) 8681 J h) 6028 J i) 4500 J
Q2 a) 675 J b) 900 J c) 428 J d) 1575 J e) 882 J f) 603 J g) 936 J h) 401 J i) 684 J
Q3 a) 17.778 kg b) 10 kg c) 62.5 kg d) 4000 kg e) 3.906 kg f) 15.625 kg g) 640 kg h) 0.004 kg i) 360 kg
Q4 a) 1.25 J b) 482253 J c) 6 J d) 181476 J e) 181469 J f) 450000 J

Page 25 Kinetic Energy
Q1

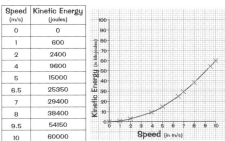

Speed (m/s)	Kinetic Energy (joules)
0	0
1	600
2	2400
4	9600
5	15000
6.5	25350
7	29400
8	38400
9.5	54150
10	60000

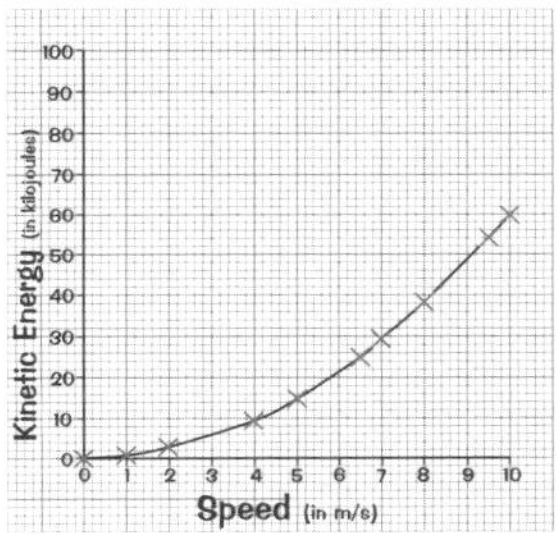

Q2 a) 4000 kg b) 908000 J c) 12 teachers

Page 26 Gravitational Potential Energy
Q1 a) 0 J b) 3750 J c) 4500 J d) 32250 J e) 1800 J f) 50250 J g) 367.5 J h) 11250 J i) 16500 J j) 1500 J k) 7500 J l) 6750 J
Q2 a) 23544 J b) 22563 J c) 147150 J d) 21288 J e) 3139 J f) 13312 J g) 21974 J h) 1472 J
Q3 a) the 1.2 kg mass b) the 14.5 kg mass c) the 3.5 kg mass d) the 4.6 kg mass e) the 37 kg mass f) the 1000 kg mass
Q4 a) 111.87 m b) 5661.46 m c) 64.87 m d) 491.15 m e) 19450.07 m f) 1.65 m

Page 27 Gravitational Potential Energy
Q1 a) 2940000 kJ b) 490 kJ c) 85 kg d) Man in locker (it fell 2.5 m — only he's high enough for that to be possible)
Q2 a) 206 J b) 28 kg c) 0.75 m d) 19 N/kg

Page 28 Work Done = Force × Distance
Q1 a) 5 kJ b) 25 J c) 1.25 kJ d) 21.5 kJ e) 100 kJ f) 3.65 kJ g) 8.85 kJ h) 67.75 kJ i) 49.325 kJ
Q2 a) 50 J b) 300 J c) 275 J d) 100 J e) 600 J f) 375 J g) 175 J h) 525 J i) 475 J
Q3 a) 3.9 kJ b) 2.775 kJ c) 5.025 kJ d) 1.8 kJ e) 3.45 kJ f) 5.175 kJ g) 1.575 kJ h) 4.125 kJ i) 5.475 kJ
Q4 a) 1.5 kJ b) 1600 kJ c) 100 kJ d) 2 J e) 10 kJ f) 180 kJ g) 4.9 kJ h) 40 kJ

Page 29 Work Done = Force × Distance
Q1 a) 1800 kJ b) 2380 kJ c) 1600 kJ
Q2 a) 6 kJ b) 5.4 kJ c) 7.8 kJ d) 27
Q3 a) 36 kJ b) 208 kJ c) 30.6 m d) 20.25 kJ each

Answers

Page 30 Power = Work ÷ Time

Q1 *a)* 5000 W *b)* 2083 W *c)* 1667 W *d)* 1754 W *e)* 2564 W *f)* 2326 W *g)* 2299 W *h)* 1912 W *i)* 3040 W

Q2 *a)* 1111 W *b)* 2222 W *c)* 1944 W *d)* 833 W *e)* 972 W *f)* 1250 W *g)* 1756 W *h)* 1428 W *i)* 2217 W

Q3 *a)* 16.7 W *b)* 50 W *c)* 33.3 W *d)* 66.7 W *e)* 21.1 W *f)* 17.4 W *g)* 74.1 W *h)* 37.7 W *i)* 25.3 W

Q4 *a)* 208 s *b)* 42 s *c)* 146 s *d)* 354 s *e)* 398 s *f)* 477 s *g)* 547 s *h)* 324 s *i)* 205 s

Q5 *a)* 60 kJ *b)* 72 kJ *c)* 96 kJ *d)* 48 kJ *e)* 57 kJ *f)* 87 kJ *g)* 109.5 kJ *h)* 64.5 kJ *i)* 82.5 kJ

Page 31 Work Done = Force × Distance

Q1 *a)* 286 W *b)* 222 W *c)* 1 hour *d)* 220 W *e)* 44%

Q2 *a)* 75 W *b)* 35 W *c)* 50 W *d)* 60 times

Q3 *a)* 3733 W *b)* 2273 W *c)* 1067 W *d)* 8 mins 20 secs

Page 32 Efficiency

Q1 *a)* 0.53 *b)* 0.7 *c)* 0.26 *d)* 0.32 *e)* 0.1 *f)* 0.2 *g)* 0.52 *h)* 0.53 *i)* 0.85

Q2 *a)* 86% *b)* 14% *c)* 98% *d)* 1% *e)* 40% *f)* 71% *g)* 89% *h)* 81% *i)* 22%

Q3 *a)* 11980 J *b)* 7047 J *c)* 23960 J *d)* 59900 J *e)* 8557 J *f)* 17114 J *g)* 14610 J *h)* 6656 J

Q4 *a)* 60 J *b)* 150 J *c)* 3000 J *d)* 204 J *e)* 486 J *f)* 414 J

Q5 *a)* 16000 J, 80% *b)* 17200 J, 86% *c)* 9000 J 45% *d)* 15750 J, 79%

Page 33 Efficiency

Q1 *a)* 40% *b)* 18% *c)* 36% *d)* 63% *e)* 10% *f)* 14% *g)* 59% *h)* 25% *i)* 72%

Q2 *a)* 5714 J *b)* 11571 J *c)* 763 J *d)* 25429 J *e)* 21437 J *f)* 31 114 J *g)* 175 J *h)* 1225 J *i)* 6961.5 J *j)* 9128 J *k)* 350 J *l)* 22428 J

Q3 *a)* 21% *b)* 40% *c)* 90% *d)* 83%

Q4 *a)* 78% – 100% not possible. *b)* 2000 J *c)* Garden lamp

Page 34 Efficiency

Q1 *a)* 500 000 J *b)* 300 000 J *c)* 40%

Q3 *a)* 900 J *b)* 225 J

Q2 *a)* 180 000 J *b)* 85% *c)* 54 000 J *c)* 150 m² *d)* 23%

Page 35 Half-Life

Q1 *a)* 384 cpm *b)* 96 cpm *c)* 24 cpm *d)* 12 cpm *e)* 1.5 cpm *f)* 48 cpm *g)* 3 cpm *h)* 192 cpm *i)* 6 cpm

Q2 *a)* 4 half-lives *b)* 0.5 h

Q3 *a)* 8 half-lives *b)* 0.75 h

Q4 *a)* 1 h *b)* 18 mins *c)* 6.25 h *d)* 10 mins *e)* 0.5 h *f)* 8 h

Page 36 Half-life

Q1 *a)* 3 mins *b)* 32 sweets *c)* 8 sweets *d)* 18 mins *e)* No

Q2 *a)* 2 half-lives *b)* 11 200 years *c)* 1 part in 80 000 000

Q3 *a)* 5 half-lives *b)* 28 000 years *c)* 11200 years

Page 37 Combining Topics

Q1 *a)* 40 N *b)* 7.5 cm *c)* 5 m/s²

Q2 *a)* 31250 J *b)* 62.5% *c)* 625 W *d)* 2.5 m/s *e)* 2 m/s²

Q3 *a)* 550 N *b)* 130 N *c)* 2.36 m/s² (2dp) *d)* 65 kg *e)* 3.54 m/s²

Page 38 Combining Topics

Q1 *a)* 7.5 A *b)* 10 A *c)* 900 W *d)* 6480 kJ *e)* 40%

Q2 *a)* 950 N *b)* 380 Pa *c)* 190 Pa *d)* 2 m²

Q3 *a)* 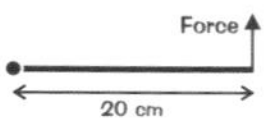

b) 30 Nm *c)* 5.024 m *d)* 753.6 J *e)* 82.8%

Page 39 Reading Graphs and Charts

Q1 *a)* Bob *b)* Rita *c)* Bill *d)* 20 s *e)* 75 s *f)* Sue, Bob, Lou

Q2 *a)* 10°C *b)* 20°C *c)* 100 s *d)* 140 s *e)* 5°C *f)* 220 s

Q3 *a)* 18% *b)* 49 % *c)* 62 people *d)* 162 people *e)* 98 people

Page 40 Reading Graphs and Charts

Q1 *a)* 40 m/s *b)* 4 s *c)* 10 m/s² *d)* 80 m *e)* 240 m *f)i)*550 N,*ii)*0 N

Q2 *a)* 5 m/s² *b)* 7000 N *c)* 160 m *d)* 2 s quicker *e)* 80 m

Page 41 Completing Graphs and Charts

Q1

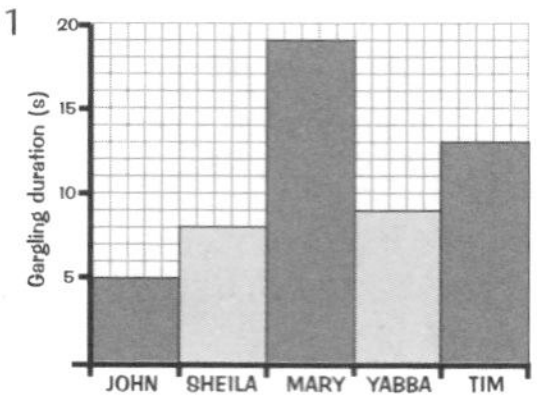

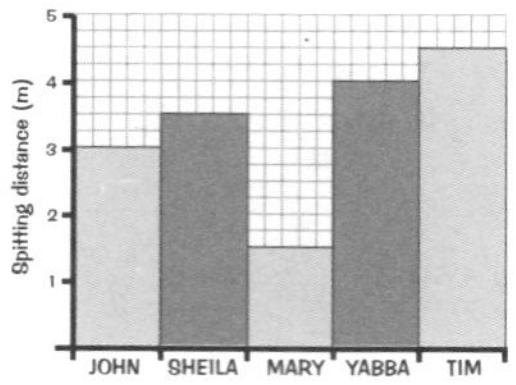

a) Tim *b)* Mary *c)* Mary *d)* John *e)* John 6, Sheila 10, Mary 12, Yabba 14, Tim 18

Page 42 Drawing Graphs and Charts

Q1

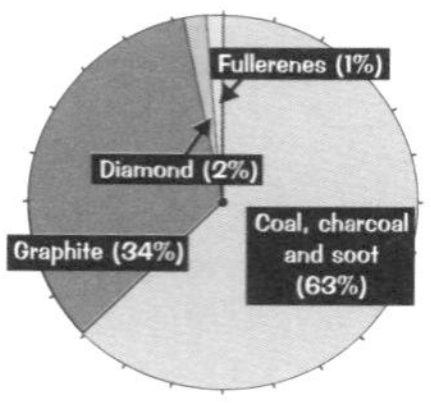

a) 34% *b)* Fullerenes *c)* 98%

Q2 *a)*

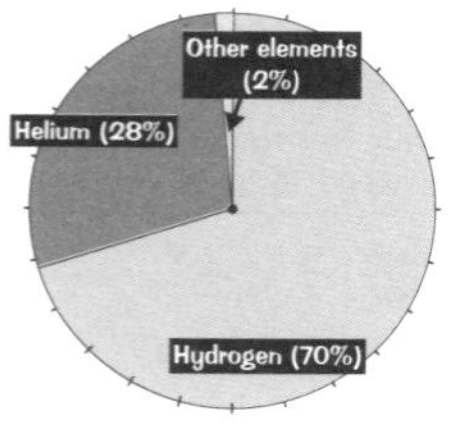

b)

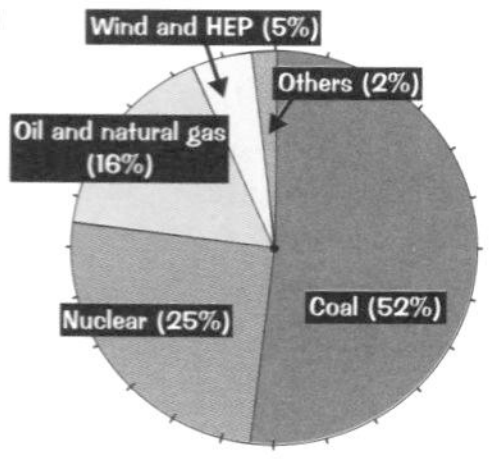

c)

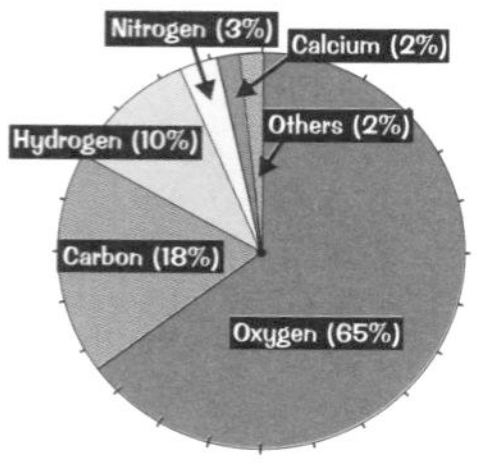

Q3 *a)*

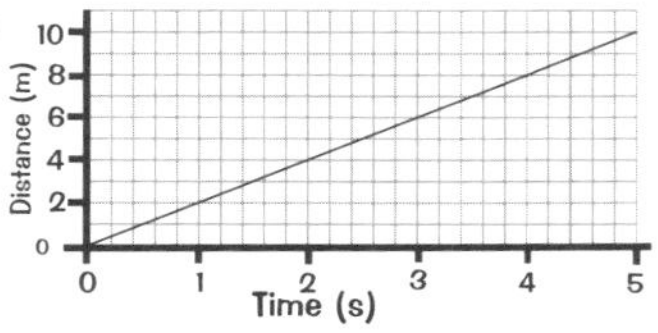

b)

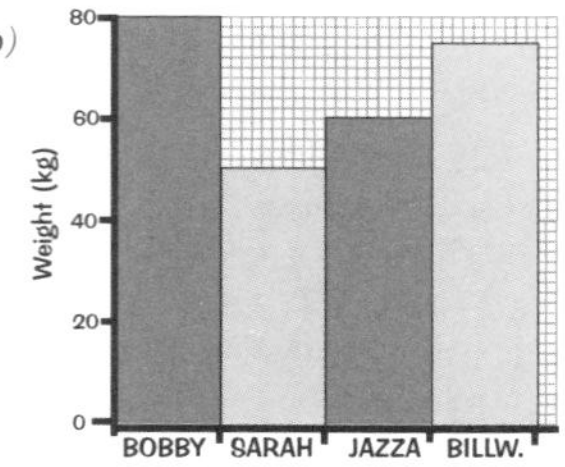

c)

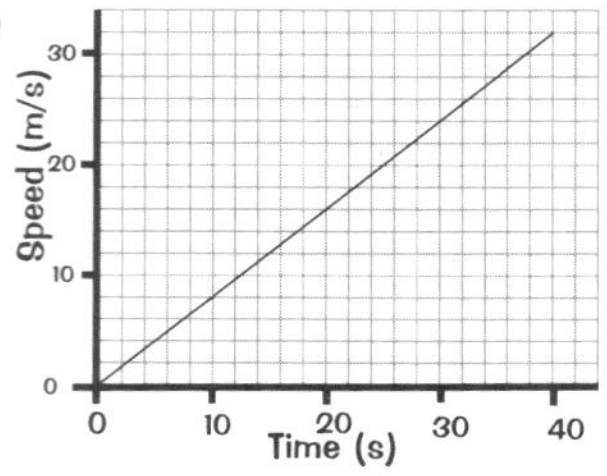

Page 43 Drawing Graphs and Charts

Q4 *a)* 2 m/s *b)* 9% *c)* 0.8 m/s² *d)* 68% *e)* 66.25 kg *f)* 9 m *g)* 56 m/s *h)* 432 N

Q5 *a)*

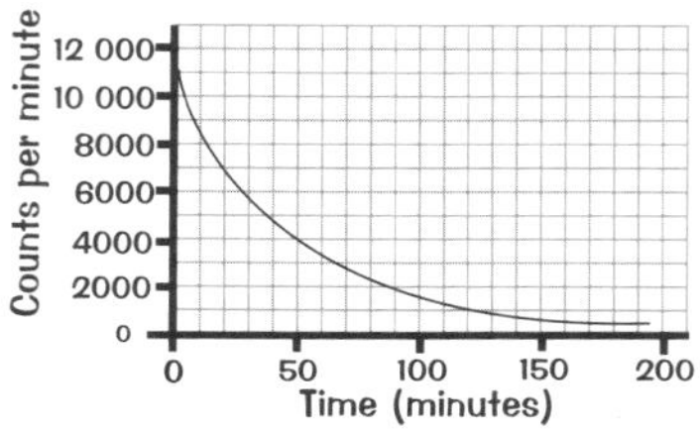

b) 36 mins *c)* Lead Pb-211

Page 44 Drawing Graphs and Charts

Q1 *a)*

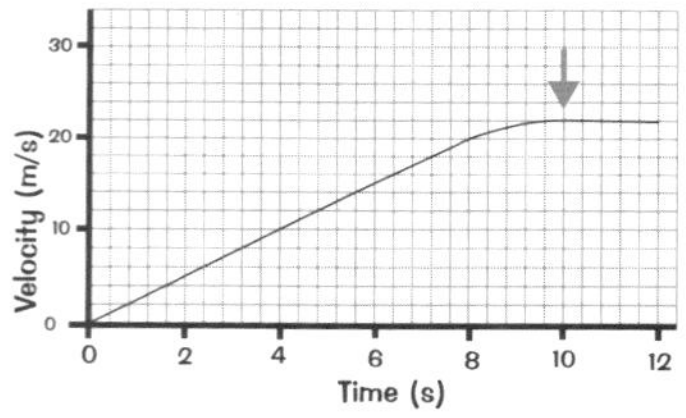

b) 22 m/s *c)* 2.5 m/s² *d)* 16 250 N *e)* 210 m

Q2 *a)*

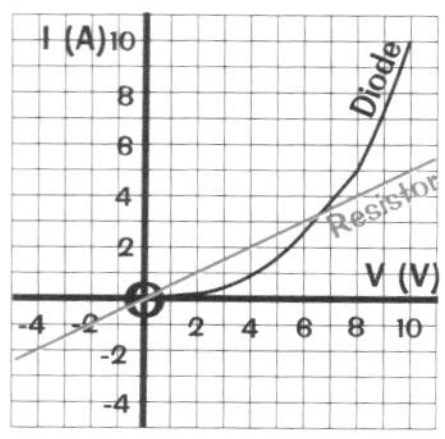

b) Component 1 — Resistor Component 2 — Diode *c)* Component 1 obeys Ohm's Law. Resistance 2 Ω.

Q4 *a)* 9 s *b)* 23 m *c)* 8.4 m/s *d)* / *e)*

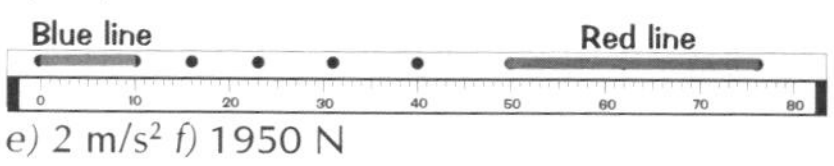

e) 2 m/s² *f)* 1950 N